AF255796

that no matter your current circumstances, success is indeed attainable through faith, focus, perseverance, patience and a balanced approach to your life and business. A must-read for our times!"

- RHETT POWER
Bestselling author, executive coach and contributing writer for Inc. & Forbes Magazines

"In the crowded literary space of 'how to create a successful business. *Lemonade!* will equip you for the peaks and valleys of any entrepreneurial journey. An important read for anyone who wants to learn from the best on how to turn even life's toughest challenges in to great triumph."

- SHANNON BOWEN-SMED
Former CEO of BOWEN Group, named one of Canada's Top 100 Female Entrepreneurs by PROFIT / Chatelaine magazines

"Lemonade! Squeeze your Challenging Life Experiences into a Successful Business" is a transformative read! Hop aboard a journey that takes you from struggling to thriving in all aspects of your life. This book is chock full of life lessons that encourage you to shift your perceptions of challenges and turn them into learning leaps. Melane's stories guide the reader through strategies that propel them forward towards success in both business and in life."

- DANETTE KUBANDA
Two-time Emmy Award winning TV producer & media coach

"As in the book of Genesis, Joseph was dealt lemons that God turned into lemonade. God also helped Melane transform her lemons into lemonade, a testimony that can be told like this: what the devil meant for harm, God will turn it around for His good. It always happens when we put our trust in Jesus Christ."

- CHRISTIAN HOSOI
Legendary professional skateboarder and former prison inmate, turned author and outreach pastor at The Sanctuary Church

LEMONADE!

LEMONADE!

*Squeeze Your Challenging Life Experiences
into a Successful Business*

MELANE MULLINGS

CONTENTS

FOREWORD

I FIRST MET MELANE ON MY BIRTHDAY IN 2008 IN CALGARY CANADA, when she attended my Success Workshop™ designed from my book, The Success Principles™. I didn't know it at the time, but I later learned that when she attended my workshop, she'd recently started her first entrepreneurial venture and had very little in terms of resources, training or support. However, she possessed something far more powerful that made up for all she lacked: She had PURPOSE. You see, knowing and working to fulfill your soul's purpose is the ultimate key to happiness, and Melane had discovered that key. She had found it where it often sits hidden in all of our lives—in our pain, the pain she refers to as the lemon experiences of our lives.

By the time we first met, she'd already defied death twice. The first time as a teenager battling leukemia, and the second, after a serious car accident that she survived months prior to our first meeting. In this book, she explains how it was these lemon experiences that inspired change in the trajectory of her life. Going from a lucrative career as a travel and per diem registered nurse leading a self-serving materialistic life, to becoming a purpose-led entrepreneur and now author, serving and impacting thousands.

Melane's first business was a recruitment firm that placed qualified and experienced, mostly international registered nurses (RNs), with Canadian hospitals and health centers in areas desperate to find staff. She came to understand that the first stage of her purpose was to help address the nursing shortage to ensure that patients that were sick and vulnerable like she once was, would receive the kind of compassionate emotional care she wished she had.

This mission was so incredibly important to her that she threw away all other alternate plans; all other means to making money. There was no plan

B. She just jumped fully into her business and was determined to make it work. And, my goodness did it ever work!

Her firm grew in size, value, and reach over the next decade—covering markets across Canada in the greatest need of RN staff. In this role, she was able to operate from her purpose. Prior to placing her nurses with her client hospitals, she first gave them additional training to prepare them to provide the kind of compassionate care she wished she'd had when she was a leukemia patient. Her leukemia lemon experience paved the way for her discovering and fulfilling her purpose. And the impact of her purpose on her nurses, their patients, the small communities where they were placed, and the health care system in those areas resulted in a far-reaching domino effect—creating blessings upon blessings and impact upon impact.

After 13 years, she successfully sold her purpose-led business. Her experiences growing it from nothing have resulted in an overflow of rich blessings for her, resulting in a truly abundant life. But those blessings are only a byproduct of her purpose, which is a result of her lemon experiences. Melane literally took life's lemons and turned them into lemonade!

The truth is that life offers us blessings and challenges equally. We've all had lemon experiences that have severely challenged our belief that we could make it through to the other side of healing and success. It may be the death of a loved one, divorce, getting fired from a job, illness, abuse, betrayal, losing your home, or even losing your business. The truth is, our gratitude for the good, bad, and the ugly, the lens from which we view our challenges and our responses to our lemon experiences are what make all the difference to our ability to transform from where we are to where we want to be.

In this book, Melane lovingly holds your hand and step-by-step lays out proven strategies that created success in her life. In part one of the book, she shares a comprehensive approach to the necessary inner work you need to do—strategies to prepare you to become the kind of business owner that can effectively manage your eventual success, without it compromising you or your business. Next she covers the outer work that will help you build a solid foundation for your successful business, so it can stand the test of time. The third part of the book covers the importance of recognizing and celebrating the fact that right now, no matter where you are, you have the seeds within you to create success in your life!

As you will see as you read, Melane's entire approach is anchored in her Christian faith, and she credits her success and the opportunity to live a truly abundant life to her application of spiritual principles to both her inner work and her outer work.

What I love about this book is the way that it reads—like a personal, encouraging and empowering note from a friend. The kind of friend we all wish for—non-judgmental, non-intimidating, understanding, encouraging, uplifting, loving, and one that sees the power in you that you may not yet see in yourself. One that believes in you more than you may believe in yourself. And one that wants more for you than what you may currently want for yourself.

I'm so happy you have this book in your possession and are about to read it. I enjoyed reading it and found it to be highly inspiring. I'm sure you will too. Make sure to read every word, take notes, do all the exercises, and, most importantly, implement the strategies she has outlined. This is a book that could change your life and propel you and your business to its highest heights. Take full advantage of this opportunity!

I wish you great success.

—JACK CANFIELD

"Life handed him a lemon,
As life sometimes will do.
His friends looked on in pity,
Assuming he was through.

They came upon him later,
Reclining in the shade
In calm contentment,
Drinking a glass of lemonade."

—Clarence Edwin Flynn, *"The Optimist"*

PREFACE

"Many people die with their music still in them. Why is this so?
Too often, it is because they are always getting ready to live.
Before they know it, time runs out."

—OLIVER WENDELL THOMAS

A SUCCESSFUL, FULFILLED ENTREPRENEUR SOLVES PROBLEMS AT A profit from the perspective of their purpose. The idea of living one's personal purpose at its best garners intrigue and excitement. At its worst, it garners fear. Living in and on purpose is freeing and foundational to living a truly abundant life. But pivoting there, if you're not on the right track, can prove daunting.

Many of us have business ideas dying inside us for fear that our age, gender, lack of education, paltry amount of capital, or a lack of direction and support will prevent us from starting and growing a successful business. Those of us lacking business acumen or experience find it especially difficult to start, fearing sure defeat from our lack of preparedness.

My journey in business started with very humble beginnings, from no business experience or educational preparation and minimal capital to the eventual growth of a successful, impactful, purpose-driven venture. My experience is proof-positive that success is not only attainable without the traditional means of preparation, but also that a particular subcategory of success can actually emerge from the most challenging experiences of our lives. I define these as ***lemon experiences***: life challenges so paralyzing that they threaten to cripple every aspect of our existence, compromising our belief that success in any direction could ever be possible.

You may be navigating through a lemon experience right now or have endured one in the past. Know that there is purpose in your pain. And if you have the courage to push through it, life will reveal a bouquet of possibilities that may include changing careers, starting a non-profit, involvement in activism, or perhaps even the launch of a product or delivery of a service offering. *Your lemon experiences hold particular power to unearth your life's purpose.* Inherent in them lie the seeds to germinate a sustainably profitable, purpose-driven venture that can impact the world! This book will encourage and empower you to view your lemon experiences as strengths rather than weaknesses and press forward with hope and tangible strategies you can implement to realize success in your own life.

THERE'S NO PERFECT TIME TO START AN ENTREPRENEURIAL JOURNEY. The conditions will never be perfect, and you'll never be completely prepared for all of the challenges you'll face. Most successful entrepreneurs, past and present, have been exactly where you are now. My hope is that, through reading this book, you'll find the courage to launch your business or entrepreneurial venture and believe that success is possible for you as well!

Full disclosure: This book is not a conventional book on business, and many of the perspectives and strategies shared here will not be found in the curriculum of any MBA or business preparatory program. This is not a traditional "how-to-start-a-business" guide, as there are a plethora of existing resources that accomplish that aim. My intent, rather, is to provide you with actionable tools on how to build *a solid foundation* for sustainable success in business, a preamble of sorts to the mechanics of establishing and operating a successful and impactful growth venture.

This book is by no means an exhaustive list of all the components necessary to build a successful business, but it is a representation of key strategies I implemented on my journey to success that were foundational to all the rest.

SO, WHY AM I A CREDIBLE SOURCE OF INFORMATION ON THIS TOPIC?

Given the statistics that only forty percent of small businesses are profitable, fifty percent fold by their second year, and only three in ten make it to year ten,[1] my journey to success was unlikely and unprecedented for someone with no business background or experience and very little capital. I started my first entrepreneurial venture just prior to the economic downturn of the Great Recession and weathered intense storms during that time, which included many victories and defeats, market changes, and a myriad of personal and professional challenges. But I eventually realized my goal to build a sustainably successful, purpose-driven business that was impactful. It positively impacted:

1. The lives of tens of thousands of people living in some of the most rural and remote areas of Canada

2. The Canadian healthcare system

3. The staff that were placed in jobs across Canada

4. Their families living locally and abroad

After thirteen years, I successfully sold my business and started my business management consulting practice, *Aere Management Consulting*, where I share my success strategies with struggling entrepreneurs and business owners. I show them how to create and/or develop purpose-driven, impactful, sustainably successful businesses so they can earn more, work less, and experience a truly fulfilling life.

Everything I outline in this book has been gleaned from all my entrepreneurial ventures, past and present, and lessons I learned from my two most significant lemon experiences. My rise to success took many years and involved a significant amount of trial and error, knowledge gleaned from over seventy-five business and personal development books, the accumulation of hundreds of thousands of dollars of debt, and significant personal sacrifices

---

1 Graham Isador, "12 Surprising Entrepreneur Statistics To Know In 2021." NorthOne, https://www.northone.com/blog/small-business/entrepreneur-statistics

to become an expert on both the process of spiritually anchoring one's business, and how to successfully build a purpose-driven venture.

In this book, I've distilled the knowledge I've gleaned and the lessons I learned into seventeen strategies, which you can now apply to your business—potentially saving you an enormous amount of time, money, energy, and heartache on your road to success.

Here, I will teach you how to build a solid foundation for your venture, as building a business from scratch is much like building a house. In order for it to stand the test of time and offer you the benefits of its intended use, it must be designed effectively, the foundation must consist of strong materials, and it must be constructed well. And if you plan to eventually sell it, staging it effectively is important too. Your business needs to be built well to stand the test of time and weather the storms that are sure to come. Building it with a solid foundation is imperative, and I will teach you how to do so effectively.

There are times when business owners and entrepreneurs become bogged down with the daily activities of working IN their ventures—making their product or delivering their service—and the activities and competencies necessary to build the business for future growth take a back seat. Here I'll help you refocus and pivot from not only working IN your business but also ON your business, a necessary component to creating a sustainably successful venture.

I also write this book with the knowledge I've gleaned from my faith, which informs every aspect of my life, solidified through my lemon experiences. Regardless of the direction of your spiritual compass, however, the underlying concepts I share are applicable to anyone's life, and, most assuredly, they can also be applied to your entrepreneurial journey.

WE ARE MEANT TO LIVE OUR LIFE'S PURPOSE. ONCE WE DISCOVER OUR purpose, we'll find a place of power, protection, provision, promise, and ultimately, peace. As the adage states: "When life gives you lemons, make lemonade!" Squeezing your "life lemons" can absolutely create lemonade (your success). Plus, your personal and professional transformation throughout your journey can positively impact those around you to step out in courage to move in the direction of their purpose as well. This cumulative effect—you living your life's purpose as well as influencing others to do the same—contains within it the seeds to germinate a changed world through your success.

"MOM SAYS IF LIFE GIVES YOU LEMONS...
GO OUT AND MAKE A FEW BUCKS!"

As you read, I encourage you to let go of your preconceived notions about how to achieve success in business and allow me to challenge your feelings about your current abilities, your insecurities, and your current understanding of the concept of faith. While there is no guarantee that you will experience success from applying the strategies outlined in this book, I encourage you to give yourself uninhibited permission to progress through a process of discovery and transformation. Doing so will open you up to more opportunities to achieve higher heights than you ever imagined possible.

I haven't been gifted with exceptional intelligence, so if I can do it, so can you! Armed solely with an understanding of *my* purpose, faith, and a recognition of the power inherent in my lemon experiences, I started and grew what became a sustainably successful, impactful, purpose-driven business. Later, I'll share with you my seventeen influential strategies for success. But first, I hope you'll gain some perspective on the power inherent in your own lemon experiences by getting to know my personal journey a bit better. So, let's get into it!

MY STORY

IT WAS MY SENIOR YEAR OF HIGH SCHOOL IN CALGARY, CANADA. AT THE behest of my parents, I was bound for university in the U.S., enrolled in a program that would lead to a career in medicine. For as long as I could remember, this had been my plan, given that either doctor or lawyer were the only two options presented. As I was preparing to take the next steps along my educational journey, however, an intuitive state of panic set in since I intrinsically knew a career in medicine was not actually my calling. This state of panic left me feeling as though I was about to experience a nightmare. Reared with a clear directive to attain a higher level of success than my middle-class parents, I felt myself buckling under the pressure to progress forward in the direction my parents had expected, despite feeling overwhelmingly torn between the options of pleasing them and staying close to home to continue exploring one of the most amazing aspects of life that had recently unfolded.

Winter had given way to spring, and Janet Jackson's newly released single, "That's the Way Love Goes," was providing the soundtrack to my life. I was completely in love with my first boyfriend, and the entire world was more beautiful as a result. Everything seemed brighter, sweeter, more melodious, and aromatic. This love and my carefree, avoidant stance at the time threatened my future that was meticulously planned to commence in the coming months more than 1,000 miles away. I was so passionate about our young relationship that I found myself sacrificing more and more of my life for him, including my three jobs, family time, study time, and exams.

As is typical with young love, concocting excuses to be with him had become the norm. On one particular occasion, I wanted so badly to get out of taking an exam at school to spend more time with him that securing a doctor's note for my excuse seemed like the perfect plan. After shamefully feigning illness, I managed to persuade my family physician to write me a note excusing me from class. For further "proof," I requested it be accompanied by a requisition for blood work. Unbeknownst to me at the time, that delinquent request would impact the course of my life.

To strengthen the veracity of my claim of illness, I decided to follow through with the blood work. Looking back, I'm amazed at the lengths I took to accomplish my nefarious means! Weeks gave way to months, and as stress mounted before graduation and my impending separation from my first love, I started to develop an actual illness. Pervasive abdominal cramping, shortness of breath, and debilitating weakness crept up on me with a vengeance, accompanied by shorter and shorter bouts of reprieve. After weeks of numerous visits to doctors and hours of attempts to draw blood from my critically dehydrated body, I was eventually rushed to a hospital unit from an emergency room, where I was quickly diagnosed with acute promyelocytic leukemia. My prior blood work provided my medical team with the information they needed to determine the quick progression of my disease, which in turn guided the course of my treatment. Within hours, everything in my life had changed. My driving force was no longer love; it was survival, and the lemon experience that would change the course of my life had begun.

AMID ALL THE SHOCK AND THE FLURRY OF CHANGE HAPPENING ALL around me, I felt a pervasive sense of stillness. To this day, I'm at a loss for words to describe it accurately. Tangibly present within me was a faith that I would ultimately survive; somehow, I just knew I would make it through. The first words I spoke to my oncologist after learning of my prognosis were, "Give me the treatment needed and let's go. I'll recover!" Despite having just completed grade-12 biology, which granted me a working understanding of the pathophysiology of leukemia, and even after hearing the stoic prognosis relayed by my oncologist, I remained hopeful, believing without reservation that God would ultimately heal me.

As months progressed, I began to develop a constant array of side effects as a result of my chemotherapy. At five feet, four inches tall and eighty-eight pounds due to rapid weight loss, the all-night nausea and vomiting sessions, inability to tolerate walking short distances, and bouts of blindness were often too much for my weak body to bear.

I was just a girl. When I saw myself in the mirror, I no longer recognized my reflection. I was physically and emotionally emaciated—confused and trying to make sense of it all. My jovial nature gave way to hours of deep introspection without uttering a word to anyone, worrying my family and medical team. I'd have frequent, unproductive conversations with multiple psychotherapists, all the while still believing without a doubt that God would see me through.

Though they were concerning to those around me, my lengthy periods of quiet introspection actually laid the foundation for one of my most effective success strategies that I would later apply to my business. During those periods, I would visualize life after leukemia: *Where would I go? What would life look like after my healing? How would my life change as a result of this experience?* Given my seventeen-year-old mentality at the time, I was mostly excited that I would no longer be forced to attend the school of my mother's choosing, but visualizing a life outside of the pain of my circumstances was pivotal to not only my transformation physically, but also my personal and the professional transformation of my business over a decade later.

I'd spent years dreaming of visiting Hawaii in my teens and used the uninterrupted, hours-long gazes out my hospital window to visualize *my* version of it. I imagined the smell, the feeling of the sand between my toes, and what the crashing waves against the beach at sunset would look and sound like. This would mesmerize me for hours, and it provided me the strength to endure the plethora of excruciatingly painful bone-marrow aspirations, a procedure where a lengthy needle is drilled into a bone in the lower back to draw out bone marrow for testing, providing medical staff necessary information on the condition of the bone marrow and blood cells. I also endured painful central line dressing changes, constant fatigue, bouts of blindness lasting for days, as well as pervasive throat, stomach, and abdominal issues. The physical turmoil of my illness was debilitating, but it paled in comparison to the emotional toll of the illness, an experience so impactful it became foundational to every major life decision I made thereafter.

DESPITE RECEIVING WORLD-CLASS CLINICAL CARE DURING MY HOSPITALizations, the emotional care I experienced was woefully substandard. Making sense of my leukemia experience was overwhelming, especially since I was a teenager at the time and did not have the benefit of access to a Leukemia & Lymphoma Society chapter or another cancer support group, as is the case for many cancer patients today. None of my family or friends had ever navigated the cancer journey either, so I felt completely alone.

It was usually a hurried exchange when the nursing staff interacted with me. A comforting, engaged connection with my medical staff was rare, which left me feeling disregarded by the people I believed would have had the capacity to understand the trauma I was experiencing. IV chemotherapy had to be calculated, hung, and infused. My dressings had to be changed, and medication had to be dispensed on time, among a myriad of other nursing duties. There seemed to be no end to the necessities of my care, and dedicated time allotted to connect with me in a meaningful way did not appear to be a priority.

One evening, during my second hospitalization, the trajectory of my illness changed instantaneously. I had contracted a potentially life-threatening blood infection and, upon receiving news of the rapid progression of my disease as a result, my mother quickly arranged an intense prayer session with leaders from our church. I was so weak and distracted that the sound of their impassioned prayers over my hospital bed, for what seemed like hours, washed over me as I felt myself falling toward warmth, peace, and a strangely invisible light that was shining in the midst of intense darkness. Slowly drifting out of consciousness, I found myself surrendering my life while talking with God, giving thanks for all the joys of life I was blessed to have experienced to that point. After declaring that I was ready "to go" in what seemed to be my last conversation with God on earth, I suddenly awoke.

It was the next day, and lying beside me in my hospital bed was my mother, calm and at peace. From that day forward, the entire trajectory of my illness transformed: blood counts quickly improved, strength welled up inside me, and weight gain proved possible. In the days prior to my discharge from the hospital, the nursing staff informed me that after that crucial night, to that date, my improvement had progressed faster than any other patient with my condition, and I've been cancer-free ever since! Faith unlocked the miracle of my transformation, and I would come to understand the power of the experience, and the reasoning behind it, more clearly in the years to come.

Years later, I graduated from the local school of my choice, albeit with the Bachelor of Science degree in biology my mother had encouraged. As it turned out, the ramifications of the feelings of panic I'd experienced during my senior year in high school eventually manifested in the reality of my circumstances after graduation. Even though it became crystal clear early in my college experience that a career in medicine was not my passion, I pressed forward and completed it anyway. After graduating with a degree I had come to realize would have no bearing on my vocational future, feelings of guilt and fear had started to set in. Although my parents were incredibly disappointed, they were overwhelmingly supportive of my desire to chart out another path toward success and gave me—a confused, still emotionally broken twenty-two-year-old—the space to figure it out.

Over a year later, while working as a microbiology lab technician, a position tangentially related to my Bachelor of Science degree, I arrived at a crossroads. Overwhelmed with feelings of frustration, while confused, unfulfilled, and directionless, I made the decision to let go to the only source of help and direction I felt I could trust to truly lead me out of this new darkness I'd fallen into. One night, I made the decision to give God the uninhibited chance to lead me into an understanding of my purpose and what was to be the next stage of my journey.

That night, after crying incessantly about the plight of my life, I came to a crossroads—a breaking point of sorts—and was overcome with a paralyzing sense of dread. Then, these words rested heavily on my heart and mind:

What are you passionate about?
If you're going to do something for eight hours a day,
it should be something you actually care about!

As night gave way to morning, the only "something I cared about" that continually pressed on my mind was my battle with leukemia and the heavy emotional toll I was still grappling with. I wanted to choose a career that would help ensure that no other patient would endure the trauma of my emotionally debilitating hospital experience. So, I decided to work backward.

I made the choice to allow my predominant passion, generated from my leukemia lemon experience, to drive my career. Since I believed that the worst of my experience resulted from my interactions with the nurses, it became crystal clear that I should pursue a career in nursing. So, I took steps to enroll at university again, on my own this time, to complete a degree in nursing.

I wish I could tell you that I experienced a steady, upward trajectory to success thereafter. However, when I started my career as a registered nurse, I quickly realized that the substandard emotional care I had received had little to do with the nursing staff and more to do with the state of the healthcare system at the time. Just prior to my hospitalization, a vast nursing shortage had crippled the healthcare system where I lived, which directly impacted the quality of care I received. Now that I was an RN myself, providentially working alongside the very nurses who had cared for me almost a decade prior, I realized that the care a nurse can provide when they have four patients is very different from the care they can provide when they have eleven. It was the system, not the nurses, that had created the compromised emotional care I experienced as a patient. With that realization, I knew that my purpose, at this stage, was to positively impact the healthcare system and create conditions by which patients could receive quality patient care, especially in regions that were suffering the most due to their critical shortages of nursing staff.

After coming to that realization, I was never at peace as an RN. I absolutely loved connecting one-on-one with patients and the opportunity to provide the personalized care I had so desperately desired during my own hospitalizations. However, years into my career, I realized that operating outside of my purpose (which I now realized was to positively impact *the system* that had created the compromised emotional care I received) only left me feeling frustrated again, unfulfilled, and yearning for more. Despite curating a six-figure lifestyle working as both a per diem RN and travel nurse, I suffered a crushing bout of burnout. I was on course—I needed to continue working as an RN to understand both the complexities of the nursing shortage and the motivations and desires of RNs—but was yearning for more and unsure of how "more" would come together. Albeit debilitating, my experience with burnout set the stage for the most pivotal stage of my journey, which would eventually lead to the start of a successful career in business.

DESPITE HAVING NO BUSINESS EXPERIENCE, EDUCATIONAL BUSINESS training, or understanding of how to start, operate, or grow a business, I set out to prove that it *was* possible to find RNs to work in the most hard-to-recruit areas, which in many cases are rural and remote regions. I planned to address the comprehensive, detrimental impact of the nursing shortage on the system, which was harmful to the nurses and, most directly, had a negative impact on patients. Never in my wildest dreams did I believe *I* could positively impact the delivery of healthcare in my area, let alone become successful doing so! Drawing on my faith that had now guided me both vocationally and through my near-death experience with leukemia, I made the terrifying decision to launch out, as the time had come to change course and start an RN recruitment firm. Despite my fear, insecurity, and a pervasive sense of a lack of preparedness to start a business, I allowed my faith and the passion generated from my leukemia lemon experience to lead me, which, incidentally, became foundational to my ability to transform my challenging life experiences into success in business.

Many of us have endured lemon experiences that, unfortunately, we've allowed to stymie our growth and belief in our ability to achieve success. Full disclosure: I haven't been gifted with any special skill or trait that sets me apart. Like me, you may have survived a near-death experience or another lemon experience that has emotionally, intellectually, physically, and/or financially paralyzed you too. Maybe you're ready to graduate high school or college and are unsure about your vocational future, or maybe you're feeling burned out, working in a career that is wholly unfulfilling. Maybe you'd rather forget about it all and just move on. You may be fearful or anxious about the future, wondering how you fit in the grand scheme of things and don't know where to go from here.

I have been you.

With no business experience or education and little capital, I started what grew to become a successful business by using:

1. An understanding of my purpose

2. Wisdom gleaned from squeezing an understanding of my lemon experiences

3. Key principles I learned from over seventy-five business books and biblical scripture

4. Lessons learned from many trial-and-error experiences along the way

…and, in this book, I've distilled all of it into seventeen strategies you can use to create success as well!

It has been said that talent is as cheap as table salt; what separates the talented individual from the successful one is a lot of hard work.[2] With drive, focus, faith, a clear understanding of your purpose, and through the application of key strategies for success, you, too, can transform the lemon experiences of your life into a successful business. Let's dive into the how…

---

2 Stephen King quote: https://www.brainyquote.com/quotes/stephen_king_16365

PART ONE

The Inner Work

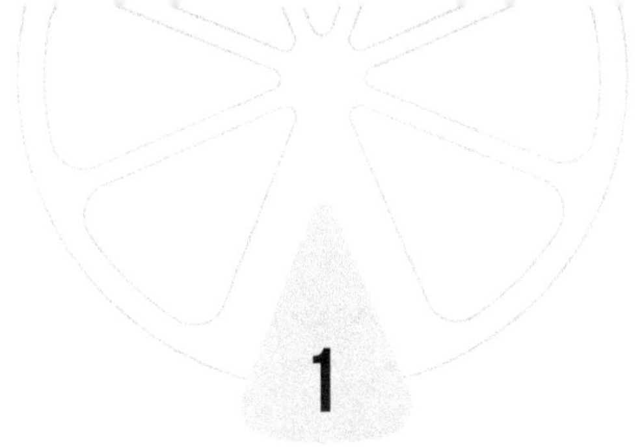

1

TELL YOURSELF THE TRUTH, QUICKLY

"Sunlight is the greatest disinfectant."

—ANONYMOUS

YOU ARE UNIQUE. YOUR SPECIFIC BIOLOGY, ALONG WITH ALL OF YOUR experiences, makes you uniquely you. No other person on earth can operate from your perspective. Why? Your life, exactly as it is, has been shaped by your environment and experiences.

We've all been through experiences that have threatened to break us. Perhaps you're still navigating your way through one right now. As I'm writing this, the world is grappling with the effects of the COVID-19 pandemic, which has indelibly impacted all of us, whether directly or indirectly. Be it a job loss, business closure, or the illness or death of a loved one, we are living in a world where the reality of transformational change, positive or negative, is all around us.

My near-death experience with leukemia changed the trajectory of my life. More than the physical challenges that accompanied the diagnosis, the emotional trauma of the experience was incredibly debilitating. Even after surviving the experience, I felt completely alone and mentally broken. The survivor guilt was confusing; at seventeen, I didn't understand why I survived over the many others that didn't, and I felt burdened by the heavy responsibility to create meaning from my life as a result. I still saw myself as that emaciated, eighty-eight-pound, weak girl in the mirror, and even though I had long surpassed that season, my eroded perception of myself continued to permeate every aspect of my life for years.

And then, during my crossroads moment, I decided to tell myself the truth.

Cancer happened.
I survived it.
It didn't have the power to change me unless I allowed it.
I was no less the person I was before it.
And God gave me another chance at life for a reason; of this, I was sure, and I was determined to find out why.

I decided to view my experience with leukemia as a *life lemon*—an event, circumstance, or experience so painful and debilitating that it can alter the course of our lives. I still feel a sting of pain as I reflect on my lemon experiences: leukemia and my journey to recovery after a debilitating car accident where I was hit by an intoxicated driver, rendering me physically unable to continue working as a floor RN. A true life lemon will invariably have the pervasive effect of a residual sting.

Learning to embrace the emotions generated from traumatizing events and experience them fully is both a blessing and a curse. A blessing, as it enables us to acknowledge our experiences so we can move to the next level of healing. A curse because staying in that emotional space for an extended period of time can lead to unintended physical, emotional, spiritual, or financial circumstances.

My crossroad moment was pivotal. It was only when I was able to fully experience my crippling emotions and tell myself the truth about my life that I was able to finally move forward. If I hadn't, I would never have been emotionally able to transition onto the road to entrepreneurial success.

The same can be true for you. The first step to turning your lemon experiences into a successful venture is telling yourself the full truth about them—and quickly. Locking painful experiences away in the recesses of your mind only gives them the power to control and suppress you, and the longer you stay in that state, the more potentially damaging the experience. In the long run, telling yourself the truth will directly impact the viability of your venture since the issues that affect us personally eventually impact us professionally.

The faster you arrive at a place of willingness to tell yourself the truth, the faster you can get on with the business of creating sustainable success.

Dealing with the emotions that result from your lemon experiences may require professional help—and that's absolutely okay! I've greatly benefited from counseling and mental health resources at key points during my journey and can vouch for how powerful and effective they can be in helping you navigate the inevitable challenges on your journey to success.

Panic attacks, along with bouts of anxiety and depression, were an unexpected reality in my early years of entrepreneurship. According to *Inc. Magazine*, thirty-two percent of entrepreneurs suffer from two or more mental health conditions.[1] Start-ups are especially rife with situations that counter advice from mental wellness experts, such as living under intense and sustained mental, emotional, physical, relational, and financial pressure. As entrepreneurs, we tend to shoulder too many responsibilities, especially in the beginning of our journeys, and operate in sustained, high-stress conditions. But one thing that sets successful businesses apart from the rest is that rather than ignoring mental health struggles, their leaders challenge themselves and their teams to face them head-on.

Whatever method you choose, be it professional help or a trusted friend's listening ear, it's imperative that you gain resolution and tell yourself the truth about not only your life lemons, but also the state of your overall health. (This will help you acknowledge the health of your venture as well.) Otherwise, your unresolved issues will invariably visit you during the formative years of your business and threaten its viability.

So, start now and tell yourself the truth about your life:
What is the state of your finances?
What is the state of your marriage or relationships with significant others?
Are you experiencing burnout?
Do you lack direction for your life overall?
Is your sense of self-worth sabotaging you?
Are your lifestyle habits wreaking havoc on your health?
Are you living a lie in one or more areas of your life?
Nothing in your life will change unless you first acknowledge the issues

and tell yourself the truth about them. The quicker you do so, the quicker you can move toward the life you envision.

So, acknowledge your life lemons, past or present.

Sit with the associated emotions and deal with them; seek professional help if needed.

Try to understand the accompanying lessons.

Then, release them and commit to turning those lemons into the lemonade of success!

THEY DID IT, AND SO CAN YOU!

Twenty-four percent of Fortune 500 companies were founded during a recession.[2] These companies persevered despite significant economic downturns; they adapted, achieved success and, to this day, continue to excel[3]:

- **Microsoft**: 1973 to 1975 recession

- **Hyatt Hotels**: 1957 to 1958 recession

- **Airbnb**: 2007 to 2009 recession

- **Uber**: born out of the 2007 to 2009 recession

- **Warby Parker**: 2007 to 2009 recession

Many start-ups experience extreme challenges in their early days. But those that endure despite extreme external pressure, financial or otherwise, develop resilience and adaptability. Your past or even present challenges provide you with an opportunity to turn your hardships into opportunities! At the time of writing, Warby Parker, an online prescription glasses retailer with an impressive corporate social responsibility footprint, is valued at $1.75 billion. Founded in a recession, Warby Parker is proof that success is still attainable in the midst of pain.

Given my lack of business experience, I was terrified to launch my business. Armed with only an unquenchable passion for addressing the nursing shortage and belief in a single Bible verse—Matthew 21:22—I set out on my entrepreneurial journey. Acknowledging the truth about my circumstances was the absolute first step in opening me up to available resources and needed help.

The same will be the case for you. According to U.S. entrepreneur statistics from 2021, fifty percent of businesses fail by their second year. By the tenth year, only 3/10 businesses that started up remain in operation.[4] The ones that succeed do so, in part, because they don't ignore anything.[5]

I beat the odds, having operated my business for thirteen years and rising through it all successfully, and you can, too! Learning to quickly and effectively spot problem areas in your business and take steps to adequately address them increases the likelihood that your venture will beat the odds, and you'll experience a state of sustained profitability or sustainable success. It all starts with telling yourself the truth about who you are and what you bring to the table—positive and negative.

PRACTICAL APPLICATIONS

One of my most trusted business associates, Tanya Stevenson, who has a change management background, taught me an invaluable concept in the early years of building my business: People typically don't change course or choose another service, product, or action until or unless they've experienced enough dissatisfaction (or pain) with their current option. My years as a registered nurse absolutely corroborated the validity of this concept. As I cared for countless patients with life-threatening conditions, I noticed that those who refused to stop a behavior—like smoking or drinking—that led to their poor health hadn't *perceived* that the consequences of continuing that behavior were serious enough to warrant a change in action. If the patient didn't experience enough pain to warrant a change of course, they continued with their behavior, even though it was slowly killing them. Unfortunately, the truth of their condition didn't matter until the pain was severe enough. In some cases, however, by the time they had experienced enough pain, it was already too late.

Telling ourselves the truth about our painful situations in life and business before circumstances become untenable is important. In business, once your target market either *perceives* or actually experiences enough pain from staying the course with their current option (current product too expensive or current service not delivering the same level of quality it once did), they will make a change. And if they then begin to purchase your product or service, that change in their purchasing behavior to now choose your option will result in a positive impact on your bottom line!

Telling yourself the truth quickly about your own challenges or pain points in your business will enable you to adapt effectively, change course, and seek options and solutions that will lead to your eventual success. Adaptability, change management, and resilience are all necessary to build a sustainably profitable venture and require the precursor of an honest evaluation of the conditions both around you and within you.

THE DANGER OF A LIE TO THE SUSTAINABILITY OF YOUR BUSINESS

If you don't tell yourself the truth, that point of deception—left unchecked—will eventually become poisonous to your venture. And a venture based on lies simply cannot survive for the long haul.

Think of the business owner who is unwilling to recognize that their employees are unhappy with their leadership, believing rather that the employees are lazy and need to go. Or the vendor that is unwilling to accept that the reason they are losing business from past reliable clients is actually the declining quality of their product. Instead, they are stuck on the belief that changing conditions within their industry or an economic downturn is the cause. Both business owners lack awareness; their actions perpetuate a lie they're telling themselves, that the issues within their organizations are someone else's fault.

The longer a truth remains buried, the more damage it will cause, and the more effort will be required to rescue the individual or business from the state of deception they find themselves in. As the leader of your venture, recognize that *how you operate personally will directly impact how you show up as a leader professionally.*

When leaders spend time rationalizing their actions and stubbornly refuse to demonstrate accountability and admit failures and shortcomings, their problems can snowball into enormous issues later, negatively impacting their business in one form or another.

The truth, and only the truth, sets us free, enabling us to show up with authenticity, energy, and the mental capacity that our ventures deserve. Seasons in your journey toward success will invariably change, and the health of your venture will depend on your willingness to adjust, look at situations objectively, own the part you play in your successes and failures, redirect resources, realign priorities, and develop perspectives based on fact.

The world is filled with people waiting for what you have to offer and teams of people looking to be involved in a venture with purpose, led by a passionate leader. Your authenticity and ability to stand in your truth amid your challenges will differentiate you from your competition and draw others to buy, invest, listen to, or join you. So, own your experiences and how they've shaped you. Make the changes necessary to heal and move forward. Even if you've contributed to the experience(s) of your life lemon(s), acknowledge it and do your inner work, which first starts with telling yourself the truth about the painful experiences of your past and maybe even your present. Experience the associated emotions generated from your lemon experiences fully, work through a process of healing and solicit professional help if you need it, then press toward the accomplishment of your goals.

"The journey of a thousand miles begins with one step."

—Lao-Tzu

If you have the courage to surrender to a transformative process of *you*, you will be led on a journey toward success beyond what you can, even in this moment, imagine possible! **There is purpose in your pain if you have the courage to unearth it.** Take the first step of the transformative process and tell yourself the truth—quickly.

So, what's your story? Chances are you've picked up this book because you've survived challenging life experiences that seemed poised to destroy you—experiences that shook you to your core and have left you yearning for a new direction and hope for the future. These life lemons, although deeply painful, are a gift; they are the same experiences that have the propensity to induce change and start your transformation from pain to prosperity.

What are your life's lemons? What are the most pivotal experiences that have shaped your life, positively or negatively, thus far? If you've already started your venture, what conditions are present within your business that have resulted in a state of stagnation or rendered you unable to transition to tangible success?

Own your story,
take a deep breath,
start now, and
tell yourself the truth.

FOR DEEPER REFLECTION...

Strategy #1: Tell Yourself the Truth, Quickly

1. What are the life lemons you've survived from your past?

2. What have you learned from your lemon experiences?

3. While it's important to acknowledge the impact your lemon experiences have had on your life and experience the emotions generated by them, it's not a good idea to stay in that emotional state for an extended period of time. Why?

4. What are the feelings that are coming up for you as you reflect on your lemon experience(s)?

5. Whom can you turn to to help you navigate the challenging emotions that may arise from this time of reflection?

6. What are the limiting thoughts you have held, or thoughts that are holding you back from fully immersing yourself in your business idea?

7. What are some of the truths you need to tell yourself about the state of your life? If you've already started your venture, what are some truths you need to acknowledge about the state of your venture?

8. There are several ways to demonstrate integrity to yourself. Some include:

   - Waking up right as the alarm clock rings instead of pressing snooze
   - Saving the right amount of money to match your budget
   - Working out for the exact amount of time intended while at the gym

9. What are three areas where you can demonstrate integrity within yourself this week?

10. How will your understanding of your lemon experiences, limiting thoughts, and the truths about the state of your life (and business) help you chart a course toward business success?

2

TWO QUESTIONS THAT WILL CHANGE YOUR LIFE... AND BUSINESS

"There is no greater gift you can give or receive than to honor your calling. It's why you were born. And how you become most truly alive."

—OPRAH

GIVEN THAT FIFTY PERCENT OF SMALL BUSINESSES FOLD BY THEIR SEC- ond year and only forty percent are profitable,[1] it's only natural to feel nervous about starting a business or concerned about your fate if you are currently operating one. Considering our definition of a successful entrepreneur—one that solves problems at a profit from the perspective of their purpose—could it be that a contributing factor to the challenging state of entrepreneurship today might lie in the owner's definition of their success, thereby impacting how they operate their ventures? Over the years, I've had the opportunity to connect with a myriad of entrepreneurs and business owners and have found that too few take the time to complete their inner work, and make the decision to operate their ventures from an understanding of their life's purpose. When businesses start with the primary goal of achieving financial freedom, power, and prestige, it is unlikely that any success achieved will lead to a sense of fulfillment or contentment. While some business owners or entrepreneurs may, indeed, beat the odds to be counted among the thirty percent that accomplish sustainable success and make it to year ten and beyond in their business,[1] nothing can compare to *purpose-driven success* that leads to peace, which is my hope for you!

Rick Warren's book, *The Purpose Driven Life*, is one of the most successful non-fiction books of all time[2]—and for good reason. Translated into 137 languages and with over fifty million copies sold, its popularity reflects our insatiable quest to find our life's purpose and how living our purpose fully can lead to a truly abundant life.

In his 1846 book, *Walden*, philosopher and poet Henry David Thoreau famously introduced the idea that most people "live lives of quiet desperation,"[3] lives that conform to the status quo while quietly and desperately yearning for more. Over 175 years later, society is still plagued by the same plight, as too many of us seek satisfaction in position, power, and prosperity in life only to find that, without purpose, success is hollow and unsatisfying.

Living from a place of purpose is an intimidating concept for many. It often conjures up feelings of fear or anxiety, and some find the pursuit of purpose overwhelming. However, if you don't explore your particular purpose, there will be a void in both you and the world that only your purpose can fill.

A life lived in and on purpose germinates hope, energy, direction, drive, and leads to true fulfillment. Without purpose, life's challenges, generated from both poverty and riches, can prove too much to bear. According to the Well Being Trust—a national foundation dedicated to advancing the vision of a nation where everyone is socially, mentally, and spiritually well—unemployment during the Great Recession of 2007 to 2009 correlated with an increase in suicide and drug overdose deaths.[4] On the flip side, the suicide deaths of famous figures like American actress Marilyn Monroe, celebrity chef Anthony Bourdain, fashion designer Kate Spade, and others show that being successful or financially wealthy does not shield one from feelings of hopelessness[5] and despair either.

Life without purpose is ultimately meaningless. Gifting ourselves with the time to fully explore the question of purpose in our own lives is key to achieving success that leads to true fulfillment and peace. In my case, telling myself the truth and gifting myself with the opportunity to fully break in my crossroads moment actually allowed for the tilling up of the stubborn, fearful, and anxious ground of my heart and mind. This ended up revealing an understanding of my purpose. Position, power, and prosperity—goals typically revered in Western societies—can indeed be the by-products of a purpose-driven life. However, if living our purpose takes a back seat to anything, we will never live to our full potential or experience a truly abundant life.

In my own experience, wealth amassed in my late twenties only ushered in feelings of emptiness, disappointment, and despondency and did not translate into the sense of accomplishment and fulfillment that I had imagined it would. My thoughts regularly pulsated with feelings of angst and frustration. I asked myself: *Is this all there is? There's got to be more to life than this!* Eventually, I came to realize that material success without a clear path toward purpose doesn't lead to fulfillment or peace. But don't lose hope! An abundant life is attainable as long as you live your life in and on purpose.

Operating from a place of purpose is freedom. And life's challenges are significantly more manageable once you understand your purpose. In business, a clear understanding of the reason for being, clearly defined goals, and the communication of tangible action plans for future growth are incredibly important. But we as business owners or entrepreneurs often don't employ the same level of specificity to chart the course of our own lives. Many don't take the time to determine their purpose. Could this be a contributing factor to the high failure rate of early small businesses and the reason why many people end up living lives of quiet desperation?

Undoubtedly, the willingness to ask and answer questions about our purpose requires courage, self-awareness, and humility. Abandoning our desire for material success to truly understand our reason for being is countercultural, especially in Western societies, but it is necessary to achieve the type of success that leads to true fulfillment and peace.

THE CONVERSATION THAT CHANGED MY LIFE

I was first introduced to the power of purpose on a first-class flight from Chicago to Paris. Exhausted from a long stretch of night shifts, I was more excited about the opportunity to sleep on the flight than the prospect of landing in Paris for the first time. But my dreams of undisturbed rest in my window seat were shattered as I was joined in my row by a corporate executive from an Ivy-League American university who talked nonstop. As I listened to her wax poetic on the love she had for her job, I began to realize the life-changing nature of this conversation.

Up until that point, I had never heard anyone speak about their work with such passion and joy. Her love for her job emanated from her, and although she humbly discussed her success, it was her sheer passion for her work that truly impacted me.

I was stunned by our exchange. I reflected on my feelings of burnout and despondency toward my own career, and after she spoke, I mustered up the courage to ask her how she arrived at this place of feeling such joy in her role.

I've never forgotten her response:

"Melane, if you're going to do something for eight hours or more a day, it should be something that you're passionate about."

It immediately resonated with the thought impressed on my mind and heart years prior during my crossroads moment, which, incidentally, directed me to pursue a career in nursing in the first place! This time, however, the idea ignited a *new* fire in me to keep going, and in listening to her, I came to realize that *passion was related to purpose.* I realized working as an RN was not the end of my journey; it was only a stepping-stone. Despite earning six figures and enjoying the lifestyle that accompanied it, the feelings of burnout and lack of fulfillment were key indicators that I was not yet exploring the full capacity of my purpose. *That* was the reason for my feelings of emptiness and despair! I was nearing the end of this stage of my journey and was ripe for a change, a reset of sorts. This conversation was pivotal to my understanding of the power of purpose. It set me on a path to realign myself and work toward turning my lemon experiences into the lemonade of my success!

YOUR PURPOSE: A CLOSER LOOK

Unearthing your purpose need not be daunting. It's simpler than you might think! The challenge lies in our willingness to surrender to the process of discovery and our openness to receive an understanding of our purpose once it is revealed.

The two questions that will change your life and business are:

What is my purpose?
How do I accomplish it?

Answering both will change your life and business by opening you up to operate from a place of passion rather than a place of duty, fulfillment rather than despondency, and abundance instead of struggle. Businesses that operate from a place of purpose are significantly more attractive to their target market and have their "reason for being" to fall back on when the going gets tough. When you understand why you are in business, that reason will propel you to push past your difficulties and persevere toward the accomplishment of your goals. The problem you are solving at a profit *needs* you and your business to operate from a congruent place of purpose, and the strength of your understanding of that need will help you develop resilience.

Furthermore, purpose is a powerful marketing, recruiting, and retention tool to help you maximize the growth of your business. When your target market understands and resonates with your reason for being, they will be more inclined to purchase your product or service. Purpose is a powerful recruitment and retention tool since the workforce today is far more inclined to choose employment or stay employed at a company that has values congruent to theirs and a company guided by principles beyond just profit.

When your team, client base, investors, and vendors understand that they are part of a worthy cause that aligns with their values and beliefs, they are significantly more likely to invest in your success, increasing the likelihood that you will achieve your goals!

Purpose is pivotal.

Accurately discerning it is transformational.

Living it leads to true abundance, wealth in many forms and, most importantly, peace.

THE ELEMENTS OF YOUR PURPOSE

When your answers to the two questions are revealed to you, they will most likely seem too obvious to be true. But welcome that! Allow yourself to think of the possibilities within them, irrespective of your education level, financial situation, experience, or anything else you think you'll need to achieve it.

Your lemon experience(s) provide clear clues, directing you to the passion that will lead to the revelation of your purpose. Even though life can be challenging, some of those difficult experiences have directly or indirectly prepared us to operate in our life's purpose. Once we've healed from the associated trauma, we often develop a sense of duty to ensure other people don't experience similar challenge(s) or a desire to help those who do, to bypass the pitfalls we've endured.

So, how can you unearth your purpose and determine your answers to the two questions that will change your life and business? I discovered mine using a simple two-step process:

STEP 1: *Define your reason for being*

Since I believe in God and trust that the Bible is a guidebook for life, I surrendered to the understanding of a passage of scripture that provides powerful clarity on this subject of purpose:

> *"For we are [God's] workmanship, created in Christ Jesus for good works, which God prepared beforehand that we should walk in them."* [6]
>
> —*Ephesians 2:10*

The understanding that we are here—we have been given the gift of life on this earth, right now—to perform "good works" *is the power behind the question of purpose.* In essence, we are here *to be of service!* Therefore, the key to unearthing your life's purpose lies in your understanding of your capacity *to serve.* In other words, what would you do for free if you could? What would you do with your days if money were not an issue? How can you best be of service to your current sphere of influence? Your unfiltered answers represent the first step to unearthing your purpose.

STEP 2: *Acknowledge your skills and your predominant passion*

Reflect on your inherent skills. What talent flows naturally from you? What are you particularly good at? If you aren't sure, ask a trusted friend or family member. Do you have artistic skills? Are you a great organizer? Communicator? Cook? Great with children? At this point, abandon the desire to go beyond the answer to this one question (*What are your skills?*) and stay present. Quiet your spirit and allow the answer to flow to you. The more you fight the process or get ahead of yourself, the harder it will be to complete the process of unearthing your purpose.

Reflect on your passions as well. Think about what irks you, what drives you to act on, read about, or invest an inordinate amount of time in. Take time to spy on yourself and notice what consumes your thoughts. Does watching the injustices exacted against others consume your thoughts and drive you to get involved in activism? Are you moved by the plight of immigrant women in your community and the challenges they face in accessing local resources to start their own businesses? Are you passionate about finding actionable solutions to address homelessness? Do you have an invention you believe will alleviate the symptoms of a particular disease? Most importantly, does your passion drive you to take a particular action? Have you expended time, effort, or money in the pursuit of this passion?

Squeezing your lemon experience(s) or evaluating them from every angle—how they drive you and have shaped you—will help reveal an understanding of your predominant passion, a component of your purpose. In my case, my negative hospital experience and the physical and emotional challenges I faced after my car accident propelled me with a fierce desire to help others. I was most passionate about ensuring my experience would not become the norm, and I wanted to be able to encourage and empower others with the tools I implemented to thrive after both of my lemon experiences. *Your predominant passion(s) will be the #1 driver toward the accomplishment of your business goals* and will help you through many a dark day on your journey toward success. This is why determining your predominant passion(s) is so key.

A DEEPER DIVE INTO PURPOSE

Take time. Step back and evaluate your life with as much honesty and transparency as you can muster. Give yourself permission to progress through a process of discovery—no judgment. Abandon thoughts like, *How would I make money on this?* or *What do I actually know about providing this type of service on a large scale anyway?* During my process, I made the decision just to let go and let God lead me into the answers, trusting that if He brings us to a precipice point in our lives, He will absolutely bring us through it.

I also realized that my passions and skills were actually God's gifts to me! Not only did I come to understand there is a precise "good work" that I am here to deliver, but I would actually like doing it because I already cared about it and possessed the basic skills to accomplish it!

Serving the world *will* fulfill you. When you surrender to the process of discovery, the answers will be made clear. Listen and watch; life will invariably reveal them.

Know that a revelation of your purpose is typically not associated with a grand, ceremonious, aha moment with angels singing. Full disclosure: I thought it would be!

The truth is you already know it.
The question is: Are you ready to accept it,
start living it,
and experience the success that will overflow from it?

For greater clarity, consider the following formula that identifies the key components of purpose:

Passion + Skills = Purpose

Let's explore each aspect of the equation:

Passion.

Think for a moment of a positive experience you've had with a vendor because it was evident that they were passionate about their craft. Did your experience render you willing to pay a higher price or tolerate inconveniences to continue to support their business? When we operate from a place of passion, the quality of our resulting work is exponentially more effective and impactful than when we work simply to work. Taking time to evaluate the activities that bring you joy, peace, and meaning will help you gain a clearer picture of your purpose and direct you to pursuits that are congruent with it.

Two bakeries, one in my hometown, Crave Cupcakes, and one from Philadelphia, Denise's Delicacies, are powerful examples of businesses that clearly operate from a position of passion. They present their creations so intricately and have excellent customer service, of course. But most importantly, you can really taste the care, attention, and passion they have for their craft. The chocolate cupcakes from Crave and the red velvet and pound cake from Denise's are second to none! Essentially, when you're operating your venture with passion, it completely shows in the quality of your product and the delivery of your service, and more often than not, your target market will be drawn to purchase from you again and again because of it. And if you are so blessed, they may even become one of your brand ambassadors as well!

NATURE'S EXAMPLE OF THE POWER INHERENT IN YOUR LEMON EXPERIENCES

Nothing is ever wasted—no experience, positive or negative—and science provides a powerful perspective to understand this concept further. According to the first law of thermodynamics, energy cannot be created or destroyed; it can only be changed from one form to another.[7,8] In essence, energy *is always conserved.*

We can use this law to illustrate the point that the energy generated from your lemon experience(s)—the strength of your pain, the power of your brokenness, anger, fear, or shame—still exists after the fact. *It's up to us* to convert that energy into another form! Why not redirect this energy and have it drive you to deliver your "good work" of service to the world? Why not allow your lemon experiences to do you and others good? You *can* squeeze the benefit inherent in these lemon experiences and use them to propel you toward success!

Skills.

One of the beauties of life is that each one of us has been blessed with at least one tangible skill, something that emanates from us so naturally that we may not even identify it as anything of consequence. You may be a master negotiator but not understand how you can use it to serve others. You may have been inventing products since you were a child, but feel that your inventions are nothing more than hobbies. You may have been told you are a great writer and feel energized when you write poetry but believe it's something just for you, not recognizing that the power of your words may bring healing and hope to others.

Look no further than Amanda Gorman for an example of the power of our skills. The poem she wrote for President Joe Biden's inauguration stirred the world, and within hours, her two forthcoming books shot to the top of Amazon's bestseller list.[9] Likewise, her book, *The Hill We Climb*, rose to #1 on the *New York Times* bestseller list and other lists[10] immediately after publication. Her skillfully written poem and masterful delivery caught the attention of former President Barack Obama, who, after the inauguration, tweeted:

> *On a day for the history books, @TheAmandaGorman*
> *delivered a poem that more than met the moment.*
> *Young people like her are proof that "there is always light,*
> *if only we're brave enough to see it;*
> *if only we're brave enough to be it."[11]*

Your strengths have the ability to positively impact others. If something as simple as a poem can resonate so strongly as to drive book sales to #1, even before the poem was created into a book, your skills can also be used to impact the world around you.

Operating out of the overflow of our skills is especially important in the professional arena to ensure maximum effectiveness and productivity. In the book *Now Discover Your Strengths*, authors Marcus Buckingham and Donald Clifton show that when employees are working in the capacity of their skills, their organizations enjoy lower employee turnover, more productive business environments, and higher customer satisfaction scores.[12] In the book, they expand on the idea that success can be realized when we operate from a place of strength. Your skills are gifts you were born with that will help you accomplish your purpose.

When you combine your predominant passion(s) with your skills, you have found your purpose. In my case, my leukemia lemon experience was my predominant passion in my youth and instilled within me an unquenchable desire to help ensure that the emotional trauma I suffered while hospitalized would not become the norm. Coupled with my inherent ability to effectively encourage, empower, sympathize, and empathize with others, along with my skill of understanding biological concepts more easily in school than others, all this helped reveal the first stage of my life's purpose—a career as an RN.

Recognize also that the fullness of your life's purpose isn't a vocation or a title; it is a specific manner in which you will impact the world *through* your work of service. Some may say *my purpose is to become a doctor*, or *my purpose is to be a stay-at-home mom*. The reality is that you were created for a good work that will come from your chosen path. A more revealing perspective to consider might be: What impact will you have on the world as a doctor? Will your presence in the healthcare system impact the delivery of services in a specific, positive way? What impact will your role as a stay-at-home parent have on your children and who they become? Are you intentional in your role as a parent to raise the leaders of tomorrow?

Think of examples around you of individuals or organizations that are clearly operating from a position of purpose. What makes you think so? Is it their level of effectiveness? Impact? Joy in their work? Likely it is all three, and when you drill down into their story more deeply, invariably, you will find something specific was driving their desire to function in their capacity, which was coupled with the inherent skills they possessed. As you evaluate your own life, both areas—your passions and skills—will reveal your purpose, and as you continue to stay open with a willingness and determination to live it, you will be internally and externally guided along the way.

Let's take our equation—*Passion + Skills = Purpose*—a step further:

Living a life of **purpose** results in **success** that leads to **fulfillment** & **peace**.

Success.

There is no one definition of success, as it takes on different meanings for all of us. But, while reading this book, try to suspend your preconceived notions about success—specifically what it means and how to attain it—and allow me to challenge your understanding. To one person, success may mean owning a mansion or living a six-, seven-, or eight-figure lifestyle. To another, success might mean raising children who are altruistic, contributing members of society. To yet another, securing their GED or becoming the first member of their family to graduate with a college degree might represent success. You get to define your own idea of success, however, recognize that it will take on a different meaning in the context of your purpose. Think of it this way: If you discern that your purpose is to help raise awareness of the plight of displaced refugees from the civil war in Syria and other war-torn countries, it wouldn't be appropriate to define success by making seven figures from your venture.

Success for you may mean a lavish lifestyle full of material possessions. But while material gain absolutely can accompany purpose-driven success, it cannot be *the driver* of it. If you are motivated by money, power, or prestige, know that your entrepreneurial pursuit is absolutely not one of purpose! If these are your motivations, tell yourself the truth and make a conscious decision to either stay the course and sacrifice your internal peace, or pivot onto the road of purpose and experience success that leads to true fulfillment.

PRACTICAL EXAMPLES

CNN Heroes, a Peabody and Emmy award-winning television show[13] in the United States, honors the pursuits of everyday people accomplishing extraordinary feats to positively impact the world around them. The awardees are perfect examples of individuals achieving success by following their purpose. Past recipients include:

- Wrongfully imprisoned former inmate **Richard Miles,** who, after serving fifteen years in a Texas prison, started a non-profit to help other formerly incarcerated individuals transition back into society by helping them obtain identification, enroll in college, and secure housing. His non-profit also provides computer and career training, financial literacy programs, and job placement services.[14]

- Former bartender **Doc Hendley,** who distributes water filters and installs wells in communities around the world through his non-profit. He's provided clean water to more than 150,000 people in seventeen countries living in conditions that lead to preventable diseases and death from lack of access to clean water.[15]

- Eight-year-old **Cavanaugh Bell**, who started a community pantry during the height of the COVID-19 pandemic. With the support of donors from all over the world, Cavanaugh and his team assisted 8,100 seniors struggling with food insecurity to access desperately needed groceries.[16]

These heroes have certainly achieved success in their pursuits to impact the world around them! They may not amass an abundance of financial wealth or power through their ventures, but the sheer magnitude of their impact renders them successful. *When you are operating from a place of purpose, your success, in one form or another, is inevitable, and with it comes a sense of contentment and peace.*

Peace.

At the core of our human desires lies a hunger for peace. But peace can escape us when we are living in conflict with our life's purpose. You can, indeed, be materially successful operating outside of your purpose, but the nagging feeling of discontent and a lack of true fulfillment gnawing away at your spirit will render it all worthless in the end.

While I was an RN, I watched countless patients transition from life to death. What tends to matter most at the end of life isn't the accolades achieved or the riches amassed, but the relationships fostered and the impact of our lives. Peace comes from a life lived on purpose and truthfully, and nothing else can adequately replace it.

"Knowing your purpose gives you something internally
you can't purchase."

—Dr. Dharius Daniels

PURPOSE: A JOURNEY OF STAGES

The full scope of your life's purpose may not be revealed all at once, as purpose is often revealed and accomplished in stages. In my case, after surviving leukemia, I believed my purpose was to become an RN to help ensure my negative experience would not become the norm for other patients. Once I became an RN and experienced burnout early in my career, I realized that working as a nurse was not the last stop on my journey. It was only when I surrendered to the full process of discovery—listened to my inner yearnings and progressed through the two questions listed on page 47—that I became cognizant of the full scope of the purpose for my life. But first, I had to progress through a set of stages:

STAGE 1: *Start my career as an RN*

A career in nursing perfectly addressed my pervasive passion at the time and adequately utilized the inherent skills I possessed to that point.

STAGE 2: *Establish my entrepreneurial venture*

My career as an RN enabled me to operate my nursing recruitment firm effectively and from a place of authenticity. As an RN myself, I knew what other RNs would be looking for in an employer and set out to create a service package that would be attractive to RNs and accepted by employers. The passion from my leukemia lemon experience provided me the fuel to accurately effect the change I was seeking, which ultimately led to my success.

STAGE 3: *Release a book about my entrepreneurial journey and develop my consulting practice*

The success I achieved with my nursing recruitment firm now provides me the platform to encourage and empower my consulting clients from a place of integrity. Through this book and my consulting services offered through my company, Aere Management Consulting, I'm able to live the fullness of my life's purpose, which involves encouraging and empowering others to start and grow purpose-driven ventures—despite their challenging life experiences—with a recognition that success is indeed attainable when you believe!

Since purpose is typically revealed and accomplished in stages, anticipate after your first step is revealed, you'll be internally led on a journey with one or more stops or stages until the fullness of your purpose is realized. Think of it this way, at stage one, you may not have the competencies or confidence to believe that your final stage is even possible! Progression through a series of stages will place you in the position to effectively live the fullness of your life's purpose later. In my case, immediately after surviving leukemia, I didn't possess the confidence or level of competence needed to start and operate a business, and I certainly hadn't accumulated enough experience to write a business success book! It wasn't time to live the fullness of my life's purpose yet. Had I not become an RN, started an entrepreneurial venture from scratch, and suffered through the process of building it to become a sustainably successful, impactful, purpose-driven business, my words here could not be articulated from a place of authenticity or integrity, and they would have little impact to create change in your life. I *had* to progress through step one, to effectively operate on step two, and so on.

Along your entrepreneurial journey, you too will build on the inherent skills that will allow you to operate effectively at stage one and develop new skills that will enable you to operate at the other stages of your purpose journey. Even mistakes and pivots away from your journey can still prepare you for success if you take the time to learn from them. Squeeze all of your challenging life experiences and use your understanding of them to propel you to the revelation of your life's purpose.

The process of discovery of purpose is just as important as the facilitation of it. Why? Because learning to use the same tools that helped you unearth your purpose—quieting your spirit to let answers flow to you and telling yourself the truth—will serve you well as you build your venture and prepare it for sustainable success.

THE POWER OF PIVOTS

After graduating with a degree that I realized would no longer directly impact my vocational future, I suffered feelings of brokenness, shame, and fear. But even though that season of my life was incredibly debilitating, it indirectly ended up propelling me to eventually achieve success. During my education for that very Bachelor of Science degree I begrudged, I learned concepts, honed skills, and developed perspectives that directly inform how I now communicate, digest, and analyze information and conduct my business ventures. That degree was instrumental in opening up pivotal opportunities and blessed me with lasting friendships that I still enjoy today. Living in and on purpose is a process, and there are stages along the way that will seem useless or unnecessary to the overall picture. But remember, none of your experiences will be wasted; all of them and the knowledge you gain from each will contain nuggets of wisdom that will prepare you for the success that lies ahead.

> *"Sometimes wake-up calls are gentle taps on the shoulder,*
> *other times they can knock the wind out of you,*
> *and on some occasions, they're bombs dropped directly*
> *over your head."*
>
> —Lisa Nichols

TWO IMPORTANT GUIDEPOSTS ON YOUR JOURNEY

As you move through the stages on the road to achieving the fullness of your life's purpose, it's important to watch for signs that you are off track or need to move onto the next stage of your journey. **Burnout,** a syndrome conceptualized as resulting from chronic workplace stress that has not been successfully managed,[17] is one guidepost that should warrant your attention[18,19] and propel you to evaluate and address its source with surgical precision.[20]

Burnout requires quick navigation, as its prolonged presence in your life can be physically, emotionally, spiritually, and even financially harmful[17] (a concept discussed in more detail in Chapter 11), which can derail or even deter you from achieving success.

Passion is your fuel. If you don't have your fuel, you'll burn out quickly. If you find yourself losing your passion at a particular stage of your journey, that is likely indicative of one of the following:

1. You are operating outside of your purpose, and are off-course

2. You are on purpose, or on-course, but eager to move to the next stage of your journey

3. There may be a mental health component at play

Your purpose, in and of itself, will not drain you to the point of despair, even in the midst of challenging circumstances. Rather, it will energize you to accomplish the specific good work you were created for. Your readiness to move from one stage to the next can leave you feeling physically, emotionally, or mentally exhausted, however. Another aspect to consider is that there are mental health conditions that present with the same symptoms as burnout. In essence, the presence of burnout is a warning sign.

Pay attention.
Acknowledge the source of your burnout.
Take the necessary steps to address it:

1. Either tell yourself the truth about your current state; acknowledge you are off course and take the time to discern your purpose

2. Stay the course, as you are on the right track, but may still have competencies and lessons to learn at the stage you're on, or

3. Secure help to determine if there is a mental health component at play and access treatment options available to you.

Another guidepost is **a lack of peace**. When you choose to move in the direction of your purpose, you will likely experience a sense of peace, often even in the presence of uncertainty and fear. That sense of security will be present with you while you are on track if you have mastered the first step of your inner work: telling yourself the truth while having discerned your purpose correctly. As you progress and remain in a place of self-awareness, your sense of peace about business decisions will invariably guide you. The more you listen to the guidance this peace brings you, the more convicted and assured you will feel about your decisions when they prove to be right. Allow the guideposts of burnout and peace to redirect you as you work toward creating your successful business. Both are key indicators that will save you time, money, and a myriad of mistakes that can threaten to derail your journey to success.

Think of the progress you've made to get to this point. Are there jobs you've held in the past that will serve to prepare you for the next stage of your journey? Are there classes you've completed or are taking now that you're not terribly fond of, but will provide you with the skills that will help you accomplish your goals? Are there people you've met in a community setting, such as a church, that could help you accomplish your life's purpose?

Remember, each stage of your life story to this point has prepared, or is preparing, you to function in the capacity of your life's purpose.

> Release to the process of discovery and transformation.
> Acknowledge that your purpose may be revealed and accomplished in stages.
> Pay attention to the guideposts of burnout and peace along your way.
> If you experience burnout, acknowledge and address its source
> and keep progressing forward!

NOW THAT YOU'VE FULLY ARTICULATED YOUR PASSION(S) TO YOURSELF, acknowledged your skills, and developed an understanding of your purpose, congratulations! You are leaps and bounds ahead of most people but are likely feeling a sense of unease and uncertainty. Thoughts like, *How can I make money doing this?*, *How should I start?*, *What are people going to think of me if I change course and move in this direction?*, or even, *I don't have what it takes to make this work!* Know that once you gain clarity at this point, or at any juncture along this journey, your faith in what has been revealed to you—the understanding of your purpose—will be tested by internal and external forces, a topic we'll dissect in greater detail in Chapter 4. So then, if you're still unsure of your purpose, be sure to take the time now to confirm it.

Ask for feedback from the people who know you well, or ask for spiritual guidance to help you unearth it and discern it correctly. *Ensure you have an accurate understanding of your purpose and start to experience the peace that accompanies it* **before** *you start or continue on your entrepreneurial journey, though.* This is a critical step, as doubt about your direction is poisonous to you and your venture. A clear belief and an understanding of your purpose will help you in more ways than one as you build your successful business.

The why of your business, and the strength of your belief in it, will draw key people to invest, support, join, and buy from you. Understanding the why of your business as you draw from your own personal skills and acknowledge your pervasive passion generated from your own lemon experiences will be one of the key strategies that will propel you to success. So, embrace the understanding of your purpose, write it down as your mission statement, and keep it in the forefront of your mind.

THE STRATEGIES THAT LEAD TO A TRULY FULFILLED, ABUNDANT, SUCCESSful life really are straightforward. There's no need to live in fear of your potential! Purpose is power, and casting a vision for your successful future is one of the most enjoyable and important aspects of the journey. So, starting now, visualize your purpose—generated from both an understanding of your skills and predominant passion(s) from squeezing your challenging lemon experiences—and allow this vision to propel you to effectively serve the world and create the lemonade of your success!

"You were created by God on purpose.
You were created by God for a purpose.
It's never too early to live on purpose.
It's never too late to discover your purpose."

—Christine Caine

FOR DEEPER REFLECTION...

Strategy #2: Discern Your Purpose

1. Take time for self-talk. Ask yourself: If money were not an issue, what would you do for free? Your honest answer will give you a clearer perspective on your purpose.

2. What are you good at? Create a detailed list of all of your skills, including areas of competency you've been told you possess.

3. Write down your answers to the following:
   a. What are you most passionate about, and how do your lemon experiences relate to it?
   b. What is one thing you could do over and over again and never get sick of?

4. Based on your answers to Questions 1 to 3, what have you discerned to be your life's purpose?

5. Review the following practical application of the principles of purpose in the fictional life of Susie:

Susie has always been skilled at styling hair and loves helping women feel beautiful. She survived a traumatic relationship that left her feeling emotionally shattered, with a compromised view of her self-worth. After therapy and intense personal discovery, she made it through to the other side of healing. She's determined that, going forward, she will make it her life's work to help empower women who are survivors of trauma to build their sense of self-worth: first, by helping them feel supported, cared for, and beautiful through styling their hair, and then by empowering them with resources to experience healing.

Skill: *styling hair*

Life lemon: *traumatic relationship*

Passion generated from life lemon:

- *To help rescue women from a compromised sense of self created or worsened by traumatic relationships*

- *To provide resources to help them escape the trauma and experience healing*

Purpose: *To help women feel beautiful, supported, and empowered with resources to escape trauma and experience healing, and to also help strengthen their sense of self-worth through styling their hair.*

Business venture: *Start a beauty salon styling hair geared toward empowering women to develop a stronger sense of self-worth. Foster a sense of community and support with clients. Place empowering quotes inside the salon. Place literature geared toward positive messaging and resources for healing strategically inside. Establish partnerships with local, vetted service providers (therapists, etc.) that can provide help escaping and healing from trauma, and provide coupons and discounts for hair-styling services to the list of service providers to give out at their establishments as well.*

Susie's understanding of her skills, coupled with her passion for helping women escape the realities of her previous experience, revealed her life's purpose. Wouldn't you support such a business, either by your patronage, referral, or direct assistance to help her in her mission? Can you see how this business, born out of Susie's passion and skills, possesses the seeds needed to lead to a successful venture? Write down each component from Susie's example (skill, life lemon, passion generated from life lemon, purpose, and business venture) and map out your own journey ahead.

6. Write down three of your favorite neighborhood shops or service providers that you believe are clearly operating from the perspective of their purpose.
   a. Would you go out of your way to purchase from them, spend more money at, or tolerate other inconveniences simply because you believe in the "why" of their business and/or what they represent? Why or why not?

*** Need more help unearthing your purpose? Email:*
concierge@aereconsulting.com

3

THE POWER OF PERSPECTIVE

"The question is not what you look at, but what you see."

—HENRY DAVID THOREAU

CONGRATULATIONS! YOU NOW HAVE A WORKING UNDERSTANDING OF what you were born to do. You can clearly articulate what drives you and what brings you joy and peace. You understand your skills and how they relate to your purpose. Now, you may be thinking: So, what's the next step? What does this discovery mean, and how can I accomplish my life's purpose? If it involves the development of a business venture, the rest of this book will provide you with foundational strategies to help you build a successful, purpose-driven business that will have an impact on your market and beyond. If your purpose involves an endeavor outside of the business realm, the strategies listed here will still serve to guide your understanding of how to progress forward in your specific area of "good work."

In the early years of my entrepreneurial journey, I lived in a constant state of anxiety and fear. I made a series of choices that I thought would prove profitable personally and professionally, but instead, several of them turned out to be costly mistakes, and I was left to endure the ramifications of hundreds of thousands of dollars of debt. Working through threatening calls from creditors all day long, along with piles of mail demanding payment, only fed my anxiety. Waking up day after day, building the business through insecurities, the chatter of the nay-sayers, and my own feelings of a lack of preparedness regularly compromised my level of overall confidence, productivity, and effectiveness. Nevertheless, I still believed I had accurately discerned my purpose and that God would see me through to a successful end eventually. In addition to a confident understanding of my purpose, what saved me during those early dark days was a clear vision of my success and a mindset that I *could* make it—others had before me—and that clear vision eventually grew into a belief that I *would* make it! This transition was partly due to an evolution of my understanding of the power of perspective. Implemented consistently and with intention, harnessing the power of perspective can help you, too, to develop a winning attitude that will propel you toward success.

In Chapter 2, we asked ourselves many questions about our skills and passions. So, once we've acknowledged our skills, determined what drives us and what we were born to do, what do the answers mean for our lives? Should we quit our current job? Change our program of study three years into our degree? Fold the business we've invested years of time and money in? **Should we completely course-correct from our current path or stay put?** The answer could be yes or no, depending on the circumstances and the stage we're at along our purpose journey. Let's dive into how both could be correct and what to do when the answer is yes or no.

Yes.

During your journey, there will be moments that will require a complete course correction for you to operate in your life's purpose. If you didn't know that to be true to some extent, you wouldn't be still reading this book! These moments will require you to commit to the understanding of your purpose now, as you pivot from your current path. In my case, deciding to leave nursing to start a business was terrifying, but it was a necessary step toward fulfilling my life's purpose and arriving at a place of peace.

You'll eventually come to a place where the status quo is unbearable, and the time will come to fully immerse yourself in a new direction—the next stage of your journey. This won't be easy! You have responsibilities, debts, fears, insecurities, and valid concerns that may be preventing you from moving forward, which may cause you to emotionally check out from even thinking about another direction. Know, however, that once you understand your purpose, you will either be given the option to pivot from your current status quo, or life will make that decision for you.

In my case, after leaving my per diem and travel nursing positions in the U.S. and relocating back to Canada, I incorporated my nursing recruitment business and was working to build it, while still working as an RN, albeit now on a transient, casual basis. Even though I had set the intention to leave the profession of nursing to start my business—and eventually did leave my full-time travel nursing and per diem positions—I hadn't fully jumped into the world of entrepreneurship out of fear. Had I not gotten into a car accident that left me unable to continue working as a casual floor RN in Canada, I may still have tried to function as an RN and entrepreneur at the same time, all the while feeling overworked, drained, and overwhelmed! In the end, life decided for me through a car accident. Thereafter, I finally, fully immersed myself in the next stage along my purpose journey, which was timely and pivotal to my eventual success.

Regardless of how you arrive at your decision, when the status quo becomes physically, emotionally, and spiritually unbearable, and your current state is robbing you of peace, take courage and let go. Trust the process and embrace your understanding of your purpose. If you don't make the decision to do so, chances are, as was in my case, life will make the decision for you.

No.

During my transition from Stage 1 to the end of Stage 2 (from page 56 & 57), I was led through an emotional, intellectual, spiritual, financial, and vocational transformation. Early into my career as an RN, I became frustrated after realizing that the issue of my poor emotional nursing care had less to do with my nurses, but was more a result of the detrimental effects of the nursing shortage. Functioning as an RN then was, in essence, no longer addressing the reason why I started a nursing career path—to do what I could to help ensure my experience would not become the norm for patients. This realization of the real reason for the issue of my poor care was daunting and directly contributed to my crushing bout of burnout years later.

Nevertheless, for me to fulfill my life's purpose, *I had to continue* working as an RN for more time to become intricately acquainted with the issues and inner workings of the healthcare system, and to myself, understand the challenges nurses face in order to be able to successfully operate a nursing recruitment firm from a nurse's perspective. I had to stay put, which was incredibly debilitating and draining at times, but had I left the profession before my time, I would have missed out on the opportunity to authentically relate to my future clients, which would have undoubtedly compromised my ability to create success from my venture.

I affectionately refer to my time in Stage 2 as my Ph.D. from the school of hard knocks, as I operated my business for thirteen years and learned the principles of success from the information I gleaned from several sources that included the Bible, a myriad of business and personal development books I read, seminars and courses I attended, the many trial-and-error experiences I endured, and nuggets of wisdom I received from my professional advisors. Even though those early days were difficult, that time was necessary to prepare me for what was to come: the abundance of the life I live now and the opportunity to consult with struggling entrepreneurs from a place of authenticity and integrity.

Since I endured the harshness of the entrepreneurial journey myself and emerged successful, as a business management consultant, I can now effectively help other business owners and entrepreneurs navigate their challenges as well. However, even though I had a clear understanding of my why, there were *many times* I almost walked away from it all out of frustration, fear, and a myriad of other negative emotions. In speaking engagements and in an entrepreneurship group coaching class I facilitated years prior to selling my business, I revealed that it took me three and a half years before I made my first dollar, and that it would be years even after my breakthrough before work came in on a steady basis. Eventually, though, after years of consistently implementing principles of success and key strategies to build a solid foundation for my business, I was ready for an overwhelming, yet steady state of work that led me to sustainable success. Had I folded during the early, challenging years, I would not be in the position now to help you squeeze your challenging life experiences into a successful business!

WHEN DRIVING IN A BLIZZARD, WE AREN'T MADE AWARE OF THE CONDITIONS of the road ahead; we're only privy to what's right in front of us and must continue the journey until we reach our destination. There are moments in your journey that will call for you to stay the course, however painful and draining, so, at times, the answer to the above question is no. You may not need to course-correct; instead, cultivate resolve, patience, and the will to persevere until the point of your breakthrough and success.

HOW DO I KNOW IF IT'S YES OR NO?

The only way to tell the difference between your "yes" and "no" moments is to take time to pull away and acknowledge the truth about what you are feeling. Ask yourself:

Why am I feeling anxious at this particular time?
Is it because I'm off course?
Or is the anxiety warranted due to a mistake I've made or am about to make?

Are you simply tired of the stage you're at and, in your itch to graduate to the next level, are feeling anxious to move on?
Or are those feelings reasonable, generated from the negative state of your life or venture?

Discern the truth of your feelings by applying the principles outlined in Strategy #1 (Tell Yourself the Truth, Quickly) to determine whether a course correction is truly valid (answer: yes) or if staying put in your current circumstances is best to hone your skills and acquire new ones to operate effectively in the future (answer: no). Graduating to the next stage of your journey before it's time can cost you in more ways than one. Properly discerning between your yes—to course-correct—and your no—to stay put—requires a deeper layer of truth-telling. It requires perspective.

THE THREE COMPONENTS OF PERSPECTIVE

In the context of success, perspective is incredibly important on your journey toward the accomplishment of your goals. It encompasses:

1. How you perceive internal and external conditions and circumstances around you

2. Your vision, particularly how you plan for your success to unfold

3. Your ability to remain focused

"Your attitude, not your aptitude, will determine your altitude."

—Zig Ziglar

First, let's dissect the concept of **perception**. Allow me, for a moment, to challenge your views on some widely held beliefs:

Perception is not reality. The sky is not actually blue. Well-hydrated grass is not green. Light hitting objects is what translates into our *perception* of color through an intricate, complicated, instantaneous interplay between the human eye and the brain. Specifically, cones, one of the photoreceptors of the eye,[1] transmit messages to the brain that produce *the familiar sensations* of color.[2] Isaac Newton observed that there is no inherent color in objects; rather, the surface of an object reflects certain wavelengths of light and absorbs all others; the one that is reflected is *perceived* as the predominant color.[3] Therefore, we see primarily with our brains, not our eyes! Let's dive deeper and consider the following:

"…We see different colours because of how our brains learn to link the signals they get from the eyes with the names of different colours.
When a baby points at a ball and her father asks, 'Would you like to play with that green ball?'
she learns to associate the colour she's seeing with the word 'green,'
and she will soon call things of a similar colour 'green' as well."[3]

As it is in our physiology, so it is in business. How we perceive something will determine how we relate to it. In essence, your view on the road ahead will greatly impact your ability to turn your life lemons and skills into a successful, purpose-driven venture—the lemonade of your success! Your perception of yourself, understanding of your purpose, perception of your venture, and abilities will all directly determine the fate of your venture.

Jack Canfield, #1 bestselling author of over 500 million books and a pioneer in the field of personal development and peak performance, wrote the most influential business book I read during my entrepreneurial journey, *The Success Principles.* In it, he discusses many principles that can help one achieve their goals. Key among them is the importance of transcending limiting beliefs as a critical first step toward becoming successful.[4]

"Amanda, you've got to get
over being shy."

Know that you are absolutely capable of achieving success in the direction of your purpose since you were created for it! Combating negative thoughts is crucial—it is precisely why determining your purpose is imperative, since feelings of doubt, fear, and other limiting beliefs can plague you long before starting your pursuit toward purpose-driven success.

Research indicates that the average person has more than 6,000 thoughts per day,[5] and, according to psychological researchers, eighty percent of those thoughts are associated with negative self-talk.[6] Try to stop the tape playing in your mind—thoughts of *I can't...*, *I'll never...*, *I'm only...*, or *I'm just...* You are never *just* anything! We are wonderfully and masterfully made to live from a perspective that is uniquely ours and serve the world with our own skills and experiences. Tell yourself the truth, and quickly, about the state of your mind when you're feeling doubtful or insecure. Rein in those feelings and press forward. The longer you allow those feelings to fester, the greater the likelihood they will infect your behavior and sabotage your venture. Left unchecked, they'll end up requiring a significant amount of energy and potentially resources to rid yourself of them.

"Whether you think you can or you can't—you're right."
—Henry Ford

At this stage, it's absolutely normal to feel overwhelmed, even terrified, as you consider the road ahead. During my journey, despite being a self-described positive person, I regularly struggled with insecure thoughts from feeling ill-prepared: *Did I bite off more than I could chew? Are passion and an understanding of my purpose really enough to get me through the dark days? Was I crazy to launch out into the world of entrepreneurship without more capital, more help, more preparation, and more education?* Yes, all those thoughts were valid and applicable if I were building a traditional business with the primary goal of making money. In my case, however, I was launching a *purpose-driven* venture to serve and impact the world in a manner that would uniquely draw from my own skills and lemon experiences.

A purpose-driven venture does not subscribe to the traditional academic principles of business growth and development. Despite my insecurities, I actually *did* possess the seeds of everything I needed to eventually succeed: drive, discipline, faith, hunger for knowledge, humility to change course when necessary, a passion to impact change in my industry, emotional intelligence, focus, and a clear perspective. These were all attributes that compensated for my lack of knowledge, experience, and even resources during the early stages. And you, too, are more prepared than you think!

The truth is, *we are what we think of ourselves.* Limiting thoughts that play in your "negative self-talk mind playlist" are normal and part of the human experience. But it is so important to learn to talk to yourself like a winner![7] You can start to do this by allowing the negative thoughts to come up and address them in truth, with a positive perspective (*I can do it!* **I am** *able to accomplish…*). You were born for this "good work" of your purpose, and your passion for it will give you no peace until you chart a course toward your eventual, successful end.

PERSPECTIVE ALSO ENCOMPASSES VISUALIZATION: THE PROCESS BY WHICH you chart a tangible path forward with clear direction on where you want to land. Your purpose will guide your overall vision, but it is imperative that you create a concrete plan in one form or another. You can use several methods to help clarify your vision, which include but are not limited to the creation of a vision board, affirmations (which we'll discuss more deeply in the next section), and a clear list of the mission, vision, and values you'd like your venture to represent. These are some of the methods you can use to help you start clarifying your vision of what you want to achieve. You may need to use more than one method to help ensure your success. The more vivid your choice of method, the greater power it will hold.

MY TOP TWO

During the early years of my venture, I found that the most successful methods I used to clarify my vision were:

1. A daily repetition of my list of affirmations

2. A daily reading of scripture

Among the countless benefits of both, reviewing scripture and repeating my affirmations each morning directly bolstered my confidence and strengthened my belief that *I could* actually squeeze my challenging life experiences and create a successful business!

Affirmations

Following guidance from the book *The Success Principles*, each morning, I would look myself in the mirror, smile, and recite my list of affirmations;

statements that describe a goal in its already completed state[7] or a phrase representing a state that I wanted to achieve.

An effective, complete affirmation statement is brief, specific, positive, and reflects you and not someone else. One type also ends with the words "or something better."

There are two types of affirmation statements that I've found very useful. The first type of affirmation statement starts with the words "I am," followed by a descriptor carrying a positive connotation for you. Examples of this type of affirmation statement:

- I am confident

- I am successful

- I am competent

Examples of the second type of affirmation statement brings together the other components:

- I am *enjoying* my new, three-bedroom, beachfront home in Maui, or something better

- I am *thankful* for my successful, purpose-driven business that I operate with joy, from which I earn six figures per year or something better

Associating your affirmation statements with the feelings that you believe will accompany the accomplishment of each goal really unlocks the power of visualization and helps to bring you to the place of success in your own mind, which actually helps prepare you to get there.

BELIEFS LEAD TO ACTIONS, THEN RESULTS

The second method I used to bolster my confidence and strengthen my belief that I could actually squeeze my lemon experiences into a successful business was the daily reading of Bible scriptures in the morning before I started work. While reading, I developed an understanding of who God is and that He is actually invested in me, cares about me, and wants me to accomplish my purpose! Belief in God and His power set in motion an eventual belief in myself; believing in the power of Proverbs 23:7—as a man thinks of himself in his heart, so is he[8]—I actually started to *become* what I was thinking! I started to become the words I was affirming to myself in the mirror every morning, and over time, I transformed into the person that embodied the adjectives I had been using to describe myself.

My changed **beliefs** about myself and what I could accomplish through the power of God led to **action**, which eventually translated into **results** for my company! Here's how the process worked for me:

- When I started to believe my affirmations—the powerful, positive words I was repeating to myself daily—I, subconsciously and over time, began to act in a manner that aligned with the words.

- As I began to act in a manner that aligned with the words, through the grace and power of God, people around me started to relate to me in the same way! Clients started to relate to me as though I was competent and trusted me to deliver the services I had been asking for years for them to give me the chance to provide. People started to relate to me as though I was successful, and long before I reached the state of sustainable success, other business owners and entre-preneurs started asking me for help and advice on building their ventures!

- All of my changed actions resulting from my newly adopted beliefs eventually translated into results for my company.

Letting go of your limiting **beliefs** and choosing to be intentional about adopting new positive ones will eventually lead to changed **action**, which, in time, will translate into **results**. Hooray for the simple strategies to achieve success!

DECONSTRUCTING BELIEF

Technically speaking, this is how this process works in our minds:

Visualizing goals as already complete and operating with the belief that we will succeed creates *cognitive dissonance* in our minds, a mental state of discomfort that results from holding two conflicting beliefs, values, or attitudes.[9,10] This state of cognitive dissonance creates an internal battle in our subconscious mind between our thoughts about our current circumstances and the ones we are visualizing,[9] eventually resulting in our mind steering us toward the positive, visualized reality.

Our subconscious mind is always aiming to pull us into a state of balance and a state of completion. That pull masterfully addresses the cognitive dissonance by helping us *perceive* our environment differently with a positive perspective, which will eventually encourage us to take actions that will turn our current reality into the realization of our vision!

I believe in God's guiding and sustaining power and the power of the mind He created within us. We can truly accomplish unimaginable feats if only we can get to the place of belief. So, make your vision of what you want to achieve for your business powerfully vivid in your mind. Beyond visualization, also use your other senses to imagine your goals as if you've already accomplished them.[11] Trust in your Higher Power and believe that by intentionally and consistently taking appropriate action to build your venture, your Higher Power acting on your subconscious mind will help you find ways to accomplish your goals.

VIVID VISIONS GAIN RESULTS

As previously mentioned, the more vivid the visualization of your success, the greater power it will hold to help you achieve your desired results. Consider using your five senses to help you to strengthen the clarity of your vision to unlock the power of visualization. To do this, think of:

What will success **sound** like to you?

Accolades?

Words of thanks from others?

The sound of crashing waves of the ocean from your beachfront property?

What will success **look** like to you?

For example, physically go to the place you envision will be the future location of your company, if at all possible. Walk around the area. Imagine yourself in your office, and think about how you plan to decorate it. Experience the feeling of what it will be like actually to be there, having achieved your goals.

If your budget allows it, maybe even purchase a work of art that you plan to hang in your future office or another item that symbolizes success for you.

To maximize the power of this strategy, repeat this exercise for the rest of your senses of touch, taste, and smell.

IF YOU'RE DEALING WITH VIABLE CHALLENGES AND CONCERNS THAT HAVE, so far, prohibited you from believing success could ever be possible for you, cognitive dissonance can provide you with one amazing source of hope! The more separated you are from your goal and the more alive, clear, and vivid your vision of success is, the concept of cognitive dissonance provides hope that you *can* actually achieve the lemonade of success you are envisioning! The greater the frequency with which you read positive literature, believe and draw strength from your Higher Power, claim your affirmations, and regularly utilize your visualization techniques, the greater the likelihood your goals will manifest through the changed actions you will invariably take as a result.

PRACTICAL EXAMPLE

I lived the power of this strategy while lying in my hospital bed with leukemia. As I attempted to move toward a state of healing, I would visualize the island of Hawaii for hours, a place I had not yet visited. I thought about what Hawaii would **look** like with its vast greenery, gorgeous island flowers, rolling hills, and beautiful sunsets. I imagined the aroma of flowers and what the salty beach air would **smell** like. I imagined the **sound** of island birds, the **touch** or feeling of having my toes in the warm sand, and how the foam of the waves crashing against my legs would feel. I would daydream with the belief that one day when I finally recovered from my illness, I would experience *my* Hawaii. And when I did visit Hawaii on one of my many trips years later, the *exact* picture I had created in my mind was realized when I walked onto the white sandy beach at the Grand Wailea resort in Maui!

The practice of visualization in all its forms is powerful. Dreaming is free, so why not try it? Many successful people, such as actor Jim Carey, former governor of California Arnold Schwarzenegger, famous talk-show host, media mogul, author, and philanthropist Oprah Winfrey, and countless others have used it,[11,12,13] and you can, too! If the founder of *1-800-GOT-JUNK?*, a \$100 million-dollar multinational company, can attribute his success to the power of visualization,[14] I think that warrants giving the practice a try!

"You want to set a goal that is big enough that in the process of achieving it, you become someone worth becoming."

—Jim Rohn

Beyond visualization, conventional goal-setting strategies can also help you map the course for your road ahead. A formalized business plan consisting of an executive summary, business description and structure, market research and strategies, information about your management and personnel, and financial documents is useful. It can assist you in creating an effective strategy for growth, identifying your future financial needs, and attracting investors or other funding.

My journey was unconventional, however. Throughout the life of my businesses, I've never completed a formal business plan document that includes the specific, traditional components of a business plan. This, however, is contrary to any directive one would learn in a business preparatory course or MBA program. Revealing this truth to folks within my business network has always been met with disdain and surprise. How was I able to start, grow, sustain, and sell a successful business without a formal and detailed business plan document? I did it by charting an exact path to my end goal.

Even though I didn't have all the components in one document, the structure of my business was constantly at the forefront of my mind and in other documents. I was constantly conducting market research and looking for ways to apply the information I was gleaning to grow strategically. I kept clear financial records and intentionally weaved my mission, vision, and values into the activities of the business on a regular basis. My plan for my business wasn't drafted on one formal document, but at the end of each fiscal year, I would write down my goals for the next fiscal year, relating them back to the overall purpose for the business, which is an important strategy to implement for growth. By the grace of God, at year thirteen, when I sold the business, I had accomplished every major goal set and can therefore vouch for the power of goal-setting and the practice of translating those goals into action items per year, per quarter, per week, and even per day.

Am I suggesting you forgo completing a formal business plan for your venture? Absolutely not! Ultimately, your journey is yours, and I believe that your purpose-driven entrepreneurial journey is solely between you and your Higher Power. Resist the need to make it make sense to anyone else.

EACH OF YOU IS ON AN INDIVIDUAL JOURNEY OF BUILDING A PURPOSE-DRIVen venture, so what makes sense for you may not make sense to another. The purpose-driven business journey is specially tailored to you. It will transform *you* in the areas needed for your personal and professional growth to allow you to serve the world through your product or service most effectively. You may decide to complete a formalized business plan and choose to hire a group of staff at the start of your venture, and another business owner may not. It does not make their journey or business less viable or less bound for success than yours. In my case, the results of following God's particular path *for me* while building my business instead of following the status quo on how to start, operate, and grow a successful venture, actually resulted in my personal and professional transformation and access to opportunities beyond my wildest imaginings!

Do what you feel led to and what works best for you. No matter what approach you choose, be sure to cast a clear vision of what you want to accomplish and write it down. Seeing your plan on paper is beneficial, as it provides an opportunity to evaluate your goals outside of your mind. When goals are written down, they become more real and concrete. Writing them down can also provide you and others with a roadmap on how you plan to tangibly progress forward, which will be important for everyone involved in your business to know. As long as you are consistently and intentionally implementing sound principles to build a solid foundation for your venture and are taking steps to learn and grow as a leader from multiple sources, don't be afraid to follow your own path and pivot as needed as you continue creating the lemonade of your success!

"This stuff isn't selling.
Maybe we should switch to Viagra."

The last aspect to consider regarding perspective is **focus**. Your ability to remain laser-focused on the vision you've cast for your venture and the specifics of what success will look like for you is extremely important.

Don't allow yourself to get sidetracked.

There are a million amazing business ideas out there, but they are not all congruent with your skills and do not draw from your pervasive passion generated from your lemon experience(s). Stay focused and squeeze dry your lemon experience(s) by applying what you've learned from them, and keep moving in the direction of *your* purpose. Fulfill the purpose that has been revealed to you at each stage of your journey before moving on to the next. When the going gets rough, redirect your focus back on your goals, those visualized and those written down. Doing so will help you press forward effectively and keep going.

Here are five steps that will help you maintain focus while building your purpose-driven venture:

STEP 1: *Identify What Success Looks Like for You*

At this point in your journey, it's not necessary to have a detailed road map on how everything will come together, but it is important to clearly identify what success looks like *for you.*

Dream, and dream big!

Start with your purpose, visualizing how you can best achieve it. Remember, the core goal of a purpose-driven venture is ultimately impact, and your success should lead to personal peace. So, think of concrete achievements for your venture that speak to your core. And don't be shy about adding some material aspects of success (car, house, places you want to visit) to the mix, too! There's nothing wrong with attaining personal wealth, which can be a byproduct of success. Your professional and personal impact should be your priority, but there's nothing wrong with curating a vision that includes aspects of material success as well.

One way to gain confidence at this stage is to practice visualization with small things. Write down something you are striving for, something somewhat attainable you've been struggling with. Place the written goal in a place where you can see it, and set aside time each day to think about (using your five senses) what it will be like to achieve it. Through the consistent and intentional completion of your inner and outer work, the day will eventually come when you start to accomplish your goals! Once you achieve your smaller goals, challenge yourself and practice this intention of visualization for bigger and still bigger goals. Your compound successes will give you the courage to believe that your larger goals are indeed attainable! Regularly visualizing a successful future and actually seeing it come together, one accomplished goal at a time, will provide you with the necessary motivation needed to keep going.

STEP 2: ***Complete a Detailed Analysis of Your Market***

Questions that arise from your research could include (but are not limited to):

Who is your target market?

What motivates them?

What is the area of their pain? (If you have followed your passion generated from your lemon experience(s) correctly, it should be similar to yours, past or present.)

What problem are you solving for them?

How will your "good work" benefit them?

Why should your market purchase your product or service offering?

Focusing on your market and understanding their needs, desires, and motivations will help you create a product and/or service offering that will draw your market to purchase from you.

STEP 3: ***Determine the Values Your Venture Will Represent***

Clearly document the "why" of your business, in essence, the purpose of it. Beyond the reasons previously discussed, the "why" of your business will become important later when you curate your marketing strategy and marketing materials.

Determine also the values that you want to define your company. Some examples of company values are integrity, transparency, and accountability. Do any of these resonate with you? Think of a set of values that will guide how you will operate your business. Relate them to your passion(s), specifically those generated from your life lemon(s). How will your lemon experience(s) impact your service and business operations? Will you operate your business differently than the other companies in your space because of your lemon experience(s)?

You may be wondering: Why would I establish my business values before I determine how to deliver the service? Since this venture is a *mission* to live according to your purpose, the "why" of what you do should absolutely be placed before the "how." Getting yourself accustomed to thinking about *your* "why" from the beginning of your venture sets the tone for how your business will operate. Remember: This venture is not about quick riches or operating solely for your personal aggrandizement. If your service addresses a real need of your customer base but doesn't adequately reflect *your* "why," you threaten the sustainability of your purpose-driven venture, as it will come across as inauthentic. Even if you do achieve success, you'll rob yourself of the peace that accompanies operating on purpose. Understanding the "why" of your business will help guide your answer to the "how."

The "why" should always come first.

STEP 4: ***Brainstorm What You Want Your Service to Look Like***

Think of how you will deliver your service or develop and distribute your product. Are you thinking of an online distribution model only, or are you planning to eventually have a storefront location? If your venture involves the delivery of a service, how will you structure your service packages, what services will be offered in each, and why?

Keeping in mind our earlier definition of a successful entrepreneur—one who solves problems at a profit from the perspective of their purpose—outline the specifics of how you envision solving the "problem" for your target market, taking into consideration your skills and passion(s) generated from your lemon experience(s). How will your product or service address your target market's problem with excellence in a manner that is unique to you and draws from your own lemon experience(s)? How will your business compare to all other businesses in the same space?

In my case, I set out to address the critical nursing shortage by delivering an RN recruitment solution to the healthcare system, specifically from a nurse's perspective. As a nurse myself, I had a solid understanding of what nurses were looking for in a position, and I also had a unique perspective, having been a patient hospitalized for an extended period of time. I knew the type of staff I would want to care for me as a patient and set out to place these types of nurses with my client organizations to help them address their urgent staffing needs. Armed with the perspective of both a patient and a nurse, when I became a recruitment business owner, I could listen to the challenges faced by health executives with a more empathetic ear and could suggest solutions that proved effective in addressing their staffing issues.

Squeezing the juice from my lemon experience allowed me to look at the nursing shortage problem from a patient's perspective first, then as an RN. Both helped me design components of my recruitment service package that would help draw more RNs to me, who would then trust me to place them with my "nurse-vetted" client organizations. In essence, your lemon experience(s) will help you focus on what's important. And if you allow it, your lemon experiences will also help you structure your service offering or develop your product with excellence.

STEP 5: *Refer Back to Your End Goals Regularly*

Now that you've completed Steps 1 to 4, you're ready to work backward from your end goals—the goals that represent business success to you—and start writing down clear and concise actionable activities that can get you there. Doing so on a regular basis (yearly, quarterly, weekly) will systematically guide your activities and help you stay on target.

After creating a list of goals for completion in the upcoming fiscal **year**, be sure to break down your goals into those you plan to complete each **quarter**. This is the start of effectively progressing through Step 5. Then, for the first quarter of the next fiscal year, break down the goals you've listed for that quarter into goals for completion each **week**. You may even find it useful to break it down into activities you plan to complete each week that will help you accomplish each goal. Repeat this exercise before the end of each quarter.

INTERNAL AND EXTERNAL CONDITIONS WILL LIKELY CHANGE; NOT EVERY-thing will progress according to plan. However, casting a clear vision yearly, quarterly, and weekly will allow you to effectively focus on action items for completion of the larger goals. Staying focused is a key strategy you'll need to master, as it directly influences your ability to create the lemonade of your success.

Here's an example of how to use Steps 1 through 5 for a sample business:

Goals list (Step 1): Become the #1 dealer of beach art in my country. Build an effective team of two full-time employees in two years. Earn $100,000 net profit within the first five years of business. Donate 10 percent of the gross profit each year to Oceana, the largest international advocacy organization exclusively working for the conservation of oceans.[15] Eventually buy a Porsche Cayenne for myself once I make $550,000 in one year in profit.

Target customer (Step 2): Based on my extensive market research, I will target purveyors of art that appreciate beach culture worldwide, those motivated by a desire to experience this culture while living away from it.

Why (Step 3): I experienced the power of emotional healing through beach art while immersing myself in island culture on a past trip to Honolulu, and I want to share my passion and artistic talent with the world.

Business values (Step 3): Exceptional customer service, timely and effective communication, timely delivery of services, commitment to corporate social responsibility; essentially, having your business give to a cause, or causes with consistency and intentionality—a concept we'll discuss in greater detail in Chapter 13.

How (Step 4): Create beach scenes using different media, connect with other artists around the world, and arrange to sell their beach art through my platform for a percentage of the profits. To start, I'll sell all art on my company website, as well as through social media and local art vendors. I'll also target celebrities, pro-surfers, and other pro-athletes that are immersed in beach culture and get my art in their hands with the goal of having them promote it.

Working backward (Step 5). <u>Goals for the upcoming fiscal year</u> could include:

1. Create a set number of pieces of beach art using different media. Projects categorized into themed works: sunset art vs. "dayscapes," pieces that incorporate surfing and boating culture. Chosen projects would be based on market analysis on the types of beach art that sell well. Also, based on market analysis, establish contact with artists around the world that are creating exceptional beach art and inquire about their willingness to have me sell their creations through my platform.

2. Decide on which and how many professional development activities I will participate in for this fiscal year. From a list of classes to strengthen my artistic skills, classes to learn how to effectively market art on social media platforms, classes to help strengthen my sales skills, and participation in networking events. Will create a plan to secure sources of funding and secure the services of a Business Management Consultant to help me build my business effectively from the ground up, one that will also help me grow as the leader of my purpose-driven business.

3. Develop an effective, user-friendly website that supports e-commerce.

4. Curate brand strategy and marketing messaging and establish a social media presence on several platforms.

5. Implement systems to ensure communication with customers is timely and effective in communicating company values, story (the why), etc.

6. Implement systems to ensure the timely delivery of art pieces and facilitate company operations.

7. Establish contact with Oceana to inform them of my company's corporate social responsibility initiative to support their organization.

8. To effectively progress through to the end of Step 5—working backward—I'll be sure to break down my goals into those I plan to complete each quarter and then each week with action items for completion. I'll be sure to revisit these lists regularly. Before the end of each quarter in this fiscal year, I'll again break down the goals for

the upcoming quarter into action items I can take each week to get me to the completion of the goals for the quarter. I know repeating this process throughout the year will help me achieve the goals on my fiscal-year list.

Map out your business goals on paper using this example as a guide. It will help you maintain focus and stay on target to accomplish your goals.

DON'T DOUBT IN THE DARK WHAT GOD HAS SHOWN YOU IN THE LIGHT[16]

Make your life lemons worth the pain you've endured by setting your gaze forward. Focus and don't look back! Circumstances that threaten your positive perspective will invariably arise, but never doubt in the dark times what you have been shown in the light. Revisit the process of unearthing your purpose and stay focused.

When challenging times arise, acknowledge the truth about why you are feeling discouraged. If your feelings are warranted as an internal or external warning sign (you actually have a tangible reason for discouragement because something is wrong within you or your business), driving you toward a particular course of action, then pivot and make the change. If your discouragement, anxiety, or insecurities are due to your own negative self-talk, commit to transcending them. Replace them with a perception of yourself as a person who is able to accomplish their goals, then re-establish focus, and move forward.

Maintaining focus is imperative, and it's one of the greatest success secrets you can adopt on your entrepreneurial journey. Focus provides you with the mental discipline to stay on task with undivided attention, which helps you complete your work effectively and efficiently.[17] Distractions draw you away from what's important and result in work that is less than your best.[18] Remain present in all your interactions: your individual work or your interactions with clients, customers, and/or your team. Giving your undivided attention is not only important for productivity, but it also helps to ensure your team and target market feel heard and appreciated. Focus on what's in front of you, along with your goals and, most importantly, keep in the forefront of your mind an understanding of how your "good work" will impact the lives of your target market and beyond.

Your journey toward success will progress through many iterations of change from inception to completion. However, understanding the nuances of perspective in the context of business success—perception, vision, and focus—will help you stay on track and chart your course toward the lemonade of your success.

FOR DEEPER REFLECTION...

Strategy #3: Cast a Clear and Detailed Vision & Remain Focused

1. To effectively turn your life lemon(s) into the lemonade of your success, you'll first need to develop a clear vision of what you are striving to achieve. List three components of your vision for your venture:

2. There were several tools discussed in this chapter that can help you visualize effectively:

   a. One was affirmations. Create a list of three affirmation statements.

   b. Create a vision board with pictures illustrating what success means to you. Ensure that they are specific, vivid, and beyond what you believe to be possible right now to effectively activate the power of cognitive dissonance.

   c. For Bible passages that can help you build confidence and visualize your successful future, go to the Resources page at: **melanemullings.com** and search for the section "Chapter 3."

3. Describe your vision of success:

   - What will it look like for you?
   - Feel like?
   - Sound like?
   - Smell like?
   - What types of foods or beverages will represent success for you?

4. What are the values you want your company to represent? Examples include: integrity, transparency, effective communication, innovation, respect, honesty, trustworthiness, and accountability. Write down a list that speaks to the values you hold dear and those you see represented in your favorite businesses.

5. Think about what you want your company to look like in terms of structure, the benefits you plan to offer your team, how you plan to integrate your business values into the delivery of your service or the

development of your product, your mission, your impact, and what you plan to achieve overall. Create a document that captures this comprehensive vision. Review it regularly.

6. What are three things you can do in your workday this week and going forward that will help you minimize distractions and maintain focus?

** Bringing all this together will provide you the tools to develop a new per-spective that will help you build a solid foundation for a sustainably successful business.

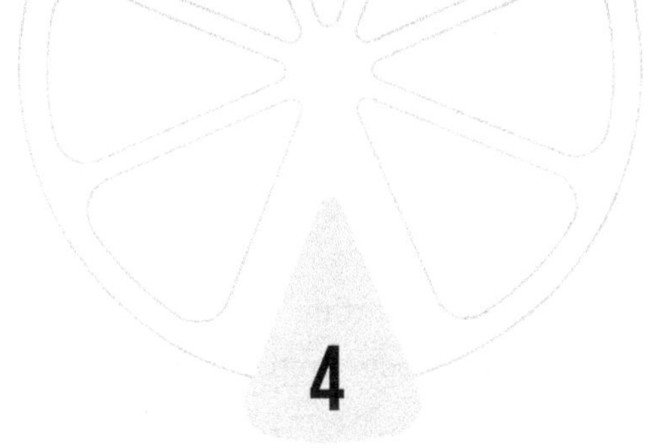

4

YOUR STABILIZING CORE

"Whatever you ask in prayer believing, you will receive."[1]

—MATTHEW 21:22

ARMED WITH A PASSIONATE BELIEF IN THIS SINGLE BIBLE TEXT, FAITH that God would keep His Word, and an understanding of my life's purpose, I set out on my entrepreneurial journey to prove that, yes, registered nurses *could* be found to address the critical RN shortage threatening to compromise the delivery of quality patient care in areas with the greatest need for nurses. My goal was to establish a successful nursing recruitment firm, built from a nurse's perspective, that would help address the RN shortage in the hardest-hit areas of Canada. With no prior knowledge of how to start, run, or grow a business, I completely depended on God to lead me, open doors for me, and instruct me along the way.

When I started, I had no formal business training whatsoever and little capital to fund my venture. My lemon experience as a patient during an intense nursing shortage was *the most* influential component of my preparation for this endeavor, and that was terrifying! I'd given up a six-figure lifestyle to follow my entrepreneurial dream, then as a result of a car accident—my second most influential lemon experience—I lost the ability to function as an RN to fund that dream, but I still pressed forward with the belief that God would see me through.

How might you ask? Well, the only reason I felt I could depend on God to lead me, open doors, and instruct me along my entrepreneurial journey was because of my lemon experiences. God had demonstrated His trustworthiness to help me survive through challenging seasons in the past; surviving leukemia and a serious car accident, where I was hit by an intoxicated driver three months after incorporating my business, sustaining injuries to my neck and back from the T-bone impact that required over three years of physical therapy. This is what gave me the will to exercise faith in Him again. I'd survived both death-defying lemon experiences by the mercy of God in the past, so squeezing an understanding of these past challenges and a recognition that God ultimately brought me through them empowered me with the strength, courage, focus, and drive to effectively operate at this next stage of my life's purpose with the belief that *I could* trust Him again.

Strong core muscles stabilize the spine and pelvis, which can aid in the reduction of lower back pain.[2] When your core muscles are strong, your body is more stable, and you can achieve better balance and posture. As it is in life, so it is in business. As it relates to your business, faith needs to be your stabilizing core. It will see you through many a dark day along your entrepreneurial journey, and it will help you maintain perspective, focus, and balance as you grow toward achieving your goals.

THE POWER OF PAST FAITH

As a result of my lemon experience with leukemia, I learned that childlike faith in God is more powerful than any medicine or therapy, any human motivation or encouragement, or any amount of conjured willpower. Although my medical team regularly communicated the severity of my condition to me, I found strength in my faith and was grounded in the belief that I would survive and live to thrive!

Envisioning life after leukemia in vivid detail, along with my belief in the power of God to heal me, helped me endure the challenges of the disease: hours-long vomiting sessions, bone-marrow aspirations where a four-inch needle[3] was drilled into my pelvis, painful dressing changes, bouts of blindness for days, and much more. Looking at myself in the mirror at the height of my illness—a frightened shell of my former self—was incredibly debilitating. But the strength of my faith that I would live to experience a full recovery and would one day see the Hawaii I'd envisioned in my mind helped me hold on.

Clinging to my faith in the midst of extreme conditions was so pivotal not only to my recovery, but also to my future as a business owner. Squeezing my leukemia lemon experience in particular—evaluating it from different angles, thinking about how I felt in the scary moments of my hospitalization, how the power of visualization helped me survive the pain of those days, and that I miraculously survived it all—is what gave me the courage to let go and trust God again during some of the darkest days of my business journey.

The journey toward your life's purpose *will* invariably stretch you beyond what you believe you can emotionally, physically, relationally, financially, and spiritually handle.

Expect it.

At some point during your journey, it will become imperative for you to give yourself permission to surrender to a Higher Power. This will help you effectively navigate the invariable challenges that lie ahead. As a Christian, I believe in the power and presence of God and His ability to transform any set of circumstances. Whatever Higher Power you subscribe to, though, recognize that your purpose-driven venture requires faith to help you avoid crumbling under pressure. Faith will be your stabilizing core, the key to unlocking your success and opening the door to a truly abundant life. Without a willingness to surrender to higher wisdom, you threaten your ability to achieve your goals.

DURING THE PROCESS OF UNEARTHING MY PURPOSE, I REALIZED I WAS granted a second chance at life for a reason; the survivor guilt would allow me no rest until I charted a purposeful course forward. This realization gave me the courage to, once again, let go and have faith that the same power that rescued me from near death before could and would guide me on my entrepreneurial journey as well.

"...He who has begun a good work in you will bring it to completion..."[4]
—Philippians 1:6

We tend to become jaded as we age, and our willingness to trust diminishes as disappointments, setbacks, and failures add up over time. As failures and disappointments stack up, we attempt to make sense of how concepts like "you can do anything if you put your mind to it" or even Matthew 21:22 (see page 91 - page one of this chapter) could ever be possible. But, rather than doubting based on past disappointments that, in many cases, contain many variables as to why situations did not come together as we would have liked, recognize that God *can* actually be taken at His Word! The question is: Are we willing to give Him that uninhibited chance to show us?

"Many of us believe in God, but not many of us believe Him."
—Anonymous

Allowing ourselves to have faith in any Higher Power can be terrifying once we've experienced enough disappointment. Chances are you're reading this book out of frustration from expending time and resources in directions that were unfruitful. You may be feeling broken and despondent, having endured life-altering lemon experiences, and are now lost on how to create meaning from these experiences. You may not even be sure you have it in you to fully give yourself to anything again after suffering defeat in the past. Trust me, I can relate!

Remember, though, that your purpose-driven venture is not merely for the sake of amassing wealth, experiencing the freedom of owning your own business, or receiving the influence and accolades that can accompany success. You were *created* for this "good work," and the sheer magnitude of the impact on those who need your service behooves you to lean on your Higher Power to guide you through. The emotional, physical, financial, and relational sacrifices you'll need to make along your journey toward success will require a force greater than you to help you navigate.

Take courage.

The success of your purpose-driven venture is imminent IF you surrender to the formative process of you *first* through the completion of your inner work—all of which is held together by faith.

"Courage is the most important of all the virtues because, without courage, you can't practice any other virtue consistently. You can practice any virtue erratically, but nothing consistently without courage."

—Maya Angelou

For some, having the courage and willingness to let go and relinquish control to a spiritual process of faith is a huge challenge. I've found that for most people, though, faith itself really isn't the issue, as all of us exercise some degree of faith on a consistent, even daily, basis. Here are some examples:

- If you've ever traveled by airplane or bus, you exercised faith that you would arrive at your destination safely.

- If you've purchased a vehicle from a car dealer and have confirmation of the completed paperwork, you have faith that you will receive your vehicle at the predetermined time.

- When you drive through an intersection, you have faith that the people who are approaching their red light will stop and not hit you as you drive through the intersection.

Recognition of the small, seemingly insignificant examples of faith you consistently exercise will serve to provide the fuel for you to believe that bigger things are indeed possible! If having faith doesn't come naturally to you, think about consistently implementing the same type of faith in your business venture as in the above examples. When you do, eventually, you will start to experience doors opening, resources flowing toward you, people connecting with you, and more opportunities for growth than you've ever experienced before!

Exercise courage and believe in your Higher Power. Believe also in your discerned purpose, and believe in yourself! Through faith in your Higher Power, you *can* accomplish the goals you're envisioning for your business, and you can squeeze success out of your lemon experiences.

So, FAITH ITSELF REALLY ISN'T THE ISSUE. *EXERCISING COURAGE* TO OPER-ate from a place of faith amid challenging circumstances is, and represents, one of the greatest stumbling blocks to achieving success, particularly if you've endured debilitating lemon experiences.

You may be jaded, bruised from past experiences when you *did* believe and were disappointed, and now you may not even be sure you can handle another setback. Just the thought of hoping for something better might leave you feeling anxious and fearful. Consider, however, this passage from Theodore Roosevelt's famous 1910 speech, *Citizenship in a Republic*:

> *"It is not the critic that counts… the credit belongs to the man*
> *who is actually in the arena,*
> *whose face is marred by dust and sweat and blood; who strives valiantly…*
> *who comes short again and again,*
> *because there is no effort without error and shortcoming;*
> *but who does actually strive to do the deeds… who spends*
> *himself in a worthy cause;*
> *who at the best knows in the end the triumph of high achievement,*
> *and who at the worst, if he fails, at least fails while daring greatly,*
> *so that his place shall never be with those cold and timid souls who neither*
> *know victory nor defeat."*[5]

Those of us who have the courage to dare greatly and take the leap into living with purpose, even if we suffer experiences that resemble defeats, live far richer lives than we would have ever lived prior! No resignation to living a life of quiet desperation, but rather persevering toward a life of purpose, meaning, impact, achievement, and ultimately, peace.

Remember, no experience you've ever endured will be wasted. If you live your life on a journey in the direction of your Higher Power's purpose for you—providing the "good work" you were created for—your success is inevitable if you believe.

If you can get to a place where you can envision better for your-self,

if you can muster the courage to believe better is possible for you and that *you can*, indeed, make it to the other side of your current circumstances…

Then invest in yourself and take the next step:

Let go, and let your Higher Power guide, instruct, provide, protect, comfort, and bless you on your entrepreneurial journey.

PRACTICAL EXAMPLES

As discussed in Chapter 3, our minds are hardwired to complete the tasks we put in front of them, whether positive or negative; the guidance provided in Proverbs 23:7 (from the top of page 75) provides an understanding of this concept. Think about it: In your own life, there have likely been instances where you've believed in something, and after having faith that it would come to pass, eventually, it did! These experiences build our confidence, which in turn helps us exercise our faith and graduate from belief in the manifestation of simple things to the belief that bigger blessings are possible, too!

The sheer act of believing is so powerful. I think of Jim Carrey, who, as a struggling Canadian comedian trying to make it in Los Angeles in 1985, wrote himself a check for ten million dollars for "acting services rendered" and kept it in his wallet, believing that, one day, he would be in the position to cash it. Five years later, he was cast in the movie *Dumb and Dumber*, for which he received—you guessed it—ten million dollars.[6,7]

Some might be tempted to chalk up instances like this one to mere coincidence. But *visualization coupled with faith is undeniably powerful.* Beyond surviving leukemia, I experienced the power of combining both many times throughout my entrepreneurial journey. One example relates to the mammoth debt I accumulated funding my dream, which constantly threatened my resolve to keep pushing forward. Sifting through piles and piles of demand letters from lenders at the mailbox and enduring the shrill and stern voices from creditors throughout my workday was an aspect of my reality during the early years of building my venture. However, I eventually learned to take a deep breath in those moments, tell myself the truth that yes, I was in debt, but as God delivered me in the past, I believed He could *and would* do it again as I worked toward living my life's purpose.

Simultaneously, I would visualize a life free of debt. I thought of the day I would be in the position to walk to the bank and pay off my last investor. I envisioned the weather, which route I would take to the bank, how I would feel getting ready to head to the bank, what I would do afterward—I formulated a specific vision of the exact day when all my debt would be paid off and replayed that vision in my head over and over again. Interestingly enough, when the day finally came, it unfolded *exactly* how I had envisioned for years that it would, albeit without the grand feeling that I expected would accompany it. Why was there no grand feeling? Because I had lived that day so many times in my mind, that when it finally happened, it just ended up feeling like any other day! That's the power of visualization coupled with faith.

Take a moment to scan the trajectory of your life. I'm confident you, too, will remember times when the level of faith you do have, coupled with visualization, resulted in the manifestation of blessings in your own life. Take time to dissect those experiences. How were you feeling before you experienced the deliverance? Stressed, anxious, impatient, fearful? When everything came together, did you think of how your visualization or beliefs played a part in surviving the experience? Reflect on these experiences and glean nuggets of wisdom you can apply to your entrepreneurial venture now. As you survived those past challenges, as well as your lemon experiences, you can squeeze your understanding of them to help you create your successful business.

LIVING THE PURPOSE YOU WERE CREATED FOR AND ACHIEVING THE RE-sults that come with it will require you to have faith in the Higher Power that blessed you with your purpose in the first place. Without trust in your Higher Power, the journey toward purpose will drain you and cost you time, energy, and resources. As your ultimate power source, your Higher Power is aware of what is ahead of you, how to direct you, whom to bring onto your path to help you, and how to prepare you to operate efficiently at each level of your journey. Faith is the stabilizing core that holds your entire venture together. Connect to your power source consistently, exercise faith, and take courage! The manifestation of your success story is just over the horizon.

THE PROGRESSION OF FAITH

As you take the leap and endeavor to graduate from the level of faith you have now to the faith to believe that *you can* indeed squeeze your challenging life experiences into a successful business, you will experience a powerful spiritual transformation, which will form the backbone of your ability to weather storms during the entire life of your entrepreneurial venture. In my case, I started with faith in who I understood God to be through evaluating my leukemia lemon experience. Based on that, as I started my entrepreneurial journey, I made the decision to build on that faith and graduate to belief in Matthew 21:22 (from the top of page 91). I then decided to give God a chance to do what *He said* in Matthew 21:22 because of what *He* previously *did* in my life.

The first stage is having childlike faith, and the second forms the reasoning behind it; the "why" of what we believe is equally as important as the "what." If you understand why you believe—in your venture, for example—that will help you believe in the "what." If the reason you believe in your venture is that you are crystal clear that it is your life's purpose and you have no doubt that it seamlessly combines both your passion and your skills, the strength of that belief will help you believe in the "what"—that *you can* create a successful business! Progression to effectively believing in the "what" requires belief in the "why," and both are imperative for you to effectively navigate all the challenges you will invariably face on your entrepreneurial journey ahead.

The one thing that is true for all of us is that we made it! No matter how close you came to death, your lemon experience(s) did not kill you. You survived, and as the adage states, what does not kill you makes you stronger. The sheer fact that you made it through your challenging life experiences, albeit in some cases, with scars, you still survived! Let it be for a reason and squeeze or evaluate your lemon experience(s) again and gain courage from the fact that you are made of strong stuff! You survived challenges before, and you can do it again.

We are all blessed with a purpose, armed with lemon experiences that reveal our passions and skills that can propel us forward. By bathing it all in faith, we receive strength, motivation, energy, and resources to effectively persevere to accomplish purpose-driven success that eventually leads to peace. Your personal growth, and demonstration of faith in your Higher Power in one area, will equip you with the strength to progress forward to manage the greater challenges that lie ahead. None of us will ever attain a state of utopia in life, a state of full self-actualization or the pinnacle of success where everything is perfect. However, striving toward the next level of growth and success will require the progressive development of our faith and a willingness to connect with our power source to get us there.

TRUST IS BUILT WHEN WORDS MATCH ACTIONS OVER TIME[8]

We can begin the process of developing faith by allowing others to demonstrate their trustworthiness, which is built when they keep their word to us over time. Should someone deserve your trust if they consistently demonstrate an inability to keep their word? Surely, the answer is no. If, however, someone demonstrates consistency in keeping their word, shouldn't they be trusted to do so again in the future?

Surely yes! If a vendor comes through and provides you the promised product on time, that experience warrants your trust and a willingness to use them again on a bigger project. If you take a chance and make the financial sacrifice to secure the services of a consultant, and they end up adding value to your business, shouldn't that warrant a referral to others within your network? If a member of your team has committed to completing an urgent project for you and they do so on time with excellence, they deserve a chance to show you they can handle bigger projects. In my case, coming to an understanding that God had proven to be trustworthy during my lemon experiences in the past is what gave me the courage to exercise faith in His stabilizing power to carry me through my entire entrepreneurial journey as well. God's past trustworthiness warranted my faith, and making the choice to believe God and hold Him to the promises included in the Bible was the single, most influential success strategy I implemented during my entire entrepreneurial journey.

It started with my review of the biblical passage of scripture Matthew 21:22, which I was reintroduced to from the book, *The Secret*. I decided to put the concept of "warranted trust" to the test and give God a chance to demonstrate his trustworthiness to me again and began to trust Him on a consistent basis. I started to claim Matthew 21:22 while requesting "little things" of God, and, after the answers to my prayers started to stack up, I began to develop confidence in the power of more of God's biblical promises to manifest tangible blessings in my business as well. The little things I asked for generated what I call "simple answers." As the simple answers to my prayers for little things stacked up, my requests became bolder, which to my surprise, generated "big answers." Drawing from the momentum I was experiencing through my faith, I decided to give God a chance to show me that He could bless me in unimaginable ways and provide "bigger answers," even through seemingly impossible circumstances in response to my audacious prayers.

For me, the progression looked like this:

Simple Answer

During my last stint of employment as a per diem RN in Philadelphia, I lived right outside the bustling area of Center City. As a night shift RN, finding parking in the morning on the street close to the apartment where I was staying was nearly impossible, and there were days I would circle around for more than an hour before finding a parking spot. Regularly working overtime after a twelve-hour night shift, then commuting home to search for parking started to become extremely tiring and increasingly unbearable. Matthew 21:22 gave me the courage to ask God for something as trite as opening up *immediate* parking for me *every* morning after my night shifts. After praying back to God His promise in Matthew 21:22 and clearly communicating my request, it worked! Until my last day of work in Philadelphia, God opened a parking spot for me on the street *immediately* upon arriving home, a feat that had proved impossible for months prior.

Big Answer

While I was working as a per diem and travel nurse, my tax return was reliably the same amount year after year. In the months leading up to my return to Canada, I'd worked a night shift and forgotten to swipe in when I arrived at work. When I recognized the error prior to leaving work for that day, I notified my supervisor, filled out and submitted the necessary paperwork, and notified Human Resources of my mistake. Despite my efforts, my paycheck didn't account for that day of work. Though I had documentation that proved I had been there for that shift, I wasn't able to convince them and recoup my earnings.

Matthew 21:22 gave me the courage to ask God to put the exact amount of money from that missed shift onto the tax return I was to receive in the coming weeks, even though past experience had reliably demonstrated that each year while in Philadelphia, my tax return would not reflect a higher amount. But when I received my tax return in the mail that year, I fell to the ground in shock and amazement. For the first time, the check amount was higher; it included the amount from my missed shift and even a few cents extra!

Bigger Answer

Three months after I incorporated my business, I endured my second lemon experience: a car accident, which required over three years of physical therapy and treatment from several health practitioners to get me fully back on my feet and functional. Due to my injuries, I couldn't work in my previous role as an RN. I had already incorporated my business prior to the accident, so my rehabilitation time doubled as an opportunity for me to build the business. But, since I had no experience or business educational training, it took three and a half years to make my first dollar from my efforts. Debt was piling up during my recovery and, at the beginning of my entrepreneurial journey, I refused to ask for outside help out of misplaced guilt and a misguided position that since I had chosen this journey, it was solely my responsibility (and God's!) to get me out of it.

The days of having money for luxurious living were a distant memory—even money for necessities was non-existent at the time. With necessities becoming scarce and fear and depression in abundance, I chose to glean strength from Matthew 21:22 again and go grocery shopping with a credit card I was fully aware was maxed out, with no room to cover even a single purchase.

I moved through the aisles of that grocery store with both fear and excitement. Fearing embarrassment, I nervously filled my cart with items I desperately needed, that I knew, without a doubt, I could not pay for. But I was also excited about the possibility of experiencing another miracle in a matter of moments, believing beyond a doubt that God would come through.

With several impatient shoppers behind me, I closed my eyes as I raised my hand to give the cashier my credit card for a purchase over a hundred dollars, ultimately believing that God would allow the transaction to clear. When I heard the "beep" on the credit card machine and saw the receipt printing, it was a surreal moment I will never forget. The transaction was approved! To the cashier, it was no big deal—just another transaction—but to me, I knew it was a miracle. Breathless, and with my eyes opened wide from shock, I packed up my grocery bags and left the store with more evidence of God's trustworthiness.

THE PRESENCE OF FAITH IS NOT THE ABSENCE OF FEAR

When you make the decision to exercise faith, that does not mean that you will never experience fear. During my leukemia hospitalization, I was, indeed, grounded in my belief that I would survive that lemon experience, even when my prognosis became grim. As my body started to lose strength more rapidly though, the foundation of my faith started to shake. One day while my father was in my room with me in the midst of my weakening resolve, I gathered strength from my emaciating body and quietly asked him, "Do you think I'm going to die?" The truth of my physical state was cracking my resolve, and I asked the question, perhaps looking for a reason to let go. Immediately he answered "No!" in the most stoic, confident voice he could muster, but his quick exit to the bathroom in my hospital suite to cry uncontrollably gave away his true feelings. A moment I will never forget.

Many times throughout my entrepreneurial journey, I walked the balance between faith and fear, belief and unbelief. The same has been the case for anyone that has accomplished any great feat. *The cumulative effect of your faith is what is most important*, however. In our humanness, even with the most steadfast determination, the greatest of techniques and all the sound wisdom in the world, you will still experience days that will shake your resolve. Nevertheless, evaluate: Are you in a state of fear *more* than in a state of faith? Are you constantly thinking of what might go wrong or concentrating on your insecurities or shortcomings as you build your venture, or do you spend more of your time believing that despite them all, you can still create the lemonade of your success? Strive to stay in a state of belief more often than not. One strategy that will help you do this is reviewing the journey that brought you to the place where you are now.

NATURE WEIGHS IN

Even in our darkest circumstances, an honest review of our lives would reveal that God *has* demonstrated His power to answer even the simplest of our requests. Recognition of this builds confidence and faith that He will come through on the bigger requests. Maybe you've experienced deliverance in the form of provisions, right on time when you were about to lose everything, or a phone call from a friend that came right when you were about to give up. Having been an avid biology student for much of my life, I've found that the intricacy of nature has always provided a powerful illustration of the trustworthy attributes of God's character, which helped grow my faith and belief that even when things got tough during my entrepreneurial journey, God would eventually see me through. Sigourney Weaver's beautiful, soothing narrative in the DVD series *Planet Earth* illustrates the point this way:

"…Winter. When the temperate seas are lashed by violent storms.
The storms are beneficial.
Turbulence stirs the water and draws nutrients up from the depths,
but nutrients alone cannot support life;
you need sunlight, too!
The spring sun will grow algae fields the size of the Amazon rainforest.
So vast that the algae produce ¾ of all the oxygen in our atmosphere."

Nature masterfully demonstrates God's power at work in challenging seasons. In winter, violent storms on temperate seas are beneficial and serve a purpose. Likewise, during your purpose-driven journey, you too will have storms to navigate that may shake you to your core. The storms, albeit stressful and daunting to sailors that may be navigating the waters, help to serve a purpose, to draw nutrients up from the depths. If you allow them, your challenges will equip you with strategies that can help you make it to the next level of your journey! When the sun eventually hits the nutrients that have been pulled up from the depths, algae fields grow, refreshing the entire earth with oxygen, which we need to sustain life. Likewise, squeezing your life lemons and learning lessons from them has the potential to not only grow you, but also impact your world as well as you walk in your purpose! Evidence of God's power in nature is on full display all around us. If God can care and provide for nature with such accuracy and specificity, shouldn't He be given a chance to show His ability to see us through our current situations and lead us along the direction of His purpose for us?

This narrative can give you courage during your business journey, as it demonstrates that your lemon experiences and the challenges of entrepreneurship have the capacity to birth beautiful beginnings that can refresh the world. Trusting in your Higher Power will help get you to a beautiful, successful end!

NOTHING ELSE WILL DO

In the early days of my journey, I read every business start-up book I could find. Acutely aware that I had no formal business training or experience, I immersed myself in literature I felt would provide me the real-world instruction I needed to succeed. I read memoirs of successful figures, business management books, along with a myriad of personal development books. I took sales courses and attended all sorts of conferences, seminars, and workshops. Yes, the information did, indeed, garner results, but only to a point. Eventually, I was left empty and spinning in circles on the same level I was at because I was constantly teetering between faith in myself, and the power inherent in the *application* of the principles I was learning to lead me to success, along with a full surrender to have faith in God that *He* would ultimately usher me to success through my personal transformation. I came to understand that *achieving success from a purpose-driven venture is unlikely without fully surrendering, in faith, to the power of guidance that brought us to our purpose in the first place*. We need an intentional connection with our power source to achieve success that flows from operating in our purpose.

So, no matter how skilled you are, how many years of business experience you possess, or how many venture capitalists are funding your business, if you don't believe in a Higher Power, you will eventually run out of the energy needed to power you through your purpose-driven journey. As you exercise your stabilizing core of faith, you will be able to effectively navigate the storms that await you on your entrepreneurial journey. Then, you'll be able to positively affect others and maintain the success that's in store for you.

***

FAITH IN YOUR HIGHER POWER ALLOWS YOU THE FREEDOM TO EXHALE, knowing that your venture is in capable hands! As your core muscles stabilize your entire body, likewise, faith holds your entire purpose-driven venture together. Commit to exercise childlike faith and give your power source a chance to demonstrate trustworthiness to you. By claiming the promises made to you, you'll be strengthened to believe *you can* actually accomplish your goals!

Faith is the stabilizing core of your business. Take courage and give yourself permission to let go of your own personal and professional transformation, and by faith, you'll eventually enjoy the lemonade of your success!

FOR DEEPER REFLECTION...

Strategy #4: Exercise Faith

1. Applying the principles and promises of the Bible helped develop my faith, strengthen and embolden me with confidence, and enabled me to accomplish seemingly impossible feats during my entrepreneurial journey. Perhaps they will prove to be a source of encouragement and strength for you as well! Head over to **melanemullings.com** and click the "Resources" tab and search under Chapter 4 at for a list of scriptures that helped solidify my faith.

2. List two challenging experiences from your past where you demonstrated faith and the situation resolved as you believed it would.
   a. Would you say that your level of faith was a contributing factor? Why or why not?

3. List two challenging experiences from your past where you demonstrated faith and the situation did not progress as you believed it would.
   a. Would you say that your level of faith was a contributing factor? Why or why not?

4. What are your current beliefs about your Higher Power? List them.

5. What are three examples you can think of from nature or in the human body that demonstrate the presence of your Higher Power at work?

6. What impact have your lemon experiences had on your faith journey?
   a. What has changed in your level of faith since surviving your lemon experience(s)?

7. What do you believe about your Higher Power's ability to provide help, strength, and guidance along your entrepreneurial journey?

LEMONADE CHALLENGE

Over the next three months, commit to spending a set amount of time each day immersing yourself in literature or other sources of information that will strengthen your spiritual connection to your Higher Power. While doing so, connect with your Higher Power and make simple requests with faith, believing that what you are asking will eventually come to pass, or something better. **Ask with patience!** Keep track of the results of your requests over time. As you experience answers to your simple requests, gradually pray more audacious prayers and continue to keep track of the results. On your list, place a colored checkmark beside each answer to see a visual representation of your faith journey.

Month 1

Prayer requests: Answers to prayer:

Month 2

Prayer requests: Answers to prayer:

Month 3

Prayer requests: Answers to prayer:

5

THE MOST IMPORTANT STEP IN CONFLICT RESOLUTION

"When they go low, we go high."

—MICHELLE OBAMA

MANY ENTREPRENEURS FIND IT USEFUL TO START THEIR VENTURES alone. Eventually, as you hone your skills, develop your product or service offering, gain confidence as a leader, and earn money from your venture, you'll need to expand your circle and develop your success team to grow. Initially, your expanded team may consist of outside professionals that include but are not limited to: an accountant, lawyer, consultant(s) and perhaps even investors. Once you've exhausted your current capacity, you'll need to take on staff or work with additional outside professionals to help you grow to the next level.

As the adage states, no man is an island; you will need others to achieve the goals and attain the success you've envisioned from Chapter 3. Faith in your power source, an understanding of your purpose, a willingness to tell yourself the truth, and an intention to operate your business with a clear perspective, laser focus, and detailed vision for the future are all key pillars to building a solid foundation for your business. Additionally, developing a mindset that will enable you to *handle* the success is also key, and how a leader manages conflict personally and professionally directly impacts the heights their business will attain.

As your venture grows, the frequency and intensity of your interactions with those around you will dramatically increase. Eventually, you'll interact with more and more clients, vendors, customers, employees, consultants, and other professionals. The larger your circle and the longer you are in business, the greater the likelihood you'll experience situations that will require you to manage people with differing viewpoints, motives, and objectives. Learning to deal with these issues effectively is one of the most important components to managing your venture successfully, and a well-managed venture is more likely to achieve a state of sustained profitability.

And how would you rate your relationship with colleagues?

Conflict is inevitable and will invariably arise within your team (as well as externally, with people who interact with your business), since people have differing personalities, expectations, and approaches. Whether they choose to articulate their concerns is irrelevant. The point is this: When you, as a leader, become aware of issues within or outside of your organization, your immediate attention and effort are required. You can manage conflict by actively listening to the viewpoints and needs of all sides involved, communicating effectively with the use of non-judgmental, neutral language, gaining clarity on the issues at play, and suggesting compromises where applicable, so as to facilitate the sentiment that each side has walked away with a win. Acknowledging the truth about the presence of issues in your business is key and will help you plant the seeds of positive resolution, which will assist you in fostering an environment where success can bloom. However, true and full resolution means eventually moving forward in a positive direction *after* the conflict, even in the midst of differing viewpoints and ideas.

In order to withstand inevitable seasons of conflict, your willingness to create an environment of openness that can handle a diversity of ideas is important. At times, however, the way employees communicate their differing ideas isn't conducive to a healthy work environment! Managing conflict effectively will require your immediate attention and systematic implementation of key strategies on a consistent basis, and it is important to recognize that after the dust settles from conflict, the resulting negative energy calls for a figurative purification of sorts. This can be accomplished through **forgiveness**—the most important step in conflict resolution—without which true progression forward and complete resolution of issues cannot take place. Should animosity and resentment fester, it will undoubtedly infect your operations and eventually impact your bottom line.

To create a positive environment after conflict, you'll need to gain proficiency in this area in your personal life *first*. Forgiveness is an important component of your inner work to build a sustainably successful, impactful, purpose-driven business. A consistent demonstration of personal competency in this area will allow you to effectively manage potential ramifications of conflict that can threaten to derail your success. Let's explore how.

FORGIVENESS AND YOUR MIND

From Chapter 1, you've progressed through the process of telling yourself the truth about your life: your lemon experiences and their effect on you, how you arrived at the place you are now, and if you've started your business or entrepreneurial pursuit, perhaps even the current state of your venture. Some part of your "truth-talk" process was probably overwhelming. It likely included the revelation of unresolved issues from your past, including people or experiences that hurt you deeply, or perhaps even scarred you to the point that you move through life differently now.

I can relate. In fact, as I sat to write Chapter 1, I needed to pause and re-evaluate areas of my life that needed fresh examination! Following our Higher Power's influence, it should come as no surprise that we ought not to live in contention with others or hold grudges in our hearts for anyone, personally or professionally. We can't be open to the positivity and opportunities we seek for our venture in a mindset of negativity or resentment; our consciences will constantly try to bring us to a place of resolution or completion. Since our brains are hardwired for completion, unresolved conflicts drain us of energy and distract us, wreaking havoc on our life and our entrepreneurial endeavors.

In his book, *The Success Principles*, Jack Canfield discusses the importance of cleaning up our messes to move from where we are to where we want to be. When our past includes "incompletes," we cannot be free to fully embrace the present[1] and, by extension, the future. Incompletes take up what he calls "attention units"[2] or daily irritants that can take up space in our minds. He suggests that one of the best strategies we can implement to move further or faster along our success path is to fix, replace, mend, or get rid of these irritants that annoy us.[3] Conflicts definitely represent one category of incompletes that takes up rent-free space in our minds. Freeing yourself of the weight of hurtful experiences is crucial to building a sustainably profitable, purpose-driven venture. No matter how deeply you've buried your hurts, avoiding the resolution of past or present conflicts will invariably have a negative impact on you and the future growth and sustainability of your purpose-driven venture.

MY EXPERIENCE WITH FORGIVENESS

In the early years of my business, I found myself struggling with bouts of depression, born out of complete frustration with the slow pace of the progression of my business. After giving up everything to start my entrepreneurial journey, and after following a systematic approach to building my business, casting a detailed vision, and bathing it all in faith, I still couldn't get to the point of transformation or breakthrough. Exasperated from feelings of defeat, I decided to communicate my frustrations with one of my then mentors, a pastor friend. His response was transformative to both my inner work journey and my business, and I suspect it will have a similar effect on you:

> *Is there an area of your life that you have not fully surrendered to God?*
> *Are you holding resentment against anyone?*
> *Recognize that doing so could be blocking blessings for your business.*

The honest evaluation of my life and relationships to that point revealed that, even back to my childhood, I'd "moved on" from hurtful experiences and, as an adult, excised people from my life—warranted and unwarranted—but I hadn't truly resolved the offending issues *within myself.* Following biblical guidance on this topic of forgiveness[4] along with advice from *The Success Principles,*[5] I decided to resolve my ***past*** issues directly with those I felt safe to do so (Group 1) and wrote letters to the others (Group 2).

For the first group, I was able to have productive, healing conversations with them that helped me let go of past hurts. For the second group, on my own, I wrote a list of all the offenses I'd suffered from them that I realized I was still carrying and how I felt about it. I wrote detailed "total-truth" letters to each person reflected on the list from Group 2 and ensured I vented everything that I would want to say to them if I had the chance, and felt safe to do so. I then gathered each of the letters in a pile, articulated my willingness to forgive them, then burned the letters outside in a safe place and let the ashes blow in the wind. This experience was cathartic and symbolized my commitment to let go of the issues and move forward free, allowing me to rid—even my subconscious mind—of the attention units I was allocating to these experiences.

You, too, may find progressing through this process alone helpful. For some, professional help will be required to navigate through past hurts effectively. Either way, tell yourself the truth and seek out support and help as needed. The benefits of full release to both you and your business are unparalleled, and only you can give yourself the gift of freedom from the burden of resentment; a gift that will set you up for sustainable success.

THE TOTAL-TRUTH LETTERS WERE EFFECTIVE IN HELPING ME NAVIGATE past hurts, but unfortunately, years later, I was faced with a situation of broken trust and deep disappointment that seriously threatened the survival of my venture, and the total-truth letter proved ineffective. The situation came as a complete surprise, perhaps because I was so engulfed in my business. The discovery left me feeling emotionally, physically, spiritually, and intellectually incapacitated. Far more damaging, however, was my consistent and pervasive unwillingness to let the situation go and forgive completely.

I was struggling, and no letter or conversation would suffice this time around as the situation was still raw and ongoing. The total-truth letter and direct conversations had worked for me in dealing with past hurts but were not proving effective in dealing with this *present* one, especially in light of the fact that the offending party refused to acknowledge any wrongdoing. I found myself unable to fully forgive, and the compromised state of my heart and mind started to directly impact how I was showing up in my business.

The sharpness of my tone with clients and the quick reactivity and heightened level of frustration on seemingly inconsequential happenings was negatively impacting my business, and the numbers didn't lie. Telling myself the truth quickly and choosing once and for all to forgive saved my business, and likely rescued me from my own self-sabotage.

God desires us to grow from one stage of life to the next. My journey of life graduation in this arena started with squeezing my challenging life experiences from my past—evaluating them, learning from them, and dealing with them through direct conversations and the total-truth letter. This time, however, those strategies would not suffice because it was a present situation. Nevertheless, I still had to come to a place of resolution and develop competency in this arena for the health of my venture. I intrinsically knew that learning how to forgive fully personally, would help me apply this principle of forgiveness to business situations that would eventually arise in the future.

To experience the full benefits of effective conflict resolution, I had to demonstrate growth *personally* and learn how to fully progress through this last and most important step of the process, forgiveness. I realized that subconsciously holding on to resentment in my personal life was taking up rent-free space in my mind, disabling me from operating my business with excellence. The freedom that comes from full forgiveness is completely transformational on every level; it especially opens doors to your creativity, productivity, and opportunities for your business that would likely remain shut otherwise.

*"Keeping resentments is like swallowing poison and
expecting the other person to die."*

—Katie Evans and J. Michael Sullivan

Unforgiveness, bitterness, resentment, and other associated negative feelings ultimately leave us damaged and compromised. They actually tend to have a more deleterious effect *on us* than the person we're meant to forgive! The energy required to hold a grudge is overwhelming to your body, and over time, it will invariably rob you of the mental capacity and focus needed for you to achieve success.

Unforgiveness—the practice of engaging in ruminative thoughts of anger, vengeance, hate, and resentment—results in unproductive outcomes for the ruminator.[6] Physiologically, perceiving we've been wronged and ruminating on the associated anger keeps us in a fight-or-flight bodily response,[7] in which the brain triggers the release of the hormone adrenaline. Adrenaline has an important function, equipping our bodies to manage acute stress or danger. It does this by increasing our heart rate and blood pressure, expanding the air passages of the lungs, enlarging the pupils in our eyes, redistributing blood to the muscles, and altering our body's metabolism,[8] all responses necessary to help us deal with acute stressful events. However, we're not meant to remain in this heightened state for long. The consistent release of stress hormones can result in anxiety, depression, digestive issues, trouble sleeping, weight gain, a weakened immune response, and even heart problems.[6] Forgiveness, yes, involves releasing the offending party from your anger or resentment, but it mostly enables *you* to be freed from the negative effects of the grudge, which ultimately allows you to bring your best, unencumbered self to your venture.

A BUSINESS APPLICATION

Unforgiveness in business can show up in many ways. Examples include:

- One of your team members shames you in a meeting in retribution for how they feel you criticized them in front of a client.

- A customer writes what you perceive to be an undeserved bad review online because your staff would not give in to their demands. You respond by blacklisting them, blocking them from all your company social media accounts, and then alerting your staff to be "on the watch" for this particular customer.

- A vendor costs you future business with one of your major clients due to late delivery of a key component of your product or service offering, despite receiving confirmation from them that everything was on track for early delivery. You respond by calling them in front of your team and lose your cool as you communicate your anger and frustration. You take it a step further, and when in conversation with others in your business network that you know utilize this vendor, you share your side of the story and encourage them to drop this vendor also.

Disappointments and conflicts happen in business. They are an inevitable aspect of the entrepreneurial journey. Some disappointments and conflicts may even end up costing you money. If you have an ax to grind against a vendor, client, customer, or member of your team, the presence of negative energy has the propensity to become kryptonite to your venture. To create a positive work environment conducive to productivity, achieved goals, and sustainable success, however, you'll need to develop your skills in effective conflict resolution right to the end of the process. This includes the extension of forgiveness and the ability to then move on from the offense in a positive direction. As the business leader, setting this tone within your organization is key, and those that negate this important last step miss an enormous opportunity for growth, without which they can stymie their progression toward impactful, sustainable success.

FOUR STEPS TO COMPLETE FORGIVENESS

So, how can one forgive completely and effectively, to the point of moving in a positive direction thereafter? Here are four all-encompassing steps to forgiveness that I implemented at key points during my entrepreneurial journey that may prove useful to you as you navigate this important process:

STEP 1: ***Make the choice to forgive and vocalize the choice to yourself continually.***

If applicable, forgive yourself first, then forgive the offending party. Recognize that you will need to continually make the choice in your mind to forgive over and over again, as emotions of the experience keep rising to the surface. In the beginning, you will find that thoughts about the situation race through your mind regularly, surprising you with how often and how significantly the situation has impacted you! Each time feelings or thoughts of the offending experience arise, though, verbally check them and set your intention by audibly vocalizing these two intentions yourself:

> *"I choose to forgive them/myself."*
> *"I choose myself."*

Choosing yourself means making the choice to go free: unencumbered by past hurts, released from all the physiological effects of the state of unforgiveness. Choose to put yourself in the position to win by setting the intention to forgive.

When verbalizing the two intentions above, practice taking a few deep, cleansing breaths. Research has found that when we breathe shallowly (and most of us do so subconsciously), we rob our bodies of the oxygen necessary for proper brain function.[9] This can lead to mood swings and depressed, anxious thoughts. Taking slow, deep breaths in stressful or emotional situations floods our brains with necessary oxygen, and the calming, mind-clearing effects are almost instantaneous.[9] Breathing this way is one of the simplest ways to manage your emotions and makes you feel better by supplying the frontal lobe of your brain, which is involved in reasoning, with the oxygen it needs to walk you through the steps toward resolution.

Forgiveness is a choice. It doesn't absolve the offender of wrongdoing; forgiveness is simply a gift you give *yourself* to free yourself from the pain, negative energy, and detrimental physiological effects of holding a grudge.

STEP 2: *Acknowledge the truth of the situation in its entirety.*

Telling yourself the truth about what happened and any part you played in the situation, if any, is imperative. If you flavor the experience(s) with exaggerations and altered facts, you'll ultimately be doing a disservice to yourself, which can lengthen the process of your eventual release. Seek guidance from your Higher Power to give you a clear understanding of the facts of the situation as it happened, and keep your heart humbly open to receive them.

Exercise restraint and refrain from allowing yourself to get caught up in the emotions conjured up by the experience. Simply tell yourself the truth—what happened and your involvement, if any—and stop there. If this experience has held you back for any amount of time, there's no need to become trapped by the emotions of it all again. Stay focused. The purpose of engaging in this exercise is freedom *for yourself* to be able to function at full capacity, personally and professionally. Simply acknowledge the full truth of the situation. Stop there, then progress forward to the next step of this process.

STEP 3: *Acknowledge how the state of unforgiveness is precisely affecting you.*

We've already reviewed the detrimental physiological impacts of the emotions associated with unforgiveness. Here's another point to consider: Medical research estimates as much as ninety percent of illness and disease is stress-related.[10] This is a staggering statistic and is a warning of the all-encompassing effect stress in any form can exact on the body. Your ability to think clearly, focus, and make sound decisions is all compromised in a state of unforgiveness. Beyond physical and emotional impact, operating your business in this state can cause financial strain, should resources be funneled to exact revenge on the offending party. So, it is important to tell yourself the truth about all the ways the state of unforgiveness is tangibly affecting your personal health and the health of your venture. A clear understanding of the all-encompassing detrimental effects of unforgiveness will provide you clarity on how remaining in this state has the potential to negatively impact your entire life.

STEP 4: ***Recognize that you cannot forgive yourself or anyone else completely on your own; you will need help from your Higher Power.***

Six of the twelve steps of the famous Alcoholics Anonymous program are linked to the recognition of God's restorative power.[11] Forgiveness, like restoration from addictions, doesn't come naturally to most of us. When we've been wronged in life or business, our natural propensity is to wish ill will toward the offending party or "pay them back" somehow. We don't have to use our energy orchestrating payback, though; we have our purpose to accomplish, and success and peace await us!

God is fully aware of what you have endured. Often, we don't want to let the anger, bitterness, or resentment go because we aren't ready, or willing to let the other person off the hook. When you're journeying toward your purpose, however, know that it simply cannot be accomplished from a heart that is resentful.

The truth is that you don't have time to get caught up in resentment! The world is waiting for you to operate in your purpose. Imagine if the women of the women's suffrage movement had been distracted by resentment; who knows when we would have gained the right to vote. Or, if the many people involved in the civil rights movement had allowed themselves to become emotionally paralyzed by the violent, inhumane treatment they experienced at every turn, how much longer would people of color in the United States have waited to receive equal rights?

Forgiveness takes courage, and the process takes time, but the only way to truly forgive is to surrender the entire process to your Higher Power. Ask for the strength to effectively progress through Steps 1 to 3 and surrender full control of the entire process with the humble recognition that you do not have the power to forgive the offending party on your own. If you did, would you not have done so by now?

When you come to a full understanding of Step 4, repeat Step 1. There may be instances where you'll find yourself audibly repeating your two intentions—*I choose to forgive them/myself, I choose myself*—several times a day, and it may appear as though Steps 1 to 3 are not working to quell your frustrations or anger. You may even feel like a fraud when thoughts like *I don't forgive them* or *They don't deserve my forgiveness!* arise. In those instances, revisit Step 3 and recognize that the state of unforgiveness is likely hurting you more than it's hurting them. Follow Steps 1 to 4 with consistency and intentionality, and you'll find that, over time, the frequency of the negative thoughts will decrease, and you'll feel the weight of the experience lift. Ultimately, you'll arrive at a place of full release.

THE REALITY OF FORGIVENESS

Again, forgiveness is a process; it takes as long as it takes. The more impactful the negative experience and the longer you've been holding onto it, the more diligence will be required to stay focused during each stage of the process.

It's also important to note that forgiveness **does not** excuse or absolve the offending party of wrongdoing. In some cases, forgiveness may not mean restoration of the relationship or trust on any level either. *It simply releases you* from the harmful effects harboring resentment will exact on your mind, body, and spirit. Recognize that *you will never be at peace if you remain in a state of unforgiveness.* Your arrival at a place of personal peace will be required to consistently bring the best of yourself to your venture. Forgiveness is a choice, one that is imperative for you to make not only for your health, but also for the health and sustainability of your business.

Forgiveness is an important component of *your* inner work, but if you believe you would benefit from professional help to effectively progress past the pain from past or present lemon experiences, by all means, seek it. At the end of the day, true progress will come down to your willingness to put the knowledge you've received into personal practice. You can attend as many counseling sessions, workshops, and conferences as you can muster and read all the books in the world, but if you are endeavoring to turn your life lemons into the lemonade of your success, you will need to systematically and consistently implement strategies for your own personal well-being and that of your venture.

THE RESULTS

Perhaps the unresolved conflicts requiring your forgiveness will be the very lemon experiences that will imbue you with a greater level of empathy toward the people you will eventually serve through your venture. Or perhaps the experience will bless you with the passion needed to propel you toward your purpose! Who you are is far more important than your operational skill, product, or entrepreneurial idea. Your purpose is not only tied to what you will offer the world, but also to *who* you are and will become in the process of achieving success. So, addressing the state of your heart and mind should be an absolute priority at all times.

In a storm, rain falls indiscriminately on everything and everyone open to receiving it. Showers of blessings, in many forms, are all around us—access to people who can help us, funding, or opportunities. People who have an umbrella up—blockages due to unforgiveness, for example—directly shield themselves from the life-giving growth benefits that come after the figurative rain. An unwillingness to do our inner work can also prevent us from receiving the full benefits of those falling showers. *You simply cannot fulfill your purpose or achieve lasting success or peace when harboring resentment.* Remember, your brain is hardwired for completion, for success! Create a space in your mind for openness, productivity, and receptivity. If you consider the intentions that will result in the resolution of an issue, your mind will find ways to accomplish it for you.

Time is the greatest commodity.
Once it's spent, it's gone.
Use yours wisely.

Focus your energies on things that will move you in the direction of your purpose and allow you to progress forward freely. Unencumbered by the weights of the past, you will be enabled to forge a path forward, toward lasting, impactful success and, ultimately, peace.

UNDERSTANDING THIS IMPORTANT STEP TO EFFECTIVE CONFLICT RESOLUTION will equip you to weather inevitable storms that are sure to come on your business journey, allowing you and your team to bloom and grow beyond the negative experiences.

Choose yourself.
Give yourself permission to progress through the stages of forgiveness and put yourself in the position to win!
Endeavor to operate from a clean emotional slate, personally and professionally, and forgive fully to experience the release that comes from living free.

"...Become complete... live in peace.
And the God of love and peace will be with you."[12]
—2 Corinthians 13:11

FOR DEEPER REFLECTION...

Strategy #5: Forgive

1. Managing conflict in any business can be challenging. Here are some strategies you can use to help you manage conflict when it arises within your organization:

   a. Determine who/what is the source of the conflict and actively listen to the nuances of the complaint

   b. Investigate the situation yourself first before weighing in

   c. Pull each person involved in the conflict aside in private, separately

   d. Discuss with them what you understand of the issue from your own investigation (not the original complaint)

   e. Give them a chance to tell you their side of the story

   f. Determine a path forward with each person to meet the common goal

   g. Agree on a solution and discuss the responsibilities of each person involved, including yourself, to work toward resolution

   h. Encourage each party to practice the steps involved in this chapter to progress forward toward full resolution of the issue

   i. Evaluate how things are progressing within your organization between the parties "after the dust settles," and take an active role in facilitating restoration

   j. Consider preventative strategies for the future

2. How do you currently handle conflict?

   a. What aspects of your conflict resolution strategies have been working well for you?

   b. After reading the chapter, what will you now change about your approach going forward?

3. As you reflect on your life, are there those you need to forgive that have wronged you? List them.

4. Is there something you need to forgive yourself for that you've been carrying?

5. Are there those you need to ask to forgive you? List them.

LEMONADE CHALLENGE

Create a plan to address the lists from Questions 3 and 5. Evaluate the best way to address each person based on your current relationship, the offense, your current emotional state, and any other factors that might affect your ability to process through the stages of forgiveness. Ask for professional help to guide you through this process as you see fit.

Using the advice from the chapter, execute your plan over sixty days, be it a direct conversation, a total-truth letter you compose and later burn, or another method that resonates with you to help bring you to a place of complete forgiveness. Journal the results of each conversation or interaction during the challenge, and review all your journal entries at the end of the sixty days.

6

YOUR PLANE HAS ASSIGNED SEATING

"Success comes with a price that's normally bigger than what most people want to pay."

—LISA NICHOLS

YOU'RE ABOUT TO TAKE OFF! YOUR BUSINESS IDEA IS TAKING SHAPE. Completing your inner work is transforming you and providing you with the tools to effectively navigate the ride of your life! I liken the entrepreneurial journey to a flight to an unknown, amazing location on your own private jet. You've made the decision to enter this figurative cabin. Once the door closes, you've set the intention to trust the pilot to guide you to your destination safely. Let excitement set in!

Know, however, that there will be turbulence on this flight. You will experience more than one instance when internal and external conditions will be so problematic that your oxygen mask will descend, requiring you to don yours before assisting others. Since you were created to go on this purpose-driven flight, you can trust that the oxygen *will* flow, the plane and external conditions *will* eventually stabilize, and your qualified pilot in the cockpit *is* trustworthy and will bring you to your oasis destination safe and sound.

Achieving sustainable, impactful success from your purpose-driven venture is incredibly rewarding and will bless you in ways you cannot even begin to fully imagine now. However, this success will come at a price—typically more than most are prepared or willing to pay.

The lesson I am about to share is heavy.

It will likely ruffle your feathers, but I care too much about you and your purpose-driven venture to forgo informing you of this key truth about the entrepreneurial journey. Ignorance of this crucial aspect of preparation nearly cost me my entire business, so I impart this nugget of wisdom to you in hopes that it will help you avoid unnecessary challenges or disappointments later.

You won't learn what I'm about to share from conventional business literature or educational programs, and too few professional advisors are willing to dispense this truth to you directly. However, it is an unavoidable aspect of your journey toward sustainable success, and preparation for it is crucial to ensure you arrive at your purpose destination intact.

SURROUND YOURSELF WITH THE RIGHT PEOPLE

Your plane has been gifted to you by your Higher Power—your pilot—and there is assigned seating on this flight. You are the host of this trip. It is important that the people who are joining you on your plane are placed in the appropriate seats, and it is your responsibility to place them there. Placement simply refers to the way you plan to relate to them and is a concept I'll discuss in greater detail in this chapter.

Your purpose-driven venture is so pivotal to your life that not everyone can, will, or should join you on this flight. There will be all sorts of people—from your past, present, and future—who will want to come along for the ride. But one of the most difficult pills you'll need to swallow during your entrepreneurial journey is that not everyone in your life can, will, or should join you. Each person in your personal and professional life who enters your cabin will need to be placed in their assigned seat if you are to make it to your dream destination intact. If they refuse their assigned seat, accept that and, with love and kindness, escort them off your plane. The longer this takes you, the longer it will take your plane to ascend and arrive at your destination.

"Guard your heart above all else,
for it determines the course of your life."[1]

—Proverbs 4:23

This concept of placing people in their assigned seats on your success plane and guarding your heart directly applies to those that you allow in your inner business circle, but also to those with whom you choose to extend your heart on any level. One of the most exciting aspects of romantic love is its ability to happen upon us at any time. Love is one of the most powerful forces in humanity. But what do you do when your significant other doesn't believe in your venture? You've discerned your purpose and have charted a course forward based on the completion of your inner work, but your significant other (and perhaps those within your inner personal circle as well) doesn't understand your journey the way you do.

In the early years of my entrepreneurial journey, I fell in love at a completely unexpected time, and after having spent several years with the business as my sole focus, I found it extremely difficult to share my mental space with another person. With little to show for my efforts beyond my faith, the direction I had received from God, and a crystal-clear understanding of my purpose, explaining why I was choosing this path of great resistance to others, especially my significant other, was incredibly debilitating.

In the early years of my business, I lived in a perpetual state of low-grade anxiety and frustration, irritable and impatient with both the state of my business and my relationship. Having given up so much to step out and start my business, I determined that failure was not an option; it was do or die, as I felt my faith and the understanding of my purpose was constantly on trial. If the business failed, then the entire structure of my faith, which had become so intertwined into the fabric of my being, would all be called into question. In the midst of all the professional and relational pressure, I began to crack, and at times, I would ask myself:

Did I really discern all this from God?

Is this really my purpose?

If I misread this, what other choices have I erroneously made along the way?

My whole life hinged on the success of my venture. In those early years, the fear and anxiety I subconsciously experienced amidst my faith and focus on my vision made it difficult to function successfully in life or business. In time, however, I came to understand the importance of putting people in the right place in my life, the high cost of purpose, and the need to consistently squeeze my challenging life experiences—such as failed and strained relationships—to learn the tools necessary to pivot and grow to attain my goal to achieve business success.

There will be multiple experiences on your entrepreneurial journey that will stretch, grow, and maybe even crush you, but learning to squeeze those experiences of the lessons they can teach you—one being to guard your heart—will help you effectively navigate your journey toward creating a successful business.

"I GUESS I SHOULDN'T COMPLAIN. AT LEAST HE HAS STEADY WORK."

Some people enjoy the presence of a robust support system from the outset of their venture. Express your appreciation. You are indeed fortunate! Still, consistently evaluate the position in which you place each member on your flight, as your feelings about them—and their feelings about you and your venture—can change over time.

As in my case, you, too, may find it difficult to secure the robust support or belief of key people around you, especially if you're making the choice to change course from a lucrative and stable career. With those who are supportive, ensure that you evaluate their feelings, potential concerns, and overall position on your purpose-driven venture and communicate your desire for their support. Clear and open communication on your part is key to accurately clarifying their willingness and ability to join you on your success journey.

When considering the skeptical position of your loved ones—those that are somewhat supportive—you may wonder: *Have I not articulated my dream well? Why do they not believe in me? Why aren't they invested in the success of this venture, too? Don't they see the immense opportunity in this or how fulfilled and passionate I am about it?* To be fair, your passions and your purpose are *yours*, and the people who love you may find it difficult to watch you endure the struggles along your journey toward success. Recognize that it's up to your loved ones to choose to believe and support you, and it's important that you respect their thoughts and decisions regarding that support. Your role is to:

1. Articulate your understanding of your journey ahead to the best of your ability.

2. Communicate your desire for their support.

3. Exercise patience and allow them the opportunity to absorb the information you share with them.

4. Listen to their feedback with love and understanding.

Then, take your understanding of their decision or feedback and internally, place them in their assigned seat on your flight, or figuratively escort them off it.

SUCCESS & FAILURE BOTH COME AT A PRICE

Relationships can be difficult when you're an entrepreneur, as they involve sacrifices for all parties involved to ensure the relationship is not compromised. However, the onus is on you to navigate your relationships effectively by communicating the nuances of your new reality. The good news is that chasing purpose is energizing, freeing, and inspiring all at the same time, and you can share aspects of your journey with the people on your flight. In many cases, that will encourage them to move toward living their own life's purpose as well!

Despite all the challenges, moving in the direction of your purpose can bring you a sense of peace and fulfillment that little else can provide. For entrepreneurs, it can be difficult to see anything beyond our own business perspective and the manifestation and realization of our goals. I've learned, however, that much of life is about choices along with sacrifices; undoubtedly, the road to a sustainably successful venture is paved with both.

Lisa Nichols, one of the world's most requested motivational speakers, bestselling author of six books, and corporate CEO of a multi-million-dollar enterprise whose global platform, at the time of writing, has reached nearly eighty million people,[2] discusses several brutal truths about success. Not readily heard, these truths are need-to-know aspects of the journey, imperative to understand before you fully launch ahead:

Success is a lonely journey.
It will cost you more than you expect.[3]

These truths are difficult, especially if you have a robust inner circle and active social life. But adequately preparing yourself for the impending sacrifices on the road ahead is crucial.

Hindsight is indeed 20/20. It's impossible to adequately prepare for *everything* that will be required of you at this stage of your journey, but this book is intended to help you prepare for key aspects of what you can expect. You *can* help those around you feel comfortable supporting you by effectively communicating your understanding of your purpose. Solicit their support, but recognize that not everyone will be capable or willing to join you on your journey, and that has to be okay with you! Placing those within your circle in their assigned seating on your flight will help make your road ahead significantly more palatable both for yourself and the people who will ride it out with you to the end. Know that there will be people that you will want to join you that can't, won't, or shouldn't, and you will need to steel yourself with the courage to escort them off your plane in truth and love.

A core group of people who support and believe in your dream will feel like food to the famished at key points during your flight. It's heartbreaking when your venture conflicts with your relationships, but know that your dream cannot survive in an environment of unbelief, whether it's coming from you or others within your circle. Eventually, a choice will have to be made. Either you'll make it yourself, or life will make it for you.

THE FIRST YEARS OF YOUR VENTURE ARE THE MOST CRUCIAL AND WILL require a significant amount of focus, energy, and sacrifice to make it through. But it will be worth it in the end! Despite immersing myself in business literature prior to launching, I still didn't fully appreciate the length of time, resources, or sacrifices (emotional, spiritual, physical, financial, and relational) my business would demand of me and, by extension, my loved ones as well. If, however, you make the choice to operate outside of your purpose and follow a divergent path as a result of pressure from others, peace will evade you.

YOU CALL THEM UP AND THEY COME ROUND AND TALK YOU OUT OF IT..

Your purpose is what you were created for, and you've been gifted with a special set of competencies and life experiences that will serve to guide you along your way. Your purpose *will* refresh and feed your soul! Should you divert out of step from your purpose out of the behest of others, however, resentment is likely to creep in.

So, guard your heart.

It truly does determine the direction or course of your life, positively or negatively. Not everyone is meant to join you on your journey. Once you have discerned your life's purpose, it is *your* responsibility to protect it at all costs. Your peace, and the impact you are to have on the world depend on it.

THE SEATS ON YOUR PLANE

No business venture will become successful without meaningfully connecting with others, whether they be professional advisors, friends, family, or associates. We were created for community, and a "good work" cannot be inherently good unless, or until, it positively impacts others. So, then, the success of your venture will depend upon your ability to effectively connect with those around you—whether in conflict or in good times. Even if you are an introvert, establishing solid connections with even a small group of others is imperative to achieve your business goals.

"Money makes you rich, but your relationships make you wealthy. Sometimes a phone call will do what a check can't."

—Dr. Dharius Daniels

In his book, *Relational Intelligence*, Dr. Dharius Daniels highlights categories of people we tend to entertain in our lives: associates, assignments, friends, and advisors.[4] **Associates** are people we connect with due to common interests or similar schedules; work relationships and social media connections generally fall under this category. Dr. Daniels suggests that a person "should be assigned to the associate category when there has not been enough time, interest, or desire to develop the kind of connection required for friendship. It is a relationship where a person doesn't prefer to, for whatever reason, engage any deeper than the surface."[4]

There's no emotional bond with associate relationships. If we're not careful, however, we can mistake associates for friends and attach expectations on them that they were never meant to meet. Generally unbalanced, the associate relationship *does* have mutual, albeit neutral, benefits compared to some of the other categories, but it's important to distinguish carefully between people who are associates and those in the other categories to avoid preventable conflict in the future.

The second category of people is our **assignments,** those who have been sent on our path to assist them on *their* life's journey. God sends people to help us reach our potential, and, likewise, He also sends us people to help as well! Dr. Daniels suggests that "assignments are people in whom you will make deposits, but from whom you will more than likely not receive withdrawals."[4] Because of the nature of this relationship, a balanced level of investment in such relationships is prudent, and the investment should be markedly different from the investments extended in the other types of relationships. Assignments are at a cost and, therefore, establishing clear boundaries is a must. Nevertheless, our assignments still indirectly benefit us, if only in the area of our own personal growth.

The next and most crucial category is **friends,** and rather than a specific person, this category refers to the strength and nature of the relationship. By distinction, friends are meant to receive all of us—an investment of our time, talents, love and resources—and we can expect the same from them. These are truly symbiotic relationships where both parties benefit, and the Bible describes a friend in several ways: one that sticks closer than a brother,[5] one willing to lay down their life for you,[6] and one that will love you at all times.[7]

Individuals in the friend category represent a trusted source of support and honesty. The relationship you have with a friend is not draining but edifying. Friends are dependable. They cheer us on, celebrate with us when we're at our peaks, and support us in our valleys. They see the true version of us and are not afraid to tell us the truth about ourselves: the parts of who we are that we don't even see, and the parts we don't openly share with others. They are in the best position to provide constructive feedback from a position of love and true concern, and are invaluable during our entrepreneurial journey.

Unfortunately, all people we attribute this title to do not operate according to this definition of friend in our lives. Rather than making the distinction between a true friend and simply a friend, think of this category with the understanding that both a friend and a true friend should really be one and the same. If, however, you find yourself questioning whether a person in your circle should really hold the title of friend according to the definition above, it's time to evaluate whether the title of assignment or associate is more appropriate based on the true nature of your relationship.

The category of friend also encompasses family members; in fact, family is represented in all four categories. For example, there are family members with whom you enjoy an associate-type relationship, where truthfully, you simply do not have the level of connection or trust required for friendship. You may have family members that function in your life more like assignments, where the nature of your relationship is more of a helping hand and a source of strength or encouragement than one where you receive support and encouragement during your challenging seasons. Family members can also function as advisors, a category to be discussed in greater detail in this chapter.

Given their close proximity to your heart, family relationships are essential to navigate effectively as you start and grow your venture. Know that *the presence of blood relation should not dictate the position where people are placed in your life*. Understanding this concept will save you undue pain, frustration, and heartache from unmet expectations that can lead to unnecessary excision of relationships from your life. Telling yourself the truth about the nature of your relationships with everyone, especially family members, and learning to manage your relationships effectively is key to your ability to build yourself as a successful leader, and protect your business from unnecessary challenges to its growth.

THIS NEW DEFINITION OF A FRIEND MAY APPLY TO ONLY A SMALL GROUP OF people within your circle, and that will need to be okay with you if you are to achieve sustainable success. With honesty, determine your current list of friends using these benchmarks. Of each relationship, ask yourself: Does this relationship result in mutual joy and benefit in one form or another? If the answer is no, reassign this person to either associate or assignment to prevent future disappointment, unmet expectations, or frustrations. If broken trust or other challenges are involved, consider if continuing the relationship in any category is in the best interest of either party.

Dr. Daniels refers to the last category as advisors. For greater clarity within the business context, however, I refer to individuals within this category as

professional advisors. Such individuals include but are not limited to: mentors, spiritual advisors (such as pastors), and business consultants, and you are *their* assignments! However, it is imperative not to confuse professional advisors with other relationships. This can lead to disappointment from unmet expectations and an inability to effectively draw from their expertise.

A set duration of time and key objectives for the engagement constitute healthy boundaries for the professional advisor relationships, since the expectation that typically accompanies these types of relationships will likely involve your request for help with a particular need, guidance through a specific situation, or assistance to help you grow to accomplish a particular goal. Without agreed-upon objectives and boundaries, however, real or perceived expectations from you (the assignment) could be regarded as unreasonable by your professional advisor, and confusion surrounding the time commitment and level of investment expected can lead to your frustration and disappointment as well. Initiating a relationship with a professional advisor by clarifying expectations (on both sides) and the time commitment involved is best practice. This allows you to maximize the benefits of the relationship by securing an advisor that is best suited to invest the desired time and resources to help you grow effectively.

I've been blessed to connect with several professional advisors during my entrepreneurial journey. They've proved to be invaluable in unimaginable ways—directly and indirectly—and without them, I may have faltered and lost my way. Their encouragement and support have been incredibly important to my emotional, spiritual, and financial health, and I'm so thankful for their willingness to invest in me and my success story.

ONE KEY PROFESSIONAL ADVISOR & THE TIMELINE TO YOUR SUCCESS

As it is a paid relationship, a professional advisor in the form of a specialized business management consultant can garner the most effective results for your business out of all of those on your success plane. A qualified business management consultant with the experience and expertise in building a successful, purpose-driven venture can significantly cut the time it takes you to rise to success. They have experience traveling the journey toward purpose-driven success themselves and can serve as templates for you, as well as catalysts on your rise to the top. They can also act as a shield, preventing you from being exposed to unnecessary mistakes, pain, and loss of time and money.

Friends, as mentioned, are indeed important on your journey and may provide you advice to help you grow your venture. However, in many cases, they don't have the professional reach to deliver effective, actionable guidance as a qualified business management consultant would.

Overall, one of the greatest benefits of the professional advisor category is that you can make *your choice* to engage them within the exact parameters that suit you! After due diligence on the advisor's skills, experience, and area of expertise, *you can choose* to initiate the relationship and outline your specific needs and expectations. Should they decide to accept your request, you have yourself a source of support that will be invaluable on your journey! A professional advisor is willing to invest in you as *their assignment*, and their presence on your success flight is crucial to maintaining balance, likely cutting the time it will take for you to reach your destination of success.

PUT PEOPLE IN THEIR PLACE

It has been said that people enter our lives for a reason, season, or a lifetime. As time progresses, you'll become more proficient at discerning who is with you for a specified reason (assignments and associates), a particular season in your life (associates and professional advisors), or a lifetime (friends). You will need to appropriately position people in your life for the health of your venture, as well as your mental health. Again, placement simply refers to how you plan to relate to those you allow access to you. Placement is an internal process, and generally, it's not necessary to share your seat assignments with the people around you.

It's important to note that people can be shifted from one category to another as time passes and relationships develop or degrade. If your relationship with a family member is draining or imbalanced, it might be appropriate to relate to them as an associate or assignment rather than as a friend, at least temporarily. Doing so will prevent feelings of disappointment or frustration when they don't interact with you in the manner you believe they should, according to the nature of the category you previously assigned them. Once you've achieved your goal or accomplished the objective that initiated a professional advisor relationship, this primary, professional aspect of your relationship should cease. However, if the relationship progresses to one of the other categories during your engagement, it's perfectly appropriate to reassign them. Should this happen—your relationship with a professional advisor progresses after the engagement ceases—and you start to view them as an associate or friend—this is the only instance where an upfront conversation of your desire to relate to them from the vantage point of one of the other categories is required to mitigate confusion or frustration due to unmet expectations later.

Take the time to repeat this evaluation process for every person in your personal orbit and determine the appropriate categories in which to place them. Also, evaluate if the current category you have them occupying should change. The resulting revelations will dictate the best way for you to relate to each person to protect yourself and, ultimately, your venture.

YOUR PLANE REQUIRES BALANCING

If you've ever boarded a flight that was completely sold out, and the contents of the plane were too heavy due to the overall weight of those in the cabin, combined with the weight of the luggage on board, likely you've heard the flight staff announce that takeoff may be delayed to allow time to rebalance the plane. According to Bill McGee—a former loadmaster on cargo aircraft who wrote an article in USA Today—"an improperly loaded and/or overloaded airplane is a danger to everyone on board."[8] He indicated that rebalancing a plane may involve *moving passengers to another seat to achieve proper center of gravity*, extracting baggage from the flight due to weight restrictions, *or even "bumping" or deplaning passengers off the plane.*

This actual practice of rebalancing a plane in the real world is directly applicable to the business context here of properly balancing people on your success flight. Should you operate your venture from a state of imbalance, it will invariably suffer. In your personal life, if you have significantly more assignments and associates than friends and professional advisors, you won't be able to sustain a balanced level of functioning for long before your imbalanced state of personal investment starts to negatively impact you, and by extension, your venture. Associate and assignment relationships require more investment than friend and professional advisor relationships, which benefit you more comprehensively. *Know that any operation that functions at a deficit is not sustainable.* You, too, will need to ensure you have a healthy balance between the people directly contributing to your life and/or business compared to those drawing an inordinate amount of investments from you. The balance between the two groups is different for every person, and understanding the balance you personally can sustain is key to functioning at your optimal capacity and potential.

THE IMPORTANCE OF BALANCING YOUR PLANE: A PRACTICAL EXAMPLE

If a professional advisor is expected to function as a friend or an assignment as a professional advisor, frustration and resentment will set in. If you attempt to squeeze someone into a different role they are not intended or willing to fill, you will invariably endure unnecessary disappointment due to unmet expectations.

In my personal experience, I came to understand the ramifications of placing people in the wrong positions in my life and the unnecessary hurt that can result after trying to squeeze them into positions they weren't intended to fill. During the early years of building my business, to help combat my feelings of anxiety and frustration with my slow climb to success, I found it incredibly therapeutic to spend time with those I knew that were talented musicians, and would attend their shows regularly as they performed around my city. Over a period of years, I attended their shows and enjoyed their amazing live music along with the camaraderie we all shared after the events. My time with them in the evenings represented a welcomed escape from my burdens, and provided a source of great joy as I connected with people around a love for live music.

Eventually, as the group of us became closer and started spending more and more time together outside of the shows, I erroneously began to relate to those I was closest to in the group as friends. When my father later suffered a serious medical emergency, I was extremely hurt by their perceived lack of compassion or desire to be present with me in my intense time of need. However, the reality was that these individuals were actually only associates, and the nature of our relationship did not lend itself to meet the expectations I had placed on them. Once I recovered from the disappointment and hurt from my unmet expectations, and became ready to squeeze that challenging life experience and extract lessons from it, I was able to internally reassign them to their proper seat on my success plane, and interact with them in a manner according to the true nature of our relationship.

We may be saddened when an associate doesn't prove to be dependable in a time of need, but remember that the associate relationship isn't friendship. Though it may be tempting to confide in them, assignments and associates shouldn't be granted access to details of your life or business, and you shouldn't expect the same, either from your associates or professional advisors. Reserve these privileges—detailed personal information on your life and business—for friends and your professional advisors only. When we operate with a thorough understanding of the four relationship categories, it decreases the likelihood of frustration from unmet expectations, which frees us up to appreciate the people in our lives with a clearer perspective.

DON'T GIVE UP YOUR RESPONSIBILITY TO YOUR PASSENGERS

You will come across people who will want to place themselves in their own seats, but remember that this is your flight! It is your responsibility to put people in their place on your flight. An associate may desperately want to be your friend, but again, it's not wise to place someone in a seat they weren't intended for, no matter how much you, or they may want this to be the case. You may not have built enough trust for them to fit into the friend category, and you may not have the capacity to operate as a friend in their life either! Take the initiative to figure out the right position for each person in your life. Developing boundaries with the people in your social circle is a necessary skill because, as you start to experience success in your venture, you'll need to be able to effectively set boundaries with your business associates, clients, and staff as well. Failure to do so can result in damaged business relationships that will not only affect your bottom line, but may also impact the perception of your business in your market.

In the age of social media, we are used to expecting a heightened level of access to each other, so it can be harder to set firm boundaries. Establish what you intend to share with them ahead of time, though, then set your boundaries, and stick to them. As you evaluate your seatmates on your plane of success, implementing boundaries and clarifying expectations will save you undue heartache and losses in terms of time, money, and resources along the way.

PUT PEOPLE IN THE RIGHT PLACE IN YOUR ORGANIZATION AS WELL

As it relates to your business, determine to hire the right people for the right positions within your organization. Plan to *hire slow and fire fast* to effectively protect the viability of your venture. This concept isn't new and it may sound trite, but it's crucial to the growth and sustainability of your business.

Take time to *diligently* screen future team members during your hiring process. Over the past several years, I've heard numerous entrepreneurs discuss the financial and emotional perils they experienced—some for many years—after making ineffective, rushed hiring decisions. Take the time to do your due diligence and hire people who have the skills, desire, personality, personal will, and character to join you on your success journey. Hire those with values that fit your business values and needs—individuals who possess key attributes to help you grow—especially at this precarious, early stage of your entrepreneurial journey.

Some key traits to screen for include:

- Skilled
- Qualified, for a specific role within your organization
- Experienced
- Committed
- Trustworthy
- A person of integrity
- Self-directed and proactive
- Friendly
- Adaptable
- Innovative
- A visionary
- Accountable
- Humble
- A team player
- Customer-centric

This is by no means an exhaustive screening list, especially for your first few hires, but it should provide you with a starting point from which you can launch.

There are so many resources available to help you effectively screen and interview candidates. If you're feeling insecure about hiring appropriately, invest in skill development in this area through the use of online or in-class recruitment tools or utilize the services of a recruitment firm or those of a specialized business consultant to help you, as hiring the right people is one of the most important aspects of an effective growth strategy for your business. Who you let on your success plane will directly determine your path on your flight to success and even the amount of time it will take to arrive at your dream destination.

Don't be afraid to hire people whose strengths are your weaknesses; those who bring skills that you currently lack will ultimately strengthen your business overall. During your screening process, ensure your core company values align, and your potential new hire demonstrates a drive beyond financial compensation, even on the most basic level. Determine from the outset to invest in your employees as future leaders within your organization, especially people who emanate positivity and who you discern will grasp your vision for success.

Beware!

Distractions and internal pervasive conflict and dissent can cause key resources to be redirected, costing you time and money. If you tolerate people on your team who are problematic or incongruent with the values of your organization, their presence will infect your corporate culture and communicate dissonance with others, both within and outside your business. The best people *want* to be part of a winning team, one that creates positive change and makes your business an enjoyable place to work. Have you ever had the experience of reaching out to your favorite service provider and having a new hire react to you in a way that was incongruent with your previous positive experiences with the company? This negative exchange likely left a bad taste in your mouth and, if it were to happen again, you might consider patronizing another service provider instead.

Plan to manage challenging teammates you employ using a predetermined process, which should first involve granting them a period of time for improvement, with clear communication of their problem areas. They may self-select departure, or you may find that they are better suited to another position within your organization. Whatever the case, strive to place people carefully in the right positions and cultivate the resolve to quickly and effectively deplane people who are not suited to your ride. Eventually, their presence will negatively impact both you and the rest of your passengers, so manage them accordingly to protect the viability of your purpose-driven venture.

THE POWER OF EXPECTATIONS IN BUSINESS

When you initiate a new business relationship with a professional advisor, potential client, vendor, members of your team, or investors, ensure expectations *on both sides* are clearly communicated and documented. This will mitigate the potential for disappointments from unmet expectations in the business setting. Written agreements will often reflect the terms of the relationship, but there are a set of expectations in many business interactions that aren't readily communicated in the beginning. As the product or service provider, deciphering and clarifying the full scope of your audience's expectations is *your* responsibility, and key to curating a successful business relationship.

One approach I find useful in deciphering expectations, especially for potential clients, is to determine the other party's expectations *of me first*, prior to communicating mine. This approach helps break defenses and demonstrates your willingness to listen and respond to their expectations appropriately, which is imperative for a successful business interaction. It also allows you to discern if your offering is the best fit for the other party prior to continuing a conversation with them.

Having the other party clarify their expectations first is also strategic. It allows you to develop your strategy through an understanding of their position, and it provides you with useful information to help you exceed their expectations. When you start your interactions by clarifying the other party's expectations *first*, you'll find that the final stage of your negotiations will likely progress forward more seamlessly, leading to a mutually beneficial end.

GUARDING YOUR HEART: A BUSINESS APPLICATION

In review, the concept of guarding your heart is useful for your personal preparedness and protection, but it is also crucial for the protection of your business. There may be moments when, if you're not careful, you may make business decisions from a compromised emotional state or heart, and these decisions are never in the best interest of your business. But, though it's important never to make decisions from a *compromised* emotional state, you shouldn't be afraid to let your emotions factor into your decision-making either.

Some of the most important business decisions you will make *will* come from a congruence of your head *and* heart. For instance, from the example listed in Chapter 5 (from page 116), you may choose to continue utilizing the vendor that missed the deadline that cost you business with a major client, after you listen to her explain that she failed you not out of a lack of integrity but rather, her father passed away in a tragic set of events in the days leading up to your receipt of the deliverables, and she was completely incapacitated by shock. She was not in a state of optimal functioning in her business at the time and profusely apologized and acknowledged an understanding of the harm the missed deadline cost your company. In an effort to make it right, she offered to extend to you a significant discount on your next order, and assured you the situation would not be repeated.

Although you may not want to give her a chance to cost you any more future business, your heart may guide you to view the situation from a more expansive lens and recognize that this vendor has indeed proven to be dependable in the past; you've had a strong business relationship with her for years, and it might be worth giving this vendor a second chance.

An important aspect of your development into a successful entrepreneur includes learning to identify how emotions of the human condition, and those generated from a compromised emotional state, play into your decision-making. If you're feeling frustrated, angry, unforgiving, or depressed, telling yourself the truth and guarding your business against that compromised state of your heart is imperative to preserve the health of your venture.

CONTINUE THE PROCESS OF EVALUATION

When you allow your Higher Power to guide you along your entrepreneurial journey, you will be led to connect with people who will assist you to your successful end. Not everyone who comes into your orbit personally or professionally should be entertained, though. Some people who desire to come for the ride are not meant to join you, and others may come to distract you or may have other nefarious motives. Both will eventually compromise your ability to maintain focus and grow your venture.

If you find yourself drained, burdened, or stressed by the people on your success plane, ask yourself: *Are my interactions with them purposeful? Is this person adding or subtracting value? Have I been directed by my Higher Power to operate in this capacity with or for them, or am I simply following what **I** believe I should do? Am I acting on autopilot or out of a lack of strength or resolve to change?* Of course, life is not all about us and our venture, and every individual with whom we connect isn't placed in our lives solely to help us achieve our goals. That's why we need our assignments; the people we are meant to assist, to bring balance to our lives! Assignments center us and push us to operate from a place of humility rather than self-absorption. However, when certain relationships are draining or distracting us from our venture and negatively impacting us emotionally, spiritually, intellectually, physically, or financially, it's time to acknowledge the truth and make adjustments to our interactions.

So, evaluate your circle. Trust your pilot to guide you to your dream destination from Chapter 3 and surrender to the guidance! Ensure you arrive at your dream destination intact with proper preparation and proper placement of others on your flight.

GET READY TO LAND!

You're about to experience combustible success, and catalysts in many forms will come to help you achieve your goals. Your purpose doesn't *need* to make sense or appear prudent to anyone other than you and your Higher Power; the purpose you've been gifted with *will* challenge you, and you'll need to lean on your faith to make it through. It is important to find people willing to support, encourage, invest in, and love you along the way though, but try to resist the urge to convince others to embark on your journey with you. The people who are meant to join you won't require convincing; watching your journey just may encourage them to embark on their own!

In the latter years of owning my business, I became significantly more proficient and efficient at placing people in their assigned seats on my success plane after squeezing my challenging life experiences with strained and broken relationships, learning lessons from them, and applying those lessons to my business. As a result, I experienced much more fulfilling relationships, void of the frustrations and disappointments that typically accompany unmet expectations. As time has progressed and relationships have evolved or deteriorated, my understanding of the concept of guarding my heart has protected my business from collapse and helped me maintain productivity, focus, and develop strength and peace. It's been freeing to realize that some of the people I previously believed to be friends were actually associates or assignments, requiring a shift in how I related to them. Likewise, once I began to communicate clear expectations in my professional advisor relationships and with clients, pressure was alleviated, allowing for more effective engagements to flourish.

My experiences have taught me that when you squeeze your challenging past or present, personal and business relationships of the lessons they can teach you about boundaries, expectations, and the level of investment both you and those in your circle are willing and able to extend, you become more closely aligned on the path to achieving success, and experiencing peace. The key is applying the lessons learned to help you create your successful business! If you strive to be a good steward of the purpose that has been gifted to you and place all the people in your life in their assigned seats on your plane, you'll eventually reap amazing results.

It's almost time for your takeoff! Get ready…

FOR DEEPER REFLECTION...

Strategy #6: Manage Your Relationships Effectively

1. What are three lessons you can learn from past relationships where you've endured hurt or disappointments?

2. How can you apply these lessons to your business and the manner in which you operate it?

3. Review your current list of associates, assignments, friends, and professional advisors. Who do you have currently sitting in the seat of:

   - Associates:
   - Assignments:
   - Friends:
   - Professional Advisors:

4. Who needs to be assigned to a different seat on your success flight? Evaluate why, then reassign them.

5. Who needs to be deplaned? Write down why, and how you plan to navigate the process of doing so.

6. Based on your answer to Questions 4 and 5, create your adjusted list:

   - Associates:
   - Assignments:
   - Friends:
   - Professional Advisors:

7. Is your total number of associates and assignments balanced with the number of friends and professional advisors?
   a. If not, what can you do to create a greater balance between the two groups?

8. Evaluate your list of professional advisors.
   a. Have you properly completed your vetting process prior to initiating a relationship with each?

   b. Are you satisfied with the nature of the relationships or results produced in your life as a result of your engagement with them? Why or why not?

   c. Have you secured the services of a Business Management Consultant that has experience operating a successful purpose-driven venture, one that resonates with you, and one that you feel comfortable with?

9. In the chapter, we discussed the characteristics to screen for when hiring candidates for your organization. Conversely, think of characteristics you should watch out for or "screen out" in employees you want to hire. How will your past or present business or personal relationships guide your list of characteristics to screen out?

10. At times, individuals you hire may not be suitable for the particular role they're in, but will thrive in another position within your organization. Other times, the employee simply may not be a good fit for your organization altogether, requiring you to terminate them. What benchmarks can you think of now to create a system whereby you reposition or deplane future employees effectively?

11. What is the state of your heart now?
    a. How has this state positively or negatively impacted your business?

LEMONADE CHALLENGE

#1: During your next three business interactions with potential clients, practice guiding them to communicate their expectations of you and your business first, prior to communicating your expectations. Journal your findings on how the remainder of the negotiations to a deal progressed. Strive to exceed their expectations as you provide your product or deliver your service offering.

#2: Research three professional advisors you'd like to connect with. Find out information about their journey to success or proficiency in the area you need help. Follow them on social media and review their content. Contact them within the next 60 days, then decide which one best suits your needs and budget. Determine their willingness to work with you, experience with growing a purpose-driven venture, level of expertise, and availability. Journal your process to their yes!

Enjoy your time with them! Journal the lessons you learn from them and precisely how you are applying their nuggets of wisdom to your venture. Journal also the changes in your business as a result. Be sure to communicate your appreciation of them and spread the word! Referring them to your network will help other business owners like you achieve success in their ventures too, and will help your professional advisor expand their reach.

*** Need help securing a specialized business consultant experienced in growing a purpose-driven venture? Email: concierge@aereconsulting.com*

7

FIND YOUR INNER FIGHT & WIN

"The difference between a successful person and others is not a lack of strength, not a lack of knowledge, but rather a lack of will."

—VINCE LOMBARDI

Chances are, at this point in your inner work journey, you're starting to feel overwhelmed. If you've already started your venture and have been at it for some time, you've likely endured days when you've felt completely exhausted and ready to just pack it all in and give up. You've given as much as you believe you can and more. There are times when you feel so overwhelmed and discouraged by the myriad of emotions pulsating through you and the mountains of work you know that's ahead of you.

You've moved in the direction you felt led and are diligently progressing through your inner work, but perhaps you're just not where you believe you should be, given your level of investment thus far. Maybe your venture isn't coming together as seamlessly as you envisioned, or the tide is taking too long to turn. You may have experienced success in one area of your life—completely unrelated to your purpose—and, now, moving in this new direction is leaving you wondering: *Why am I choosing to experience this stress anyway? Why don't I just go back to what was working? This is all too much!* Or perhaps you feel shame or embarrassment for quitting your job or investing in this new direction when others around you told you just to stay where you were. Now, you're in a situation that seems untenable and bound for failure.

There will be seasons, especially at the beginning of your entrepreneurial journey, when you'll feel like throwing in the towel, overcome with thoughts that it's all just too much. Likely you'll feel alone, like a salmon swimming upstream. You're doing your best. You're following your purpose, and you've completed the painful work of sitting in your truth and acknowledging the pains of the past. You're taking tangible steps forward, but you haven't yet seen success. Perhaps debt from past business mistakes has piled up, and you feel as though neither you nor your business can survive the impact of another mishap. You're at your breaking point; one more disappointment could push you over the edge.

I've been there.

Many times throughout my entrepreneurial journey, I struggled with thoughts of giving up, despite understanding that I was walking in my purpose and that all my lemon experiences had prepared me for this moment. Even after implementing the knowledge I was learning from the many seminars, workshops, and conferences I'd attended, as well as information from the business and personal development books I was reading, there were *still* moments that tested my resolve. After absorbing blow after blow, I found myself spiraling into the abyss of self-pity, discouragement, depression, and despair. In the early days of my business, my perfectionist tendencies placed me in this mindset more often than I'd like to admit. But I was able to gain strength through my complete surrender to God while maintaining a preparatory stance to fight, and persevere forward amidst the challenges of the entrepreneurial journey. And now, I'll teach you how to do the same.

THEY DID IT, AND SO CAN YOU!

During your entrepreneurial journey, lemon experiences will arise that will test the very fiber of your being, but know that it's all a *normal* part of the journey on your path to success.

You're not alone! Even some of the most successful entrepreneurs and business gurus have experienced similar emotions—prior to and during their business journey—and had to push forward amidst debilitating circumstances and potentially limiting mindsets. Examples include:

- World-renowned billionaire[1] entrepreneur, author, producer, director, screenwriter, and philanthropist **Tyler Perry** was physically and sexually abused growing up, kicked out of high school, and attempted suicide twice.[2] Since then, he's achieved unmatched success, carving out his own lane in Hollywood, with ownership of it all.

- Self-made shapewear billionaire **Sarah Blakely** failed the LSAT twice, then sold fax machines for seven years before hitting it big. When she started her entrepreneurial journey, she said, "Most doors were slammed in my face. I saw my business card ripped up at least once a week and even had a few police escorts out of buildings."[3]

- Prolific inventor **Thomas Edison**, who was expelled from school for being unteachable, was unceremoniously fired from his first jobs because he wasn't productive enough,[4] and famously made more than ten thousand attempts before finally succeeding at creating the light bulb.[5]

Nothing worth achieving comes without perseverance and sacrifice. There will always be external factors that will test your resolve and commitment to stay the course. However, it's not the external factors or lemon experiences themselves that will threaten to derail your success; it's the level of your sheer tenacity and inner will to win despite it all. To achieve success from your purpose-driven venture, you'll need to squeeze dry your lemon experiences and find your inner fight, to be able to stand up in the greatest battle you'll ever face on your journey—the battle waged within your own mind.

AND A CHILD SHALL LEAD THEM

New York Times bestselling author Malcolm Gladwell masterfully articulates this concept of finding your inner fight in his book, *David and Goliath: Underdogs, Misfits, and the Art of Battling Giants*. In it, he highlights the story of David and Goliath from 11th century B.C.[6] and discusses the probability of improbable events; that *you can* actually accomplish seemingly impossible feats! He takes his readers through stories of underdogs who wind up beating the odds and offers strategies the reader can use to find their inner fight and win at life.

David, of the historical account of David and Goliath,[7] was an unassuming, young, Israelite shepherd boy. Rugged, seemingly naïve, and with all the assurance that comes with bold, childlike faith, he dared to have a conversation with the then Israelite king about their current adversary, Goliath, who was threatening to destroy the Israelite nation.

He'd just come from bringing lunch to his brothers serving on the battlefield. They were soldiers in the army, and they, and their fellow soldiers, were paralyzed with fear after looking at the sheer menacing size of Goliath and listening to his rumbling taunts.

Goliath was a warrior who fought with the Philistines, the Israelites' mortal enemy, and scholars believe he was a mammoth figure: over nine feet tall.[8] Pompous and intimidating, Goliath taunted the Israelite army day and night. Understandably, thoughts of defeat started to take root within the Israelite camp until young David sauntered onto the scene. Unaffected by his older brother's disregard for him, David voiced his request to speak to the king about his desire to fight Goliath. He mustered up the courage to fight, remembering how he had fought and killed lions and bears to protect his sheep in the past. *He believed* with the help of God, he could beat the terrifying giant facing their nation. In the end, David—the underdog—did indeed defeat the mammoth Goliath in an unconventional way by using just a sling, a stone, and his faith.

THE POWER OF "YOUR WHY" TO YOUR INNER FIGHT

The underdog story of David defeating Goliath may leave you with questions such as:

- Why did David, a simple shepherd boy, believe he could defeat Goliath?

- Where did his strong conviction and courage come from?

- What could make someone—a child even—so confident in their success against a foe that had incapacitated an entire army and emotionally paralyzed a king?

…and how do the answers to all these questions apply to my life and business?

The answer is this: David's courage came from the depth of his sense of *knowing*.

1. He evaluated his past, challenging life experiences and recognized that by God's sustaining presence, he was able to single-handedly kill lions and bears to rescue his sheep from their hungry grips.[7] If he was able to do that with God's help before, he believed he had the capacity to beat, yet another seemingly insurmountable foe again too!

2. David knew his why—that God had made a promise to give the land Goliath was protecting to his people, the Israelites.[9]

3. He also intrinsically knew God would help him because he had faith in God's character—a character he had come to trust in the past.

As discussed in Chapter 3, your beliefs lead to actions, then results. David believed in the promises of God so fully and became so intertwined with belief in them that it translated into confidence—a sense of knowing—then action. Also, by squeezing his challenging life experiences with lions and bears, he was able to extract an understanding that if God helped him beat insurmountable foes before, he could do it again! David intrinsically reached a place of *knowing* that there was no way Goliath could defeat him, and that guided the actions he took thereafter. This is how David was able to find his inner fight and win.

"If you think you are too small to make a difference, try sleeping with a mosquito."

—Dalai Lama

So, how does this apply to your life and business? As with David, you will experience many "Goliaths" on your journey to success. They will appear completely insurmountable, seemingly rendering you powerless to defeat them. Expect them; however, first and foremost, remember your purpose— your why. Since you were created for your "good work" of service, there can be no failure when you follow it, and consistently and intentionally complete the components of your inner and outer work. If you've accurately discerned your purpose, your Higher Power *will* continue to equip you with everything you need to accomplish it. Believing that will help you find your inner fight, and win.

God will not drop you! No matter the size of your Goliaths—educational ability, gender, sex, amount of capital—know that your consummate understanding of your purpose and belief in your Higher Power's promises will help you slay your Goliaths and will lead you to ultimate victory!

MAKE THE EXECUTIVE DECISION TO BELIEVE

Belief is a choice, just as forgiveness is a choice. No one who has experienced impactful or long-lasting success has achieved it without fighting inner doubt, fear, and external obstacles along the way. A practice I implemented during some of the most challenging days of my entrepreneurial journey was to audibly vocalize the following words to myself:

I make the executive decision to believe!

By saying this to myself, I was setting the intention, as the leader of my business, to make the choice to believe in my venture in that very moment of doubt, believe in my ability to rise through my challenges victorious, believe in the power of my God, and believe in my revealed purpose. These seven words helped push me through challenging tasks in front of me, and empowered me to believe in the eventuality of a positive, successful outcome.

As the adage says, "If God brings you to it, He'll bring you through it." You'll need to recognize, however, that even with your Higher Power's guidance, your journey will not be easy. The road to lasting and fulfilling success is not upwardly linear, but developing your inner constitution bathed in faith and a clear perspective will help see you through.

Stand up, shoulders back, and lift your head up even when you feel bruised or defeated.

Speak strength to yourself! As the leader of your venture, make the executive decision to believe!

Speak courage to yourself.

Speak confidence.

Despite the challenges that will invariably pepper your path, find your inner fight and make the choice to believe. Then persevere and press forward. In addition to setting the intention to believe, find your inner fight by looking for examples of inner fight all around you. You may find them in the most unexpected places.

FOOTBALL RESCUED MY INNER FIGHT

It is well known within my circle of friends that I'm an avid football fan. One of my favorite National Football League players of all time is Peyton Manning, former quarterback of the Indianapolis Colts and the Denver Broncos. I wanted so badly to see him play before he retired and sensed early in the 2015 season that that year would be his last. As the season progressed, I could tell he was struggling from the after-effects of his 2011 neck surgery, and I couldn't bear to watch him play badly. Shamefully, I admit, after watching the beginning of the Broncos November 28 game against the New England Patriots—a game I was sure they'd lose—I allowed my personal and professional frustrations of the moment, along with my resignation to the Broncos' sure defeat, to stop me from watching the rest of the game, and football altogether for weeks.

On January 3, the last game of the regular season, I was still feeling defeated after waiting for months for a major deal I'd proposed to come into fruition. With no news or update in sight, frustration yet again started to creep in. That Sunday, however, I felt compelled to check out the teams that were playing, only to find that not only were the Broncos doing well, but they had beaten the New England Patriots in the November 28 game

I had been so afraid to watch! They were now #2 in their conference. I was originally saddened to see that Peyton was the backup quarterback for that January 3 game due to poor performance in previous games, but I was delighted when he was put back on the field and ended up winning it for the team![10] With Peyton at the helm, the Broncos not only won that game, but they rose to the #1 spot in their conference and ended up winning it all at the Super Bowl that year!

However trite an example, those November 28 and January 3 football games reminded me that it's never over till it's over. A win can be pulled out of any set of circumstances—even more so when we move in faith and the direction of our purpose. Despite the obstacles, our gifts and passions have equipped us for our journeys, so our success is imminent! But at times, you'll need to be able to encourage *yourself* to be able to make it through to your win.

Why? Because the journey toward purpose-driven success is ultimately between you and your Higher Power, and it *will* stretch you. It encompasses your spiritual, emotional, intellectual, financial, and relational growth out of your comfort zone. Your ability to draw from what your Higher Power has placed within you—power, skills, courage, passion, vision, confidence, hope, faith—and use each to persevere. This is one way your Higher Power trains and transforms you, which will become invaluable as your level of impact expands.

While it's true that you cannot achieve success in a vacuum—a topic we'll review in later chapters—before you draw from others, you'll need to develop the skill of drawing out what is already within you: your inner fight and the will to win.

To find your inner fight:

1. Get Rest and Replenish

Pull away and allot yourself a set amount of time to completely disengage from the situation, or challenges at hand within your business.[11] During your time away, include constructive, rejuvenating activities, such as sleep, exercise, connection with your support network, prayer, and perhaps even a hobby you enjoy. When you're ready to return, the break will provide you with much-needed perspective on your challenging circumstances.

2. Tell Yourself Truths About the Situation in Front of You and Separate Fact from Emotion

Some of us are prone to exaggeration, which requires an important internal check: *Are your circumstances really as bad as you believe them to be, or are you confabulating a reality to suit what you are feeling? Are your feelings an accurate reflection of your actual need to beware, stop, or pivot from your current direction, or are they born out of an internal struggle?* Tell yourself the truth and check your own motives. Inflation of facts will cloud your judgment, and any decision or path forward charted from a place of fear, despair, anxiety, or compromised motives is likely not a good one.

Your emotions can be, but are not always, reflections of truth. Just because you *feel* that people around you think you're ill-equipped to function in your role doesn't make it true! For example, you may feel you aren't an effective public speaker, so you shy away from presentations as much as possible. But just because *you feel* you can't publicly speak effectively doesn't make that true! Another example: You may feel you don't possess the negotiation skills or level of confidence to land a coveted client for your business. Just because *you feel* that way doesn't make that true either!

Our perception isn't reality. As we discussed in Chapter 3, we see with our brains first, not our eyes. If you apply this concept to your business, recognize that your perception of any given issue is a result of several factors that include: how you analyze and process information presented to you, the state of your mind and how much you actually believe in your venture (purpose), the level of belief you have in your Higher Power, and whether or not you believe you can actually create a successful business.

If you allow untruths to fester in your mind, they will manifest into an altered reality constructed purely out of fear, which will pollute your perspective. This compromised state will invariably move you to make poor decisions and take unadvisable actions that can be detrimental to your business.

Guard against this.

At times during your entrepreneurial journey, your emotions will hijack you, causing you to believe untruths about your circumstances, the people around you, or even your Higher Power. *You can't effectively fight a foe you haven't accurately assessed in your mind from a place of truth*, however. If you are fighting against the foe of doubt that is coming from the fact that you are indeed, for example, unprepared for a meeting, then you can fight it by addressing the issue head-on and giving yourself the time to adequately prepare next time. If you are fighting against the foe of insecurities that are indeed paralyzing your success, you can fight it by telling yourself the truth about them head-on and taking steps to manage or overcome them. However, if you are fighting against a foe from a place of misplaced ideas or constructed realities based on insecurities and misguided emotions, your venture is in trouble.

Emotions are typically a warning sign of either real, current, or impending danger, or our own personal hijacking that can overtake us for several reasons. Developing self-awareness and learning to tell yourself the truth about the situations in front of you by separating fact from fiction will give you the fuel to find your inner fight, helping you to address your personal and professional challenges effectively to win.

3. Remember Why You Started

David's experience with Goliath underscores the power of belief and the importance of knowing your "why" and how it enables you to find your inner fight to win. You'll have to believe in your purpose without reservation. Just as you know you have ten fingers and ten toes, you'll need to believe your purpose is 100 percent true, and undeniably yours.

Why? Because when doubts assail you—from outside sources and from within—you'll need to be able to remember that your entrepreneurial journey is what you were created for; there's no turning back since you've become so consummated with the fact that your journey is *completely congruent* with your purpose. Maintaining a strong belief in this—your truth—will help you find your inner fight.

4. Pull Items from Your "Comeback Closet"

At this point in your journey, you know that you've been prepared for this moment with specific skills, passions and, yes, even those lemon experiences—all to help you fulfill your purpose. You've survived your past challenges; you're still here! Recognize that you *have* accomplished victories in your life too. Large or small, they represent key moments and examples of your Higher Power's presence, protection, and power.

You might even have tangible proof of this guiding presence and your victories. I still have the central venous catheter that was used to administer chemotherapy to my body during my leukemia lemon experience, and one of my first business cards with my breakthrough goal written on the back of it. To encourage me during the most challenging days of my journey, I would look at cards, emails, and gifts sent from nurses my company had worked with, sent years later, expressing their appreciation for our services and the heights they achieved personally and professionally since. I would review my prayer-walk journal,[12] chock-full of entries chronicling the experiences when God provided me with financial help and other blessings at precisely the moment I needed them. Keep such mementos in your comeback closet, tangible or figurative, to be drawn out during difficult times. They serve as reminders of your successful past, your ability to achieve your purpose-driven goals, and your Higher Power's propelling presence in your life and venture.

5. Stay Open and Listen

You've likely experienced moments where ideas have come into your mind, leading you to connect with certain key people that have helped you along your journey. Or perhaps you've felt an impending sense of doom when you were on the wrong path, or when danger was around the corner. Ultimately, receiving this direction brought you peace and provided for you, or saved you from a sticky situation. Not only have you been given a gift in the form of your skills and passion(s) that now propel you along your journey, you've also been gifted with an inner guidance system from your Higher Power—your conscience—that will lead you along your way. As you learn to quiet your spirit and listen to the guidance of your conscience, the impressions you receive on your mind and spirit leading you will become stronger in your life. And the peace brought to you by your Higher Power's presence will create the strength within you to fight on to victory.

"Life isn't about waiting for the storm to pass.
It's about learning how to dance in the rain."

—Vivian Greene

Fortify your inner constitution. Whatever you choose to call it, be it dance or fight, know that the accomplishment of your goals will, in part, depend on your ability to endure and persevere.

WHILE IT IS IMPORTANT TO BUILD A ROBUST SUPPORT NETWORK OF friends and professional advisors to help you personally and professionally as you grow your venture, there are days during your entrepreneurial journey when you'll need to find your inner fight to push forward. Especially in the beginning, you'll be particularly vulnerable to feelings of doubt and fear, and you'll feel the compelling draw of stability and security you left behind. In these delicate moments, being able to encourage yourself and find your inner fight will become imperative.

Ultimately, the heights you'll attain in your business first start with seeds germinated in the soil of your own mind. What you believe about yourself, your purpose, your business, and the capacity of your Higher Power will be made manifest in your results.

I've learned that in God's economy, you cannot fail when you're living your purpose, are moving forward in truth, are exercising faith in Him, and living in obedience to His Word. Trust that your success is imminent when you're operating from your higher purpose and press on to victory! Find your inner fight and believe you can win!

FOR DEEPER REFLECTION...

Strategy #7: Find Your Inner Fight & Win

1. What are your top three greatest fears in life and business? Acknowledging and articulating them will help decrease their power over you.

2. What three truths do you need to tell yourself about how you're feeling about your venture right now?

3. Are you secretly sabotaging yourself out of fear of what it will mean if you succeed?

4. List items from your comeback closet. What do they remind you of, and how do they encourage you?

5. Think of three instances when your conscience has guided you into something that led to a benefit for you, or steered you away from something that saved you. List them.
   a. Write down, as clear as you can remember, the impression(s) that you received from your conscience from the three instances above. Becoming clear on how your conscience leads you specifically will help strengthen your ability to recognize the guidance quickly and act according to its leading.

LEMONADE CHALLENGE

Journal your entrepreneurial experiences; the challenges you are facing, successes you are experiencing, and even your overall thoughts about your business. Do so at least once a week for a period of three months. At the end, review your entries for a reminder of how you've been led and how you're progressing through your journey. It can be hard to assess your progress objectively, but I'm confident that you're stacking up victories that aren't at the forefront of your mind, and when you look at your entries collectively, you'll see instances of hope, help, and blessings along your way.

The Outer Work

8

GET READY FOR THE ONSLAUGHT!

"Success occurs when opportunity meets preparation."

—ZIG ZIGLAR

A T THIS POINT IN YOUR JOURNEY, YOU'VE TAKEN THE TIME TO SQUEEZE your lemon experiences by evaluating them, healing from them, learning from them, and consistently and intentionally applying the lessons learned to help you create success from them. You've learned to become intentional about telling yourself the truth quickly about all aspects of your life and business, and how to use those truths to operate your life and business more effectively. You've progressed through the components of your necessary inner work, and as such, you've discerned the higher purpose for your "good work of service" venture, and your perspective and vision of the type of business you want to create is clear. You've committed to surrendering to a transformative process of you, by working to develop thoughts that progress to new beliefs that lead you to execute actions that will result in your success.

You understand the importance of having balanced relationships in your life, while also recognizing the need to draw from your inner fight to make it through as well. You've become intentional about placing the people that surround you in the right positions in your life, and trust that your pilot is absolutely willing and beyond capable of seeing you and your business through to success.

Now, you're ready to take all your efforts from the progression through your inner work and start squeezing them into the lemonade of your success—a successful business! Since you've:

- Squeezed your life lemons and have started the process of healing from them

- Developed a new way of relating to them

- Squeezed them dry of all the lessons and perspectives they can teach you

- Allowed them to propel you to a new way of navigating your life and business

…you're now ready for the second aspect of your journey toward creating a successful business, the completion of ***the outer work***: *actionable strategies you can implement to help you build a solid foundation for sustainable success.* And the first step of the outer work involves taking tangible steps to get ready for a breakthrough in your business and, ultimately, the onslaught of blessings, even beyond what you've envisioned in Chapter 3!

AS YOU FUNCTION IN THE DAY-TO-DAY ACTIVITIES OF YOUR VENTURE (FUL-filling orders or delivering your service, conducting your ongoing market analysis, developing your marketing and branding, communicating with clients, conducting meetings, forecasting, hiring staff, interacting with vendors, consultants, and/or investors), the aspects of your outer work enable you to carry out these functions effectively. Your inner work enables you to implement the strategies of the outer work, which will help you build a solid foundation for your business as you carry out your daily functions and plan for growth and development. *Systematic and intentional implementation of the aspects of your outer work directly prepares you to experience combustible success.* And it begins with effective and comprehensive preparation for the onslaught of blessings coming your way!

LESSONS LEARNED FROM GETTING READY

As is the case for many successful entrepreneurs, the early years of my first business were very arduous and represented the most difficult years of my entire career. Those first years were an absolute grind, full of ten- and eleven-hour days, missed holidays, and a myriad of other physical, emotional, relational, and financial sacrifices. As previously revealed, it was only after working for three and a half years, overtime and on overdrive, that I finally made my first dollar. Nevertheless, all of my blood, sweat, and tears (which I eventually recharacterized as my *investments*) paid off in the end. Not only in the success I've achieved and the positive impact of my businesses, but also, and far more importantly, it's paid off in the person I've become through enduring the entire process.

Am I advocating for missing holidays, shouldering crushing debt, or sacrificing relationships or your health by referring to these sacrifices as investments? Absolutely not! In hindsight, I've chosen to recharacterize that incredibly stressful season of my life as a time of investment—choosing to look at it with a positive perspective—and my hope is that this book will prevent you from having to endure the depths that I sank to on your rise to creating the lemonade of your success.

"I can't remember—do I work at home or do I live at work?"

I'm a firm believer that one of the worst phenomena a new entrepreneur or business owner can experience is quick or early success. Both are detrimental, as they can serve to lull a leader into a false sense of belief that this success will be the norm. To create a sustainably profitable venture, it is imperative to develop the business and its leaders into forces that can not only achieve success, but also sustain it.

Athletes spend countless hours training and conditioning their body, mind, and spirit for their chance to win. You, too, will need to prepare for your breakthrough by systematically and intentionally implementing key principles of your outer work, which we'll discuss more deeply later. Implementing key principles of your outer work will provide both you and your business a foundation for success and a template to navigate future challenges. Whether your business is thriving or progressing through a season of stagnation, you'll find that daily disciplines of your outer work provide you the necessary tools to successfully navigate what lies ahead.

THE FLYWHEEL AND YOUR BREAKTHROUGH

In his book, *Good to Great*—in my opinion, one of the most prolific and influential management-related business books ever written—Jim Collins introduces the concept of the flywheel and reflects that no transformation from good to great happens in one fell swoop. Instead, it's likened to the turning of a flywheel:

"In building a great company or social sector enterprise, there is no single defining action, no grand program, no one killer innovation, no solitary lucky break, no miracle moment. Rather the process resembles relentlessly pushing a giant, heavy flywheel, turn upon turn, building momentum until a point of breakthrough, and beyond."[1]

The rise in social media has demonstrated that quick success is indeed possible, but *maintaining* success is an elusive feat for many. Jim Collins' perspective likens achieving a business breakthrough to the turning of a heavy flywheel because it involves a daily grind, a daily turning that builds momentum, turn upon turn which will set you up to experience your breakthrough and combustible, sustainable success.

The daily grind necessary to bring you to the point of breakthrough involves a constant commitment to implementing the knowledge you've learned from squeezing your lemon experiences and a commitment to honing your talents and skills. It involves constantly checking your thoughts and beliefs and telling yourself the truth about how they invariably impact your business. The turning of your flywheel involves telling yourself the truth about the state of your mind, body, and spirit, and yes, even your heart, and guarding your business against compromised emotional states. The turning of your flywheel not only involves your intentional recognition of how your inner work prepares you to function effectively in your business, but it also involves the implementation of the aspects of your outer work that undergirds your ability to effectively execute the daily activities of your business.

There are so many aspects to the turning of your flywheel that help you build momentum to prepare you for your breakthrough. I've discovered that the best way to turn your flywheel effectively is through continual review of your inner work, which prepares you to implement the key principles of the outer work, which in turn, helps you build a solid foundation for your business. Doing so places you in the best position to ensure that the state of sustained profitability your business attains will be maintained over time.

AN EDUCATION FROM THE "SCHOOL OF HARD KNOCKS" IS ENOUGH!

In keeping with my perspective on the sheer magnitude of the power inherent in passion and purpose, I suggest to you that the standard MBA, academic approach to business development—while effective in equipping leaders to master the *administration* of a business—is not built for growth companies, especially those that are purpose-driven.

Entrepreneur magazine proposed that the Master of Business Administration (MBA) graduate degree is less suited for entrepreneurial growth endeavors, but useful for more predictable, scalable, process-driven ventures.[2] While it's effective in helping leaders achieve a modicum of success (as compared to our holistic, all-encompassing definition of success that stretches beyond material gain, power, and position to include contentment and peace), it is deficient in adequately preparing leaders to achieve success driven predominately by purpose. Purpose-driven pursuits are typically guided by a subset of principles deemed countercultural and counterintuitive by many business elites. However, these principles are imperative to cement and undergird the necessary technicalities of operating a growth business. You can't teach drive, passion, courage, will, or faith; they are an extension of a person's belief in their purpose and are crucial to achieving success in any entrepreneurial growth venture, especially if it's purpose-driven.

Since your purpose-driven venture is one of impact, it absolutely *is* a growth venture, so a traditional approach to "administering" your business will not suffice here. If you're insecure about your level of educational preparation to start or run your purpose-driven business, take heart. According to a CNBC/SurveyMonkey Small Business Survey, fifty-six percent of entrepreneurs have not completed a college degree.[3] The study also revealed that entrepreneurs who did not attend or finish college outnumbered those with higher-education degrees across both genders.[3] While a solid education can provide you with the skills, tools, and connections that may help you make strides within your business, a college degree absolutely isn't necessary for attaining success from your entrepreneurial venture.

So, don't allow yourself to get distracted by what you possess or don't possess. Your life experiences, talents, and completion of your inner and outer work are preparation enough for success from your purpose-driven venture. Use your time and resources wisely and get ready for the onslaught—or overflow of blessings for your business—even beyond the manifestation of those you've envisioned in Chapter 3. Graduate yourself from the "school of hard knocks." Commit to continuous learning and become a student of business success. Squeeze your life lemons, apply the lessons learned, and get ready for overflow!

SO, WHY PREPARE FOR OVERFLOW?

In my own personal experience and review of biblical scripture, God has been known to release blessings in abundance or overflow.[4] Therefore, I suggest preparing *in advance* to be able to effectively manage the potential overflow coming your way, which is typically extended to us as increased business, extra funding, and unexpected support, to name a few. So, for your purpose-driven venture, prepare yourself to receive, even in excess of your requests! I am living proof that God can, indeed, facilitate the attainment of your business goals if you trust in Him.[5]

By the time I sold my first business, I had accomplished every major goal I had set, as astronomical as they were. Through effective preparation, especially in the early season of your venture, you, too, have the ability to achieve success in your purpose-driven venture—far beyond what you now even envision is possible.

"Shoot for the moon. Even if you miss, you'll land among the stars."
—Norman Vincent Peale

While I implemented much of what is considered standard business practice to establish and operate my business, in the early days, much of my attention was focused on preparing *myself* to receive precisely what I was asking for and more—a concentration on my inner work. This underscores the reason why clarifying your purpose in the beginning is such an integral part of building a solid foundation for your business; it is the necessary fuel to power your journey. You will inevitably experience moments of uncertainty, market changes, ebbs and flows, and peaks and valleys in your business. Preparation, clarity of vision, and a clear understanding of your goals are among the most important indicators that will help you *maintain* success.

But *you cannot effectively prepare for success you haven't clearly defined*. Defining what you intend to offer and why will help you steer away from opportunities that might lead you astray. In my case, I was presented with more than one opportunity, all potentially lucrative, at a time when my efforts had not proven profitable as yet. Though I had accumulated a significant amount of debt while waiting for my breakthrough, my clear understanding of my "why" and my disciplined focus to prepare precisely for what I had envisioned emboldened me to disregard the distractions and press forward to prepare for the onslaught.

Preparing for the onslaught or overflow of blessings actually gave me something to do during my years of wait! That pivotal season was a blessing in disguise; it granted me focused time to develop systems and processes to eventually deliver my service offering with excellence based on sound business doctrine from the books I was reading, research, direct advice from experts, and wisdom gleaned from the many courses, seminars, workshops, and conferences I'd attended. Most importantly, preparing for the onslaught allowed me the time to concentrate on my inner work, preparing me to grow into a business owner who could *handle* the success I was envisioning and more. Had I not invested the time to intentionally develop my business while also developing *myself* as an entrepreneur, I would never have been ready for my breakthrough moment, which happened during one unassuming, morning phone call.

THE BENEFITS OF PREPARING FOR OVERFLOW: A PRACTICAL EXAMPLE

My first few bouts of client business were incredibly sporadic and couldn't alleviate the heavy physical, emotional, spiritual, and financial toll I was bearing. In an exasperated gasp of desperation, I defiantly informed God in prayer that I could not go forward any longer. I had, in effect, emotionally given up, despite having clarified my vision for the business with a solid recognition and understanding of my why.

I was hanging onto my faith by a thread, and despite my belief in the power of God and the direction of purpose He had rested upon my heart years prior, I was completely exhausted and toyed with the option of packing it all in. I felt I had given every bit of myself to my business and believed I had nothing more to give. Despite all my intellectual and spiritual reasonings, my heart had simply given up.

Boldly, I gave God an ultimatum: an actual date to manifest the deliverance, or I would fold. By the grace of God and His humoring my desperate musings, days before my ultimatum date, I received a phone call from a health executive I had cold-called more than a year prior. At that time, she had been gracious enough to extend me the opportunity to introduce her to my business but, after a series of meetings, she decided to utilize another service provider. At that point, she kindly communicated to me that if the alternate option they had chosen was unsuccessful, I would have an opportunity to discuss my service with her further. Discouraged from the years of mounting, daily rejections, and in complete exasperation and sadness, I'd resigned myself to the likelihood that this conversation would be the last I would ever hear from her.

I'd spent years turning my flywheel by cold-calling hundreds of organizations, developing operational systems, carefully curating service packages, and completing a myriad of other tasks, all of which took a toll on me. But the years of preparation ended up paying off in the end!

Days prior to my ultimatum date to God, amidst a cloud of discouragement, fear, and exhaustion, I answered a phone call from my assistant informing me of a call she was about to transfer. The name of the caller rang a bell, but in the midst of my despondent state, I could not recognize it. Nevertheless, I allowed my assistant to transfer the call. "Do you remember me?" the voice on the line asked. As she continued to speak, I realized she was the executive I'd written off over a year prior. However, this time, she asked if I was still placing RNs as she needed several, and she needed them fast. If I had qualified, screened staff willing to work at their organization, they would take them right away! If I hadn't prepared diligently during the years prior to this call—turning my flywheel even when it seemed unbearable—I would never have been ready to take advantage of this breakthrough opportunity!

Hindsight is indeed 20/20. The time of sporadic business was actually God's grace in painful disguise, allowing me the time and opportunity to prepare for the onslaught. I had very specific business goals in mind, but to adequately handle the blessings I was asking of God, I had to mature into the entrepreneur that all my skills, passions, and lemon experiences had prepared me to become. All the activities I was engaging in on a consistent basis to turn my flywheel prepared me to operate efficiently and with excellence when the time came for me to deliver.

During the call, the executive sternly informed me that if I was not ready to present their organization with the number of qualified candidates they needed straight away, she wanted to know upfront. If not, they would seek another option that could deliver quickly. My breakthrough opportunity knocked at seemingly the last second for me, but I was ready. This marked the turning point for my business, and served as a catalyst to power the manifestation of all of my major business goals accomplished thereafter.

"Do not despise the humble beginnings, for the Lord rejoices to see the work begin."[6]

—Zechariah 4:10

The preparation for the onslaught of blessings is time for you to develop into the entrepreneur who can handle the success you envision. Most of us would welcome success with little effort or quick riches, but neither will last. Your journey isn't only about serving your target market; it's also about transforming *you*, which takes time. As you squeeze your lemon experiences and learn from them, go forward with courage and prepare for bigger blessings than even what you're asking for, as success is born from preparation *prior* to your breakthrough. Without your growth and evolution, your purpose-driven venture will not stand the test of time or reach its full potential.

Too many entrepreneurs press forward with only a great idea, competence from their education, a mass of capital, or an inflated sense of self. But the way you build your business rests primarily on who you are, and the single greatest determinant of success is YOU.

WHATEVER YOU'RE STRIVING FOR, YOUR OUTER WORK STARTS WITH ACTIVE *preparation* toward the achievement of your clear vision, and beyond. Active preparation for the onslaught of blessings involves preparing your business operations to handle an influx of business. For you, it may involve taking classes or attending workshops to help you improve your sales and business communication skills. It could also involve investing in the services of a business management consultant to help you address specific challenges in your business, one who can provide you with resources and assistance to grow effectively, and help you avoid costly mistakes. Whatever activities you choose, make sure you set yourself up to win! Your success is imminent, so actively prepare for the onslaught!

FOR DEEPER REFLECTION...

Strategy #8: Get Prepared for the Manifestation of Your Vision, and More!

1. Overflow blessings can be extended to us in many forms. Some include blessings of opportunities coming from various directions, access to people who can help you, more funding than you need, extra bursts of energy, and insight to complete tasks. What are seven examples of overflow blessings you've experienced in your life thus far? List them.

2. Do you believe you can accomplish the clearly stated goals you're envisioning from Chapter 3? Why or why not?
   a. If yes, do you believe in the possibility of an onslaught of blessings more than your clearly stated goals from Chapter 3? Why or why not?

3. What are three things you're doing right now in your business to get ready for an onslaught of blessings? List them.

9

PRACTICE ACTIVE PATIENCE

*"It is easier to find men who will volunteer to die
than to find those who are willing to endure pain with patience."*

—Julius Caesar

During my formative years, my mom could regularly be heard saying, "Good things come to those who wait." She would typically say this when I was begging with urgency for something that she was getting ready to give me, something I likely felt entitled to. The concept of delayed gratification is so pivotal to success, but it's unfortunately lost on many people, especially those who are embroiled in "get rich quick" schemes in our increasingly impatient society. Unfortunately, patience isn't a naturally occurring skill, especially among those of us that are driven, focused, goal-directed entrepreneurs and business owners. However, to develop a successful venture built on sound principles, effective processes, and strong leadership, patience isn't just required; it's imperative.

During the life of your business, especially in the beginning, many of your goals likely won't come together exactly *the way* you envisioned or in the time you expected. Of course, success isn't linear; you'll inevitably progress through diversions along with periods of peaks and valleys, with the valleys, at times, seeming to last longer than the peaks. Transformations aren't always quick, and there will be times when the delay is unfortunately a result of our own doing. Nevertheless, learning to wait—and wait well—will be a necessary skill to develop to successfully navigate your journey toward the lemonade of your success.

"Let's face it, if we were getting
any customers they'd have been here by now."

RENAME THE CHALLENGES

When you're moving in the direction of your life's purpose, internal and external forces will undoubtedly challenge your resolve. They may come in the form of family, business associates, life events, trends within your industry, people disguising themselves as friends, and even your own critical inner voice. However they present themselves, learn to view these challenges as gifts; they're meant to strengthen you, not break you.

When you make the choice to perceive your challenges as a gift—an opportunity to steel your inner constitution—you're well on your way to transforming into someone worth becoming! In life, there are simply lessons we learn best in times of calm and others in times of storms. But I believe that most of us, unfortunately, learn the bulk of our most enduring, pivotal lessons in times of storms. So, don't be surprised when your testing seasons come. Ask for the strength to persevere through them, remain patient for your day of deliverance, and press forward.

What you do as you wait and *how* you wait both directly correlate to the rate, or even likelihood, that you experience personal and professional transformation at all. You can *choose* to fight the seasons of waiting by complaining, by spiraling into despair, or by deciding just to give up, or you can *choose* to view the challenging seasons as a gift, the perfect time to complete your inner and outer work.

CONDITIONS MAY GET WORSE BEFORE THEY GET BETTER

Three months after I incorporated my business, I was involved in a serious car accident with an intoxicated driver—my second lemon experience. Injuries I sustained to my neck and back from the T-bone impact, requiring over three years of physical therapy, rendered me unable to continue working as a casual RN while I built my venture. Building a business through excruciating pain over a sustained period of time isn't a fate I would wish on anyone. Yet, after four years of legal wrangling with the intoxicated driver's insurance company and their lawyers, the financial settlement we agreed upon *was **more** than I would have earned working as an RN during that same time*! These funds provided me a much-needed buffer to continue in my pursuit toward the lemonade of my success. So, although it was an excruciatingly painful journey, physically, mentally, and financially, I chose to view this lemon experience as a gift that gave me the necessary time to develop both myself and my business. And in my day of financial deliverance, I was blessed with overflow!

This recharacterization, along with strength gained through prayer and study of God's Word, are what helped me to effectively press forward as I waited on my eventual breakthrough and combustible success thereafter. As you progress in your journey, recognize that you too may have navigated through past lemon experiences that got worse before they got better. And at times, this happens around the time you set the intention to complete your inner and outer work.

Anticipate this, and don't allow yourself to succumb to frustration.

When you make the decision to exercise patience in your lowest moments and surrender to the transformative process of you, you will eventually arrive at a moment of deliverance with an accomplished purpose.

"Would you please hurry and get ready?"

WAIT WELL

At some point, the valley experience will pass. Waiting anxiously, fearfully, or angrily won't serve you or your business well at all. Have you ever seen a child wait anxiously for something their parent was getting ready to give them? What emotions did that conjure up in you? Now, imagine yourself as a business leader and having your team watch you wait angrily or fearfully for something that eventually comes together in the end, say, a major business deal, for example. After it all comes together, your feelings of shame, embarrassment, and regret would definitely be warranted.

Strive to wait and wait well. Worrying will not change your circumstances in any way. It only ends up negatively impacting you and potentially those around you as well. Patience is an important aspect of your outer work, which will help you build a solid foundation for your business.

You have a choice. Standing upright with confidence in the valleys of your business journey is not an easy task. Believe me: I know! However, I've come to learn that doing so requires a reserve of emotional and spiritual maturity, in which you don't ask to be rescued; rather, you ask your Higher Power for the strength to make it through. I've personally experienced the truth of the concept "your attitude determines your altitude," popularized by prolific motivational speaker and author Zig Ziglar. If we have a positive attitude toward our circumstances, that will invariably impact how we show up in the world. If we have a negative attitude, it will pollute everything and everyone around us.

In addition to exercising greater patience with yourself and your business, I encourage you to consider the attitude you bring to your time of waiting as well, since *how* you wait directly impacts your ability to achieve your goal of sustainable success that leads to peace.

A LESSON *EARNED* IS A LESSON "WELL LEARNED"

Unfortunately, there are those of us that endure sustained or repeated valleys, or even lemon experiences, because we do not readily learn from them, and keep making the same mistakes that may have led to them in the first place. Think of your own life. Have you endured a negative experience over and over again? Are you willing to acknowledge that there is a pattern or core issue at play, which might be revealing itself in different forms in your life? Is the same friend, significant other, job situation, or financial condition "presenting itself" time and time again, leaving you wondering why you fall for it each time?

Don't worry; there's hope! When you learn specific lessons from challenging experiences, apply what you've learned to your life, and move forward in a new, positive direction. The next time the situation presents itself, you've overcome and *earned* the lesson. This *earning* graduates you to the next level of your development and, by extension, the eventual development of your successful business.

Commit to *earning* lessons from your mistakes. Know that when you've correctly discerned that your venture is the purpose you were created for and the reason behind your lemon experience(s), **in time**, as you consistently and intentionally complete the aspects of your inner and outer work, the lemonade of your success is inevitable.

MAY FLOWERS GROW FROM APRIL SHOWERS

As the rainy seasons bring about growth in nature, so is the case for your development and the development of your business. The stormy valley seasons in the life of your venture can cause you and your business to grow more than any peak season ever could, since you'll be earning lessons that will help you navigate your venture more effectively going forward. Patience in these seasons isn't easy, but you're not alone! There are so many successful entrepreneurs and businesses that illustrate the power of patience and perseverance. Some include:

- **MailChimp**, the marketing platform targeted at small businesses, endured *seventeen years* of ups and downs before maintaining profitability. However, through learning and persevering during that period, they've become one of the major business success stories of our time. At the time of writing, the company continues to grow by more than $120 million per year, with more than 14,000 customers signing up every single day.[1]

- **Colonel Sanders** was rejected 1,009 times before successfully selling his Kentucky fried chicken recipe, after failing at every job he'd tried prior. He was seventy-five years old before he finally sold his successful business, Kentucky Fried Chicken, and he ended up being the face of a billion-dollar brand.[2]

- **Jack Ma**, founder of multinational technology conglomerate Alibaba Group, survived countless rejections and failures only to get back up and brave every storm. Despite being rejected from Harvard ten times and finding himself on the verge of bankruptcy in the 1990s, Ma was never defeated. He put one foot in front of the other until he finally made it, with the creation of a company worth, at the time of writing, $453 billion.[3,4]

The entrepreneurial journey requires a significant amount of internal strength to endure the valleys, those of our own making and the circumstances beyond our control. Though if we allow them, these valley seasons can transform us into a person who can handle the success we are striving for. Developing patience is key to seeing you through. So, do your part and ask your Higher Power for the strength to wait, and wait well.

THE TEACHER IS ALWAYS QUIET DURING THE TEST

There were times during some of the darkest periods of the thirteen years I owned my first business when I would arrive at a standstill, and would pray for more direction and help (to be discussed in greater detail in Chapter 15) to get me to the next level of growth, but I would not get it. In those moments, I felt alone, frustrated, and even panicky at times since I'd come to depend on the "carrying" presence of God through my inner guidance system that would empower and progress me forward. In these moments, however, I had to realize that the time had come for me to actually *put to use* **all** the information I had earned from past experience, along with information learned up until that point from professional advisors, courses, seminars, conferences and workshops, and information from the business and personal development books I was reading. *I had already possessed all that I needed to make it through*, but I had to set the intention to use it consistently, and then exercise patience thereafter. I needed to lean on the character I had built through the completion of my inner work, then do my part to pass this testing season.

The teacher, or your Higher Power, will not keep carrying you through your entire journey by sending you resources, people to help, funding when you need it, and so on. Yes, that can and does happen, but remember, your entrepreneurial journey—your purpose-driven venture—is also designed to transform YOU, and learning to pass the tests along the way is part of your transformation and growth.

In those dark moments of silence from God, among the greatest lessons I learned was the power of choice. I had to *choose* to step out of panic mode and systematically progress forward using the tools I already had available to me. In the moments that test you the most, you too may notice that your inner guidance system is quiet and that the confirmation, encouragement, guidance, and resources you had become accustomed to receiving from your Higher Power has ceased, leaving you to fly on your own. The keyword here is "fly!"

Birds are provided with all they need to develop to a certain level: food, their mother's care, protection from predators, and more. At some point, though, they must learn to fly to survive, and they won't survive by staying in the comfort of the nest. Some species of birds are even pushed out of the nest by a parent![5]

As it is in nature, so it is in business. There are some lessons in business that you'll never learn without a challenging season. Learning to put all your knowledge into practice builds your confidence and skills to tackle larger tasks. If you don't fly on your own, you'll always be leaning on someone else, and you'll never fully develop into the leader you've been called to be. Being patient with yourself, the growth of your business, and even learning to be patient with your Higher Power will transform both you and your business, which will set you up to achieve your goals, and beyond.

PATIENCE THAT YIELDS RESULTS: AN ACTIVE PROCESS

Effective waiting is not a passive endeavor. Simply doing nothing during your seasons of wait won't help you survive and can actually be counterproductive. Key activities discussed in Chapter 8 will help you while waiting for your breakthrough. Additionally, you can engage in five specific activities that will serve to embolden you to wait, and wait well during the moments of your entrepreneurial journey that call for sustained patience.

You can practice active patience by:

1. Revisiting Your Agenda

Actively review the "why" of your journey, as well as your notes on how you arrived at a place of confirmation to move forward. Famous German philosopher Friedrich Nietzsche reminds us that understanding or knowing our "why" will help us *bear* or endure the questions of how things will come together.[6] Your challenging seasons require bearing, endurance, and patience; possessing the knowledge and understanding of your "why" will provide you with the necessary fuel to endure the "how" and the strength and perseverance to continue driving toward the accomplishment of your "what."

2. Acknowledging Your Current State of Being

Take inventory of what you're feeling as you wait. Be it frustration, fear, anxiety, anger, or panic, as previously discussed, your negative emotions are an indicator of the state of your mind and heart, and they impact the way you interact with those around you, both personally and professionally. No matter how hard you try to shield co-workers, vendors, and even clients from this compromised state, it will eventually seep into your communications, body language, and even business decisions, with potentially detrimental effects. Actively set aside time and find a place where you can pull away and think about your feelings in these seasons and determine to wait well—void of impatience, anger, frustration, and all their cousins.

3. Reevaluating Your Strategies & Strategic Decisions

Draw from your inner work and tell yourself the truth about how you arrived at this moment. Did you contribute to a lull in your business? Have you made erroneous decisions that have led to the season you're experiencing? This process of self-evaluation isn't passive. If done correctly, it will require an active review of your entire business: your communications, policies, strategies implemented, products developed or services provided, the absence or presence of members on your team and their placement in your corporate structure, vendors chosen, and various other aspects of your business that impact its effectiveness.

Go through your emails. Look at the correspondences sent and evaluate if you communicated your ask as effectively as you could. Look at your strategic plan for this fiscal year and your goals from Chapter 3. Have you, and are you executing them as effectively as possible? Is there something you need to add, change, or stop doing that can help propel your business growth? Go through an active process of reevaluating your strategies for growth implemented to date, and think about the strategic decisions you've made. This reevaluation is an active process, requiring a deep dive into your business activities which will help you audit mistakes or adjust your approach to set you up for success going forward.

4. Continuing Your Preparation to Accomplish Your Business Goals

Adequately preparing for your breakthrough will help you effectively manage the potential for an onslaught of blessings, even beyond what you're envisioning. As mentioned, I liken the process of building a sustainably successful venture to building a house. It takes time and the right materials, put together in the proper manner before a house is ready for presentation to the market. You don't want to be building your proverbial business house while the buyers are coming to collect the key!

Mishandling your "big break" and a lack of preparedness will be devastating to your venture, and it may be a long time before your next opportunity to redeem yourself. It's important that you maintain the level of grit, sheer will, and desire to prepare that you demonstrated prior to your breakthrough after you "make it," even though your preparation or daily work will now take on a different form. Planning, improving, reevaluating, forecasting, goal setting, and innovation should never cease within your organization; they should evolve to meet the new challenges presented by your organization's growth. This is how you can actively wait by continuing the work of preparation to accomplish your list of business goals from Chapter 3.

So, keep pressing forward with the same tenacity, drive, discipline, and precision you used prior to your breakthrough. Although the work you execute in your business will likely have evolved after your breakthrough, the attitude you bring to your business should not.

5. Implementing Measures to Strengthen Your Body, Mind, and Spirit

Exercise, in and of itself, is very important to our overall health—a concept we'll explore further in Chapter 11—and has implications on our physical ability to remain calm in times requiring patience. Furthermore, as discussed in Chapter 4, for us to stand up, run, or walk effectively, our abdominal muscles need to be strong and intact.[7] So remember to think of your spirituality and the development of your faith as your core, as discussed in Chapter 4. Every aspect of who you are and who you will become is anchored in your spiritual identity. As strengthening your core improves your balance and stability in your body,[8] strengthening your faith muscle will also help you become stable and balanced in your business allowing you to wait well.

Guard the gateway to your mind and heart from getting impatient, anxious, or panicky by strengthening your spirit. When you feel discouraged, implement the following constructive strategies to strengthen your body and enhance your faith; they will help you wait—and wait well—and will also improve your state of mind.

Choose to think positive!

Of course, this doesn't mean that your whole existence and perspective should reflect rose petals and bubblegum on a sunny day! But training your mind to absorb the positive, the constructive, and the edifying things of life will help strengthen your internal constitution rather than weaken it. Become intentional about removing yourself from anything that draws you into a depressive, angry, impatient, or negative state, especially in your challenging seasons. Don't feed the beast within you, who is already anxiously awaiting release! In my experience, I asked God in prayer to release me from my fears, anxieties, doubts, and impatience and took steps to intentionally remove myself from negative influences. The results were astounding! You, too, can draw from the power of this strategy and protect your positive mindset by spending time with trusted, supportive people. If you don't have these people in your life, ask to be led to sources of encouragement and strength to help you along your way.

Review historical examples of people that endured

The most valuable approach I implemented, which directly taught me how to wait well on my journey to success, was a daily review of the biblical promises of God and learning from the experiences of growth of those in the Bible who, just like me, had endured challenges.

There's nothing new under the sun. Though it was written at a different time, the Bible includes many examples of people who faced the exact pressures, insecurities, and challenges we experience today. Learning from the failures and triumphs of those like Joseph, Moses, Elijah, King David, and King Hezekiah, to name a few, can serve to empower you with the recognition that you are not alone. If other people throughout history have accomplished seemingly insurmountable feats for a larger purpose, so can you!

Draw from nature's well

Immersing myself in nature is another strategy I found useful for strengthening my faith and improving my state of mind during stressful times of waiting. On some of my most frustrating, exhausting days, walks through my neighborhood park immediately calmed me and helped me gain desperately needed perspective. If you live near a park, forest, or another natural area, set aside concentrated time in your workday to take a break, breathe in the fresh air, debrief with yourself, and decompress.

If you live near a body of water, allot time to sit close and enjoy it. Studies show that moving water, such as rain showers, rivers, crashing waves, and waterfalls release negative ions into the air.[9] Once they reach our bloodstream, these negative ions are believed to produce biochemical reactions that increase levels of the mood chemical serotonin, which helps to alleviate depression, relieve stress, and boost our daytime energy.[10] All those great benefits, just by sitting next to water!

Nature is powerful. Charge up from its power to help you wait well.

Exercise

Beyond the benefits to your overall physical health, thirty minutes of exercise that gets your blood pumping and heart rate increased—at least three days per week—is also a great way to improve mood and decrease stress. When you exercise, your body releases chemicals called endorphins that help increase your mood, leave you feeling more energetic, trigger positive feelings, and also reduce your perception of pain.[11] Exercise can also help improve your focus and the quality of your sleep.

Strengthening your mind, body, and spirit during your times of wait can help you develop a good attitude. Be confident that doing so will eventually increase your altitude.

WHETHER YOU CHOOSE THE METHODS LISTED ABOVE OR UTILIZE YOUR own, recognize that there are tangible activities you can add to your daily routine to help you effectively manage stressful seasons that require sustained patience. Strengthening your mind, body, and spirit, continuing your preparation to achieve your goals, reevaluating your strategies, acknowledging your current state, and revisiting your agenda are all active processes. They help you build endurance and provide you with the tools to practice active patience.

All of this requires specialized action, and you've already taken a major step in the right direction in your decision to read this book! You are passionately driven to accomplish your purpose, so it's already unlikely that you'll want to simply sit around and wait. These five key activities will help you practice active patience, propelling you toward your transformation and that of your business. Put them into practice consistently and intentionally, and you will reap exponential rewards.

THERE'S POWER IN PEACE

We've established that patience is essential to your success and that *how* you wait is of equal importance. When navigating your challenging season, know that there's also power in *choosing* to operate from a place of calm and peace.

Once you've taken steps toward active waiting while perceiving this season as a time of formation for both you and your business, all that's really left to do is to *choose* to operate from a place of peace. Being able to stand up in the face of your challenges and maintain your peace is absolutely not easy, but the ability to do so is the highest level of patience, which heralds a major shift in your personal transformation. To achieve this state, continue trusting the formative process, and have faith that the One who has prepared you for this journey will indeed make all things beautiful in time.[12]

Stay the course.
Practice active patience.
Make the decision to operate from a place of trust and peace.
Experience the power inherent in that state of being,
and continue pressing forward toward the lemonade of your success!

FOR DEEPER REFLECTION...

Strategy #9: Practice Active Patience

1. I've come to learn that God has made promises to those that commit to living according to a higher purpose for their lives. Head to my website: **melanemullings.com** and look under the "Resources" tab for Chapter 9 for a list of promises from the Bible you can claim to give you the courage to expect deliverance from your valley experiences and success from your purpose-driven venture.

2. What are three mistakes you've made in recent years that have taught you valuable lessons? List them.
   a. Was impatience a contributing factor to the mistake?

3. How can your understanding of these lessons be applied to your venture?

4. Think of an example when you waited for something but did not wait well, and the situation ended up working out in the end. List it.
   a. How did you feel about your impatience after the situation was resolved?

   b. What three lessons can you learn from this experience about waiting more effectively in the future?

5. What are three areas in your business where you currently need to exercise patience?

6. What are three activities from the chapter that you plan to commit to trying, in order to practice active patience going forward?

LEMONADE CHALLENGE

#1: If you feel anxious or stressed about the things you're waiting for, think of a list of reasons why you may be enduring this season of wait. Journal them, then revisit your list periodically.

Surrender your list in prayer, with faith, to help you gain release from anxiety and fear. Share your experiences through this process with a friend or one of your professional advisors, and gain strength through this support system. While you wait, remind yourself of the successes you've accomplished to date and revisit the principles discussed in Chapter 7 at least once a week. Be proactive and write out your prayer of thanksgiving in advance! Your seasons of waiting are preparing you to deliver your "good work" to the world, and are preparing YOU to **become** the best version of yourself; one that can handle the success you're striving for. Stay the course, anticipate a positive resolution, and wait well![13]

#2: Strengthen Your Core
For the next thirty days, implement a minimum of three of the strategies listed below at least three times per week:

- Review of biblical promises
- Take a walk in a local park or nature area for twenty minutes
- Sit by a body of water for thirty minutes
- Exercise for thirty minutes
- Listen to a presentation from a motivational speaker

At the end of the thirty days, journal the changes you experienced personally and professionally after implementing your three strategies consistently. Share them with a friend or one of your professional advisors.

10

STAY HUNGRY
EVEN WHEN YOU FEEL FULL

"A worker's appetite works for him; his hunger urges him on."[1]

—PROVERBS 16:26

YEARS AGO, I HEARD A SPIN ON THE ABOVE PASSAGE OF SCRIPTURE THAT I found endearingly cheeky. Instead of "his hunger urges him on," it was, dramatically, "his hungry belly urges him on!"

Think of the discomfort and the pangs you feel in your stomach when you're hungry for a sustained period of time and, for whatever reason, cannot access food. If you're anything like me, the aggravation would have you ingest almost anything to quell the vexation of the moment! Invariably, your quest for food intensifies the longer you remain hungry. Conversely, however, if you've eaten to the point of feeling stuffed, your desire for more food understandably decreases. Don't allow this to be the case for you as you grow your entrepreneurial venture. Even when you begin to enjoy increased business and feel that everything is starting to come together, be sure to stay hungry! Keep planning, stay diligent, and keep pressing forward using the strategies that landed you to this point, and build on them. Staying hungry in the good times will help you ensure that the success you're tasting will keep feeding you for the future.

Once you start reaping the benefits of your breakthrough, it'll become tempting to rest on your laurels and sit back and enjoy the feeling of satiation or arrival. After all, you've worked so hard for so long, and you deserve a sustained break to enjoy the moment, right? While celebrating your successes is vital to effective growth and development for both you and your business—a topic discussed more deeply in Chapter 17—maintaining the drive that propelled you to the point of breakthrough is essential to help ensure you reach a state of sustained profitability.

THE DANGER OF ENJOYING FEELING "FULL": A PRACTICAL EXAMPLE

One of the greatest mistakes I made after my breakthrough moment was to allow myself to slip into a state of complacency. I'd sacrificed so much for so long that seeing all the zeros in my bank account thereafter lulled me into an unfortunate season I refer to as exhalation. This was unfortunate because, instead of continuing to breathe life into my business, I chose to manage the mammoth responsibility I had been given all on my own, simply by staying the course. The truth was, the responsibilities I had now been gifted from my breakthrough moment *were actually too much for me to handle on my own*, and I would pay a price for deciding to shoulder it all myself. In doing so, though, I *earned* a very important lesson for the future.

Unfortunately, everything in my life after my breakthrough centered around managing the moment; delivering on the service I had been contracted to provide. On the surface, I was right to do so, as I felt a strong sense of duty to be a good steward of the breakthrough blessing God had entrusted me with. I worked tirelessly to execute my services and overdeliver as often as I could. Unfortunately, while doing so, I began to lose focus on building a solid foundation *for future growth* beyond this breakthrough client. A closer look would reveal that my frantic, overdrive pace to effectively execute the deliverables negatively impacted other aspects of my life. And one by one, everything in my life beyond the business began to suffer.

I felt a sense of relief and accomplishment to be able to finally operate my business on a larger scale, but I also felt overwhelmed regularly. Relationships started to suffer, along with my health and overall sense of peace. I earned a very valuable lesson during that season: exhale and enjoy the opportunity to work IN your business, yes, but simultaneously keep breathing life into your business by working ON it.

TOO OFTEN, THE USUAL

Too many business owners and entrepreneurs *start* their ventures in a state of exhalation and concentrate on doing the "sexy" stuff first; they complete all the activities that represent the "show" of a business (like printing business cards and other marketing materials), come up with content to launch a snazzy business website and carefully curate their social media presence all without doing a comprehensive market analysis, or their inner and outer work required to operate effectively. In essence, *they complete the tangibles of running a business before actually building it on the solid foundation of the outer work that draws from the completion of their inner work.* They work IN their business but not ON it. Their ventures are pretty on the outside but shallow on the inside, with no true substance or solid foundation to survive and thrive beyond quick success.

In our increasingly impatient society, too few business owners and entrepreneurs take the time to build a solid foundation for their ventures. How do I know? Because the business activities they find themselves engaging in on a day-to-day basis give them away.

If on a regular basis you find yourself:

1. Spending your workday solely completing tasks for clients,

2. Starting your workday with the goal of figuring out how to survive it unscathed,

3. Unaware which of the activities you engage in are the most profitable and which are the least,

4. Lost, with no plan for the completion of a clear set of goals for your current fiscal year, or actionable items to complete each quarter,

5. Operating without a clearly defined budget that allocates funds to set business objectives,

6. Making financial decisions solely from the perspective of addressing immediate needs for your business,

7. Operating without a clear plan for growth, set of values, purpose, or objectives beyond making money

...then, likely, you're stuck in the cycle of working IN versus ON your business, and you're seriously in danger of stunting your growth, preventing you from achieving a state of sustained profitability beyond your breakthrough.

Remember the statistic from Chapter 1: fifty percent of businesses fail by their second year, and by the tenth year, only three in ten businesses that started, remain in operation.[2] Of interest as well, only forty percent of small businesses are actually profitable! Of the sixty percent that are not, thirty percent of them are breaking even financially, and the other thirty percent are actually losing money.[2] Something is going terribly wrong, and in my experience interacting with several business owners and entrepreneurs over the years, I would venture to say that a vast majority of the sixty percent of businesses that remain unprofitable for a significant period of time are led by owners that are spending a majority of their time working IN, versus ON their businesses, and are operating from a perspective outside of their purpose.

You may have already started your business, and, as was the case for me after my breakthrough, you understand the reasoning for staying hungry even when you feel full—to ensure you have business beyond your breakthrough client. Maybe you haven't hit the point of breakthrough yet, though. You're receiving sporadic business but are stuck in a rut of concentrating more on working IN your business versus ON it, because you're so overwhelmed by all of the pressures, internal and external, to deliver. Whether you've experienced breakthrough business or not, feelings of overwhelm are natural when building a business. It's also natural to feel like "exhaling" for a moment to just enjoy your breakthrough season since you've worked so hard to get there. However, if you stay in either state too long—exhalation or working hard and overwhelmed—it can result in poor execution of the deliverables, or mistakes that may include overpromising and/or underdelivering. Eventually, this will compromise your integrity in your market, damaging both your reputation and that of your venture, which may prove challenging to regain.

HOW TO WORK "ON" YOUR BUSINESS: PART 1

Once the wheels of your business are turning, it does become increasingly difficult to work ON your business while effectively working IN it, yes, but commit to building a business that represents all the sacrifices you've made to start your venture. Deliver with integrity and excellence *every time* while seeking to innovate and adapt. Get help, and delegate away aspects of your business that do not draw from your core competence to those that love what you loathe doing for your business. Start building a solid foundation for your business NOW even as you work in it. A home built well can stand for decades, even amid internal and external pressures. Strive to build your venture effectively by completing your inner and outer work with spiritual anchoring to your Higher Power, and you will greatly increase the likelihood of sustaining your breakthrough level of success and beyond.

HOW TO STAY HUNGRY

So, it's important to build on the process that brought you to the point of a breakthrough by staying hungry. Learning key lessons from your breakthrough—how you managed it, what worked well, what didn't, and what you could do better going forward—and building on them to grow your venture into a sustainably successful one, is an important strategy to implement during the life of your business. Regularly audit your journey. Determine a set time each quarter to evaluate the positives and negative results of the choices and the decisions you've made for your business. Start innovating, create efficiencies, adjust your service or product, and reach out to new markets to find more avenues to scale your business to create impact. No matter the stage of your business, like a plant, if it's not growing, it's slowly dying. Set yourself and your business up to win in the future. Continue to water and feed it by staying hungry.

In review, preparing for the onslaught involved preparing your business to function proficiently once you arrive at the moment of your breakthrough, which is inevitable if you have discerned your life purpose correctly. Staying hungry encompasses preparing for *future* growth after your initial breakthrough and beyond. Staying hungry will ensure you stay a step ahead and on the road to sustainable success.

Some of the ways you can stay hungry include:

- Over-delivering on the products and/or services promised to your breakthrough client(s)

- Executing efficiencies at every turn to operate effectively

- Becoming an eager student of the developmental business process

- Creating systems to track your progress and growth

- Consistently implementing the seventeen strategies from this book—working on yourself to show up effectively in your business to build a solid foundation for it

- A commitment to continuous learning

Staying hungry not only encompasses your engagement in activities that will grow your business while delivering your service, but it also includes your diligence to continue your inner work, which is necessary to function proficiently as a leader at each stage of your journey. During your peak success seasons, it can become easy to allow yourself to be consumed by the blessings of increased business and ignore yourself and your needs in the process. However, accomplishments without balance are not true success—a concept I'll explore more in Chapter 11—and learning to manage your success effectively is key to its sustainability.

SLOW AND STEADY WINS THE RACE

After your breakthrough, plan to implement strategies to help you grow slowly and effectively at a rate you can realistically manage. This will allow you to maintain a standard of excellence in your service that will expand your current client base.

How you grow your business is of equal importance as the growth itself. When businesses bite off more than they can chew, it shows. I've witnessed a plethora of business ventures grow quickly, only to experience a fast or slow burn. Think of examples from your own experiences. When companies you like start cutting corners on their quality or customer service, how does that make you feel? Personally, I've found it incredibly irritating when I started to depend on a product or service, only to find the quality steadily or abruptly decline.

When organizations make decisions that compromise the quality of their product or service, they communicate the low value they place on customer satisfaction and demonstrate an unwillingness to conduct their business with excellence. This perspective erodes brand loyalty. Eventually, the resulting disappointment in the market will impact their bottom line.

One great example is a local dry-cleaning company in my old neighborhood. Although they've been in business for over twenty years and had built up a robust client base through innovative programs such as pick-up and delivery of laundry at no extra charge, birthday cards mailed out to repeat customers with discount coupons for future services and regular in-store draws for free services, their business started a rapid decline with a change in management. Garments I'd dropped off for alterations would come back incorrectly altered, clothes would come back clearly still soiled, and mistakes made on receipts became regular occurrences. Even complaints from staff about management *to me*, a regular customer, were jarring, yet not surprising given the clear decline of their business from within. Although I had sung their praises for years as a "best-practice business," their compromise of quality and poor customer service demonstrated by a lack of immediate willingness to make their mistakes right, ended up costing them business, along with my patronage as a loyal brand ambassador for years.

Strive to write your ending differently. Commit to delivering your product or service in a manner that respects both the endurance of your lemon experience(s) and all you've sacrificed and invested in making it to this point. Stay hungry in your business by committing to grow slowly, effectively, and with excellence at every turn, and you'll be on the road to enjoying the lemonade of your success.

A BUSINESS APPLICATION

The best example of the benefits of growing slow and steady, and the most impressive company I worked for prior to starting my first entrepreneurial venture, was WestJet Airlines. I was a call-center employee when the company earned its first million, and, in those early years, I directly experienced WestJet's insatiable appetite for excellence, and commitment to growing slowly and effectively despite external pressures.

Their values were not simply disseminated in a business communique; instead, they were tangibly modeled in leadership at every level, and weaved into the company's business operations and corporate culture. At the time, it was evident that the leadership was intent on growing slowly and effectively amid sustained pressure to fill a gap to replace Canada's second major airline, Canadian Airlines, which had been acquired by Canada's mammoth crown corporation, Air Canada. This merger left only two major airlines in Canada, WestJet and Air Canada. At the time of the merger, Canadian Airlines had over 40 percent of the domestic passenger market share,[3] so, for any company, the temptation to ramp up operations to absorb that vacant market share quickly would be compelling. Nevertheless, I witnessed WestJet stay true to its core values, and its leaders remain steadfast in their determination to grow slowly and effectively—an experience that indelibly impacted airline travel in Canada, as well my personal business journey for years to come.

How you stay hungry will be a determining factor in your ability to sustain success for the long haul. Beyond the heights that WestJet Airlines—now a multi-award-winning, worldwide airline[4]—has attained since, the fact that it also directly inspired a nursing student to, years later, make her own first million says something. Now, that's a company with impact!

HOW TO WORK "ON" YOUR BUSINESS: PART 2

My introduction to the concept of staying hungry in the months after my breakthrough probably saved my business. Over time, I discovered key strategies to work ON my business while working IN it, which set the stage for my modus operandi going forward, ultimately helping to propel me to success. You, too, may find it useful to use a strategic approach to avoid complacency in your business. Try the following strategies as you look to create an environment that will breed sustainable success for your venture as well:

1. Refer back to your yearly and quarterly goals list regularly

Adapt to your new positive reality, but make sure to keep your eye on the prize. As discussed in Chapter 3, continue to work backward regularly to ensure you are on course to achieve your goals. In review, you can do this by taking the following two steps:

a) Before the end of each fiscal year, develop a set of goals for the upcoming year and break them down into goals you plan to accomplish each quarter

b) You can then take your quarterly goal list and break them down into actionable steps for each month and each week. And if you are so inclined, plan each day to include items for completion that will bring you closer to the accomplishment of your quarterly goals

As conditions change in your business, you'll need to demonstrate agility and adjust your business priorities accordingly. Adapting to changing conditions will clearly impact your set timeline for the completion of your goals, but still, stay diligent in revisiting your plan for completion of your quarterly and fiscal-year goals. Operating with a planned, disciplined approach throughout your fiscal year will help you stay on track for success.

2. Build your success team

Having enjoyed the benefits of delivering your product or service to your target market—whether it be a result of sporadic or breakthrough business—plan to allocate funds from your new income to invest in the growth and sustainability of your venture. One of your key objectives should involve delegating tasks outside of your areas of expertise to other skilled professionals. This allows you to concentrate on delivering your product or service with excellence to your new client(s). The best leaders acknowledge their weaknesses and hire accordingly. If you haven't already done so, make it a priority to assemble your success team to set yourself up to achieve your goal of sustained profitability.

Investing in the services of a qualified business management consultant who understands the complexities of operating a purpose-driven venture is key at this pivotal stage of your business. We can help you stay on track, forecast effectively, and help you streamline the delivery of your product(s) and/or service(s) to meet and exceed your objectives. Organized operation of your business is paramount to ensure repeat business; it will help turn your breakthrough client(s) into "client brand ambassadors"—clients who fall in love with your brand and spread the news—who will become key players in your success story.

YOUR NETWORK = YOUR NET WORTH

Client or customer brand ambassadors are among the most powerful forms of increased business, and arguably carry the most weight to encourage potential customers to buy your product or utilize your service. This is one of the reasons why it's so crucial to grow slow and steady, to ensure you can develop a quality product or deliver your service with excellence. Not only are your brand ambassadors' referrals based on their personal experience of actually utilizing your product or service, but their referral or recommendation of your business is also free!

Client or customer referrals offer the most effective marketing return on your investment of growing slow and steady. Their willingness to speak on the benefits of your service can do so much for the growth of your business where traditional marketing such as websites, brochures, billboards, signs, or even TV or radio slots may fall short. Working with excellence to create client or customer brand ambassadors as a part of your success team is key. Doing so will directly help you stay hungry, and continue tapping into this free resource that comes from a love of your quality product or amazing service.

Your success team includes your client and customer brand ambassadors, a business network of professional advisors, as well as other professionals that work with and for you. Your personal and professional investments to ensure a steady stream of each of these three sets of individuals on your success team is pivotal to your ability to accomplish your goals more speedily, and even surpass those goals for your purpose-driven venture.

Additional help in the form of consultants, accounting services, freelance administrative assistants, legal services, and more can be hired on a contingency basis, and there are several options you can locate online. Customer relationship management (CRM) solutions represent an option that can help you streamline your operations and free up valuable time, allowing you to concentrate on activities that draw from your core competence.

I've developed a system of allocating at least sixty percent of my time each day to specific, predetermined activities that are known to generate income for my ventures; activities that draw from my developed areas of core competence which include organization, planning, execution of goals, managing client relationships, and so on. The remaining forty percent of my time is spent on projects to improve myself and the business, and delegating tasks to other competent professionals.

However you choose to divide your time, become intentional about structuring your days with more activities that will eventually increase your business's revenue. You can determine this by telling yourself the truth as you conduct a regular audit of what is generating revenue for your business and what is not. Learn to focus your time, energy, and expertise on efforts that will give you maximum return on your investments. As you continue to recognize the value of delegation, you will benefit from others' skills, which can help you achieve your objectives, freeing you up to bless your business with the best of you.

3. *Develop a system for securing new business*

Conduct a detailed review of the strategies you implemented on the road to your breakthrough. What worked well for you? What strategies did not? Debrief in the weeks post-breakthrough, while the information is still fresh in your mind. Develop a system by learning from your own process, and building upon the information you gleaned from your research on best practices in business development. I benefited greatly from telling myself the truth and learning from my own successes and mistakes when attempting to secure new business. When in doubt, implement the strategies you utilized to bring you to the point of breakthrough and ask for guidance from your professional advisor(s); even ask your Higher Power where you are going right and/or wrong. And remember, practice active patience! You have the seeds of all you need to make your purpose-driven venture successful. Quiet your spirit and allow the answers to flow to you while doing your part to grow your business.

Additionally, if you haven't already done so, invest in developing your sales skills. The area of sales skill development is vast, and there are a plethora of free and for-a-fee online, and in-class programs that can help you strengthen your sales skills. No matter the nature of your venture, you will invariably be "selling" your idea to your clients, customers, team, vendors, consultants, potential investors, and more. Learning to sell effectively is necessary for your professional development, which will ultimately help your business grow.

4. *Innovate*

It is possible that there are more effective ways to develop your product or deliver your service than what you are using now. Make it a priority to continually improve and innovate in your business by gleaning information from: research, best practices in your industry, trends, your competition, your team, as well as your clients and customers. Demonstrating adaptability and agility to market trends and conditions within your business is essential to your success. Still, it will be your commitment to staying hungry by innovating at every turn to become better that will help you stay a cut above the rest.

Complacency for a sustained period will lead to stagnation, so never allow yourself to get comfortable at any stage during your journey. The truth is that you'll never land at a place personally or professionally that will warrant a state of complacency. Even the most successful among us understand the value of continuous learning and growth.

The human brain has the capacity to continually learn, explore, adapt, and innovate. However, our human nature is constantly fighting against consistency, intentionality, and the will to keep pressing forward amidst challenging seasons. On the surface, it would seem like a utopia to achieve our goals and then just sit back and enjoy the fruits of our labor, perpetuating the idea that we'll be full and happy when we get "there." From my own experience, however, I've discovered that *there* isn't actually a destination; it's a state of mind and a journey to becoming. Commit to staying hungry even when you feel full and persevere toward continual growth. Who you become in the process of achieving your goals is the real success, and the continued application of the principles that landed you at your breakthrough, along with the willingness to continue evolving, innovating, and adapting, will allow you to surpass your breakthrough moment and keep growing your sustainably successful business.

FOR DEEPER REFLECTION...

Strategy #10: Stay Hungry

During my business journey, I learned of promises that God has made to those who stay hungry. Head to my website: **melanemullings.com** and look under the "Resources" tab for a list of biblical promises you can claim to gain a greater perspective on this topic.

1. At this stage of your business journey, are you predominantly working IN or ON your business? How do you know?

2. List three ways you can work ON your business during your next quarter.

3. What are some of the conversations you need to have with your team and/or yourself on what is working in your business and what is not?

4. Write a list of your areas of core competence within your business. Create a second list of roles that you currently assume that are not your core competence. Create a plan and a timeline of when you plan to delegate away items on this list.

5. How can you create a brand ambassador as you create and develop your product or deliver your service(s)? In what ways can you go the extra mile that will make your clients and/or customers unable to resist telling others about what you have to offer?

LEMONADE CHALLENGE

Prior to the end of your current fiscal year, list seven goals you would like to complete in your next fiscal year. Break your list of goals down into categories for completion for each upcoming quarter. While you are in your quarters, endeavor to break your list down further into goals to accomplish each week. Chart your progress and audit your successes and failures. Revisit this list often and add or subtract to it as conditions change within your business. Evaluate the lessons learned and earned as you progress, and be intentional about pivoting from strategies that are not serving you or your business to propel you to experience future success.

11

MAINTAIN BALANCE

*"So many people spend their health gaining wealth,
and then have to spend their wealth to regain their health."*

—A.J. REB MATERI

ONE OF THE HARDEST CONCEPTS TO MASTER IN LIFE, ESPECIALLY FOR an entrepreneur, is balance. Many of us are seemingly hardwired to be "on" at all times. I joke that I have only two settings: 1. off and 2. as fast, and as best as I can! Striking a balance between the polarities of life and business—research and execution, work and play, investing and spending, speaking and listening—isn't typically an easy feat for those of us who are passionate about one side or another. We tend to live in extremes more often than we're willing to admit.

As covered in Chapter 8, much of your business success will be attributed to timing and your readiness for your moments of opportunity. However, miscalculations caused by a lack of balance can cost you business, time, and money. For example, instead of immediately engaging a client in excitement after a monumental presentation, you might give them time to review your proposal before making a decision. This requires patience, of course, as well as an understanding of the importance of balance; the client needs time to digest the concepts you've presented, and your eagerness to contact them too early could be misconstrued, potentially costing you the deal.

Mastering balance in your personal and professional life is the work of a lifetime. Recognizing the importance of this concept is one of the key strategies you'll need in order to build a solid foundation for your business. Implementing balance will ensure you not only achieve sustainable success, but will also be able to enjoy the journey along the way!

THE POWER OF YOU

As an entrepreneur, your business venture starts and ends with you. In the beginning, you are your greatest asset; your energy, ingenuity, skills, discipline, and more will set the tone for your organization's future growth. Of equal importance to your tangible personal investment in your business is your intentional and consistent investment *in yourself.*

It's easy to become completely engulfed in the process of building your business. Naturally! Cognizant of the weight of your journey thus far—the lemon experience(s) you've endured and how your whole life has uniquely prepared you for your business—walking in your purpose now has the power to relegate all other priorities in your life to second place. Typically, those of us who choose to dive into the waters of entrepreneurship tend to be driven, focused, goal-oriented, hardworking, and internally motivated, especially when our purpose is revealed to us. Interestingly enough, however, prior to my first lemon experience, I wouldn't have described myself as particularly driven! The impact of my leukemia lemon experience was so all-encompassing that I felt an unquenchable drive that continues to motivate me to this day: first from my career in nursing, all the way to my business management consulting company and completion of this book.

Often, effort is needed to pull the purpose-driven entrepreneur away from working toward the success of their venture to maintain balance in their lives. This pull may come from family, friends, professional advisors, teammates, or business associates, or if the entrepreneur is highly self-aware, they may intentionally regulate themselves. Since you are your best asset, and you're the only one charged with your unique purpose, learning to be a good steward of *yourself* is one of the most important success strategies you can apply to attain and effectively maintain the lemonade of your success.

HOW TO ACHIEVE BALANCE

So, how can you achieve balance, and what are some tangible strategies you can implement to ensure you're creating appropriate boundaries to enjoy balance in your life? First, acknowledge what requires balancing.

Create a list. Abandon the fear that a life of entrepreneurship will rob you of your time to engage in your other passions. Write down the people and activities outside of your business that are important to you. Perhaps you wrote down the names of your close friends and family and activities you enjoy engaging in either with them or alone. Maybe you enjoy playing the cello or painting. Or, maybe, activities like hang gliding or golfing relax you and fill you with joy. If you find yourself thinking about how you could possibly carve out enough time to enjoy these activities, stop those thoughts right in their tracks! Don't worry; just write.

Now, create another list of everything *you need* to function at your best. How many hours of sleep per night *do you need* to function optimally? What type of diet and how many hours of exercise per week *do you need* to feel your best? Tell yourself the truth—what amount of time with friends and family fulfills you? What amount of time are you willing to devote to your hobbies each week or month?

Evaluate both lists. Then, tell yourself the truth here, with no judgment as to whether you are effectively balancing both now, or adequately gifting yourself with the things you need. Recognize that the key to functioning at your own personal best is balance. You will never achieve sustainable success that leads to peace if you're unwilling to give yourself what *you need* to function optimally; time to spend with important people, or time to engage in the activities that fulfill you.

WORK/LIFE BALANCE IS MORE THAN A CATCHPHRASE

I made the mistake of working in an imbalanced state for far too many years in my business. This ended up compromising my physical and mental health, relationships, and even finances. I eventually came to realize that a significant source of my anxiety, fear, depression, lack of restful sleep, and more came as a result of my perpetually imbalanced state of being. Like many business owners and entrepreneurs, I wore my tired, stressed, over-worked state almost like a badge of honor. As a result, in the early years, I suffered the consequences of poor productivity and wish for you a smoother journey to success.

I cannot overstate the importance of work/life balance in developing your ability to achieve your business goals, and surpass them. There are aspects of your personal and professional life that will require your systematic, consistent, and intentional application of this concept of balance to operate effectively, rendering you able to achieve success and arrive at a place that leads to peace.

Recognize that you will need to be diligent in maintaining balance in many areas, from the amount of time you work to the amount of time you spend enjoying your life outside the office. Whatever activities you enjoy, give yourself permission to keep doing them by allocating time in your schedule for them. Not only will the time you spend away from your business refresh your mind, but doing so is also extremely important for your overall well-being.

Success that leads to fulfillment and peace will not require you to sacrifice your health, family, hobbies, or anything else that is important to you. But those of us who are internally driven often tend to give these things up freely! It may sound counterintuitive, but it's important to maintain balance in your life as you work to achieve your goals, so you'll still have the capacity to enjoy your life and business once you taste the lemonade of your success.

Imagine achieving your goal only to have lost your health or compromised valued relationships in the process. No amount of success will make either of these things worth your accomplishments in the end.

FOUR STRATEGIES TO HELP YOU MAINTAIN BALANCE

A strong and balanced body, mind, and spirit will help you operate your venture effectively over a sustained period of time. Here are four key strategies you can implement to help you achieve a state of balance for your mind, body, and spirit that will help you build a solid foundation for sustainable success:

1. Take breaks daily, weekly, and yearly

Take time **daily** to unplug, quiet your spirit, and detach from the pressures that come with the life of entrepreneurship. Intentionally recharge by taking a few moments from your day to disconnect from your work. You can do this by periodically getting up and walking around your desk or room. Draw from the benefits of nature and give yourself permission to take a break by walking around outside, as discussed in Chapter 9. Walk around and take in deep breaths of the fresh air around you. Deep breaths refresh your mind with the oxygen your brain needs for effective reasoning. Since the brain requires about twenty percent of the body's total oxygen (and even more when the brain is in overdrive[1]—engaged in intense activity, and/or concentrating or reasoning through complicated concepts for a sustained period of time), it's extremely important for us to provide our bodies with what they need to give us what we need to show up effectively when it's time to work: focus and productivity. While taking your walks, pay close attention to the aspects of nature that embody the spirit of balance, and enjoy the time away to rest and rejuvenate your body for optimal overall functioning.

One activity that is imperative to our optimal functioning—which, incidentally, is also of great importance to God—is rest. Rest is so important that God admonished humankind to be intentional about allocating a specified day **weekly** to rest. Lack of consistent, adequate rest is not only robbing you of your ability to function effectively, but it's also compromising your ability to fully enjoy the fruits of your labor! Losing sleep, overextending yourself, risking your health, and sabotaging your relationships due to a constant state of imbalance doesn't serve you or your venture well either. Furthermore, your venture will never achieve its maximum impact on the world if it flows from an empty, depleted vessel.

Forbes and *Inc.* magazines indicate that rest is a fundamental part of success, health, and happiness and list the following benefits of adequate rest[2] along with scientific reasons why a regular rest time *every week* works[3]:

***Physical Transformation*:**
- Time out reduces stress
- Completely divesting from your work on a regular basis reduces inflammation and the risk of heart disease
- Getting away from work to rest boosts your immune system

Mental & Emotional Transformation:
- Taking regular time away from work restores mental energy
- When you take time for yourself, you're more creative and productive
- You'll focus better at work if you take weekly rejuvenation time
- Your day off will improve your short-term memory and enhance your decision-making skills

There are so many direct benefits beyond even these listed that warrant taking time out to rest, but unfortunately, many entrepreneurs and business owners keep pressing forward, working extra-long hours with the thought that doing so will ultimately benefit their ventures. The reality, however, is that working in a compromised state personally eventually wreaks havoc professionally. Our bodies simply cannot function effectively for a sustained period of time without adequate rest. Our mind, body, and spirit require us to rest and rejuvenate one full day weekly, and many of the most successful among us—those that have achieved great feats in business—strongly advocate for the need to allocate a weekly day of rest as well.

In *The Success Principles*, Jack Canfield lists the following on the concept of rest:

*"The most successful people I know create superior results, yet still maintain a balance among work, family and recreation in their lives. To achieve this, they use a unique planning system that structures their time into three very different kinds of days... to assure the highest payoff for their efforts... (the) three kinds of days: Focus days, Buffer days and **Free Days**."*[4]

The Free Day "extends from midnight to midnight and involves no work-related activity of any kind. It's a day completely free of business meetings, business-related phone calls, cell phone calls, emails or reading work-related documents. On a true Free Day, you're not available to anyone for any kind of contact except for *true* emergencies... you have to set clear boundaries."[4]

If you want to be around to experience the manifestation of your business goals, and be in the physical, mental, and spiritual health required to maintain an optimal level of functioning while doing so, *taking one designated, twenty-four-hour period of time each week to pull away and rest is key.* And when you emphasize the value you place on your designated weekly rest day to the people around you, two distinct benefits result: One, the people around you become more self-reliant, and two, their self-reliance frees you up to enjoy more days to focus on your venture and, potentially, more Free Days as well!

If a successful entrepreneur and bestselling author, and several of his successful friends corroborate the importance of a designated day to rest, I say it's worth a try!

So far, we've discussed the importance of pulling away to rest periodically throughout your workday and also once per week. Recognize also that it's important to become diligent about planning a **yearly** getaway as well.

In the early years of my business, I didn't have the time or money to allocate to a true vacation, but I did schedule time off around professional development activities—courses, workshops, and conferences that I attended away from home. To get my yearly break in, I would take time to rest and rejuvenate before the event I'd traveled for by sightseeing, or spending the day in the hotel enjoying the amenities. Or, I would take one or two days to enjoy the host city after the meetings just to relax, decompress, and rest. We'll discuss the importance of these professional development activities in greater detail in Chapter 12 but for now, consider the importance of scheduling "play time" each year; whether that be a "staycation" at home or a vacation away from home, a time to rest once per year is also important to achieve an overall state of balance as well.

I'm confident that taking my intentional breaks—**daily, weekly, and yearly**—kept me fresh, focused, and able to put my best foot forward while working in and on my business. Although I did not become intentional about taking all three types of breaks consistently until many years into running my business, once I did, I reaped the benefits of rest and rejuvenation to my mind, body, and spirit, which positively impacted my ability to operate effectively as a leader. Strive to make it a point to take these three types of breaks consistently, and you too will reap exponential emotional, spiritual, physical, and relational benefits that will eventually become evident in your bottom line.

2. Exercise

The second of the four strategies you can implement to help you achieve a state of balance for your mind, body, and spirit is exercise. As discussed in Chapter 10, thirty minutes of exercise that increases your heart rate at least three days per week is a great way to improve mood and decrease stress. Beyond the benefits to your overall health, exercise is a natural stress reducer that improves mental capacity while also increasing your energy levels, which helps stop the so-called "afternoon fatigue slump" right in its tracks, which some of us may struggle with. Exercise has also been known to help improve the quality of our sleep, which is an issue for many struggling and stressed entrepreneurs and business owners. A free and natural sleep aid and productivity booster, exercise, is a great way to help you function optimally in your business, allowing you to accomplish more each day while you're working.

When exercising to increase productivity, progress and consistency are more important than anything. You're exercising to increase mood and energy, not strength, so shorter bursts of exercise in your daily routine are easier to stick to; you want to do just enough exercise to refresh your mind.[5] A groundbreaking study showed that when participants took a break to exercise during their workday, there was a seventy-two percent improvement in time management and productivity on days when they exercised at work over days when they did not.[6] This further demonstrates the importance of taking a break daily and building on that, filling that break with some form of exercise. This study shows that doing both will have a cumulative effect to further increase your productivity and even increase your ability to manage your time more effectively.

The bountiful benefits you'll glean from exercising are so far-reaching. So, give yourself time to disconnect from the intensity of entrepreneurship and exercise. You'll reap returns on your investment in the form of increased productivity, mental acuity, focus, and much more.

3. Balance your diet

In addition to regular exercise, a balanced diet is imperative to ensure optimal physical and mental functioning. Unhealthy eating patterns can cause mood swings, and in recent years, evidence has shown that food can contribute to the development, prevention, and management of mental health conditions such as depression and anxiety.[7] Our mind and body simply will not function optimally without a balanced diet. If a diet is not balanced with a variety of healthy foods (fruit, vegetables, proteins, and whole-grain products) and minerals, along with an adequate consumption of water each day, we compromise our personal health, and by extension, the health of our ventures.

The *National Council For Mental Wellbeing* tells us that "if you reduce the variety of foods in your diet, it can be more difficult to get all the essential nutrients you need. Low levels of zinc, iron, B vitamins, magnesium, vitamin D, and omega-3 fatty acids are associated with worsening mood and decreased energy."[7] Consistently missing meals to work might seem like a good idea to finish a current pressing project or service that one last client, but doing so can result in low blood sugar levels, which over time will leave you feeling tired and weak. Working long hours may seem like the right thing to do when you have looming deadlines and clients waiting to receive their products or services, but operating from a weak, tired, and compromised state does not serve you or your venture any good.

Additionally, a diet high in unhealthy, processed carbohydrates, such as white bread and pastries, can cause blood sugars to rise and fall rapidly, which can also lead to low energy and irritability,[7] again compromising your ability to give your best to your business. Becoming intentional about balancing your diet to include healthy foods and consuming adequate amounts of water each day is so important to functioning at your best in your business. And I learned the value of both, especially the consumption of adequate water and its power-packed, unexpected benefits during the years of building my business. I strongly suggest giving it a try to help improve your focus, mental clarity, and productivity throughout your workday.

❋

I LEARNED THE POWERFUL BENEFITS OF CONSUMING ADEQUATE AMOUNTS of water each day while studying to become an RN, but I didn't take full advantage of its benefits until I began my entrepreneurial journey. A diet that includes sodas, stimulant drinks, juices, and other beverages needs to be balanced with the intake of just water alone. Pure water helps carry nutrients and oxygen to your cells, control your weight, normalize your blood pressure, stabilize your heartbeat, cushion your joints, and protect your organs. And, yes, it even balances your internal levels of electrolytes,[8,9] which play an important part in concentration, mental acuity, and effective brain functioning, which is clearly crucial to operating your business effectively. If you don't drink enough water alone each day, you risk becoming dehydrated, which can cause serious health risks that can lead to hospitalization. And what a waste to compromise your business as a result of poor health due to dehydration! This simple strategy of drinking water throughout your workday is packed with so many overall benefits, especially benefits to your optimal brain functioning.

Despite common misconceptions, there's no one-size-fits-all amount of water each of us should consume each day. For me, the perfect amount is fifty to sixty-five ounces or 1.5–2 liters a day. I've been drinking this quantity mostly every day for the past fourteen years and can absolutely vouch for its benefits. This advice may seem trite and misplaced in a book about business success, but I strongly encourage you to give it a chance, and you'll experience vast benefits to your overall health—especially mental acuity—that will help you show up more effectively in your business.

Moving from the importance of balance to our overall physical and mental functioning, let's now review another aspect of balance as it directly relates to your business.

4. Balance your income

In my experience consulting entrepreneurs and business owners at various stages of their ventures, I've discovered a widely held view that a majority of the money generated by a business should be invested back into it until the venture becomes sustainably profitable. While it may seem as though this practice would propel you to the next level quicker, think of the message this sends *to yourself* about the value you place on your own effort and time. Keep in mind that one of the greatest challenges to your business success will be your sense of self-worth. Don't underestimate the power of your self-perception and how it can affect the way you show up in your business.

---

*"When you undervalue what you do,
the world will undervalue who you are."*

—Oprah

One of the best ways to demonstrate value in yourself is to **pay yourself** the very first time you start making money from your venture. This will set a precedent *for yourself* and help you more quickly quell inevitable thoughts of self-doubt that are sure to plague you. The more you demonstrate to yourself the value you place on yourself, your efforts, and your time, the quicker you'll be able to rebound in challenging times. Consequently, you'll become more effective at communicating your value to your customers as a result.

I directly benefited from paying myself a portion of my company's earnings right from the start, and I now encourage my consulting clients to do the same. In my case, I always viewed my business as a separate entity employer, so as I would expect any past employer to pay me for my time, I expected that my business would also compensate me for my sacrifices and investments. Choose an amount to pay yourself that is appropriate for your business budget, and diligently implement this practice *from the very first time* your venture earns money, regardless of outside factors. If you've already started your venture and have not implemented this practice, be sure to start now. Know that if you don't place value on yourself, others likely won't either. Even if they say they do, your lack of self-worth will compromise your willingness to believe it.

THE POISONOUS PERSPECTIVE OF LOW SELF-WORTH

Many financial experts suggest varying numbers of categories in which to divest your money or allocate to spending, specifically, categories in which one can place their money to achieve financial balance between saving and spending. While these strategies have proven to be effective in increasing wealth for many, such categories don't fully encompass the realities of the entrepreneurial journey, or consider the values typically held by those who are building an entrepreneurial venture.

Several popular strategies encourage the creation of a category for financial freedom—for stocks, bonds, or other forms of investments, for example. If, however, you are currently in debt, the likelihood you'll be allocating any money toward future financial freedom is relatively low, as was the case for me. Once your venture becomes sustainably profitable, though, it's absolutely prudent for you to diversify your money into their suggested categories and adjust the percentages allocated to each to suit you. However, for the purpose-driven entrepreneur in the early stages of success, I propose the following five categories, with percentages, listed in ranking order of importance:

Donations (10%)

The concept of balance also applies to your money. As you receive blessings throughout your entrepreneurial journey, it's important to give back in thanks for everything you've received and allocate this money *first*. When you're building a purpose-driven venture, blessings may come to you in many forms. In my case, they included business opportunities for growth, unexpected people who encouraged, supported, and assisted me in building my business, unexpected funding, increased focus and productivity, energy, support from family and friends, and so much more! Throughout my journey, on more than one occasion, family and friends contacted me unsolicited and offered me over $23,000 in loans to help me fund my dream! I directly attribute this to my belief and faithfulness to God's ask:

> *"Bring the full tithes into the storehouse, that there may be food in my house;*
> *and thereby put me to the test, says the Lord of hosts,*
> *if I will not open the windows of heaven for you and pour down for you **an***
> ***overflowing** blessing."*[10]

God promises us an *overflowing* blessing—more than we expect—if we exercise the faith to tithe! We see here that giving back in this way, interestingly enough, ends up benefiting us in an overflowing, abundant way. The biblical concept of donating a tenth of our increase[11] (ten percent of your gross revenue) is actually a practice adopted by many of the world's richest people! Jack Canfield writes about the power of tithing in *The Success Principles* by stating:

"Tithing—that is, giving 10% of your earnings to the work of God—is one of the best guarantees of prosperity ever known. Many of the world's richest individuals and most successful people have been devout tithers. By tithing regularly, you, too, can put into motion God's universal force, bringing you continual abundance."[12]

When you tithe, it not only helps others, but it actually benefits you in the end! During one of the most pivotal seasons in my business journey, I made the decision to tithe more than just my income. I made the commitment to give my time and talents intentionally and consistently to causes that were important to me. So, I began volunteering at a local homeless shelter and started volunteering my time at church in various leadership capacities. Once I became intentional about giving back my time, talents, *and* resources (money), everything within my business changed. Thereafter, I experienced miraculous, exponential business growth and became debt-free quickly thereafter. Turning my flywheel to get to my place of breakthrough and implementing the other strategies of the outer work on a consistent basis, all worked together to bring me to a place of success, but it was shortly after I made the commitment to tithe consistently that I saw tangible results from all my years of efforts.

I experienced a plethora of unexpected blessings once I became intentional and consistent about giving back. If you hoard what you have, you don't leave any room to receive more! In the admonition from God to tithe lies the promise of a reward. Disciplining yourself to donate ten percent of your financial resources during the formative, most crucial, and even the most stressful seasons of your business journey might represent a huge sacrifice to you, but your faithfulness to grow yourself and your business God's way will pay off for you in the end.

Essentials (50%)

Pay yourself from the first time you receive income from your venture, at whatever amount from this fifty percent you see fit. As mentioned, respecting yourself and your effort from the beginning is an essential component of your business's foundation. Next, allocate money to pay your bills and essentials—housing, utilities, food, insurance, and debt payments—and strive to do so on time. Demonstrate integrity by keeping your commitments and, if you're struggling to do so, live in the truth and contact your lenders ahead of time to make payment arrangements. Remember, this venture is your purpose; it's transforming *you* into someone who can handle the full culmination of success when it comes. Revisit your inner work from Chapter 3 and recognize that your understanding of a situation is anchored in how you *perceive* it. Do your part and pay your essentials with honesty and integrity, and believe that the purpose-driven venture you've started will eventually experience success.

Rewarding Yourself (15%)

As we've discussed throughout this chapter, striving toward balance is imperative not only for your overall well-being but for your venture as well. If you operate from a miser state—saving profusely, paying your bills, and only spending on your business—when you eventually *do* receive a mammoth payday, the likelihood you'll splurge is extremely high, which can have a devastating effect on both you and your business.

Give yourself a pat on the back and enjoy the fruits of your labors as you go. Get accustomed to rewarding yourself for accomplishing your goals along your journey, even those that are seemingly insignificant.

Your reward doesn't always have to involve money, but the bigger the accomplishment, the greater the reward you should draw from this fifteen-percent pot. If you make all the calls you intended for the day, reward yourself with one extra hour of downtime. If you accomplish your quarterly goals, celebrate by taking yourself out for dinner. As long as your reward is within the constraints of your fifteen-percent budget, enjoy it!

Give yourself permission to splurge. You've worked hard! Rewarding yourself is an act of balance important to your well-being, and by extension, the well-being of your venture.

Professional Development (10%)

We'll discuss this in greater detail in Chapter 12, but for now, know that allocating a specified amount of money to develop yourself as a leader is vital to the success of your business. Set aside these funds as savings for your professional advancement each time your business earns money. It's one of the most fruitful means to invest back into your business.

Savings (15%)

It's important to set aside funds for a rainy day for both you and your business. Become intentional about saving at least fifteen percent of what you earn for emergencies, and to help pay for your business tax liabilities at the end of your fiscal year. Keep in mind that as your venture grows, your tax liability will require you to save a greater percentage of your business income beyond this fifteen percent to pay your taxes. (For my North American readers, a great bonus to donating ten percent of your income is that you can claim this amount on your taxes. This represents a tangible, financial benefit of giving back in addition to all the emotional, physical, and relational benefits you'll receive that we'll explore more in Chapter 13.)

Drawing from your savings to fund your venture will, at times, become a necessity but leaving your money untouched for as long as possible will help maintain a state of balance while you work toward financial freedom. In the early days of your venture, engaging in activities to secure funding in the form of grants, loans, or money from investors, should be a regular fixture on your yearly and quarterly goals list. This will allow you to secure additional capital to help you continue growing your business. (And on a side note: Any reputable investor who is considering investing in your venture will want to know the amount of money you've personally invested beyond your sweat, equity, or labor, as it's an important indicator of the value you place on your business.) Even in extreme times, carving out savings demonstrates fiscal responsibility: a character trait necessary for you to develop to maintain the success you envision.

Mastering the discipline of balance is, indeed, the work of a lifetime. Simply put, you won't achieve optimal effectiveness in any area of your life without intentionally seeking balance. And it's crucial to develop this discipline in preparation for challenging times. When you're in the hospital suffering a heart attack, stopping smoking at that point won't save you. Similarly, if you become intentional NOW about moving toward a state of balance by implementing the four key strategies listed—take breaks daily, weekly, and yearly, exercise, and balance your diet as well as your income—you'll be building a solid foundation for your business that will set yourself up to effectively manage both you and your business now, and for the long haul.

DON YOUR MASK BEFORE ASSISTING OTHERS

If you've traveled on an airplane, you know that, in an emergency, if the oxygen masks descend, you are advised to put on your own mask before helping others. If you collapse from oxygen deprivation while assisting someone else, what good are you to the person you're attempting to help? Similarly, you simply cannot show up effectively in your business if you don't adequately care for yourself *first* and demonstrate the value you place on balance, even in extreme times. Don't sacrifice yourself in the pursuit of your purpose. Your Higher Power can provide you with what you need to accomplish your purpose-driven goals; you don't have to wear yourself out trying to make it the hard way. Trust that!

In his book, *Good To Great*, Jim Collins reminds us that breakthrough transformations from good to great in business happen through disciplined people generating disciplined thought by executing disciplined action.[13] On its face, it may seem counterintuitive or counterproductive to discipline yourself and take additional time out of your busy schedule to implement strategies to institute balance in your personal and professional life. But doing so is necessary for optimal overall functioning.

We aren't machines, even if we tend to operate like them at times! Know that right now, as you're reading this book, you are in the process of transformation. In my experience, I've realized that whatever God calls you to, He equips you for, so move forward in faith and set the intention to be a good steward of all the people, resources, opportunities and experiences you've been gifted with along your journey. Most importantly, be mindful of being a good steward of *yourself!* Surrender to the process of becoming and, as you continue to work toward the manifestation of your purpose, take time to invest *in yourself,* and become intentional about operating in a state of balance, personally and professionally, even in extreme times.

FOR DEEPER REFLECTION...

Strategy #11: Maintain Balance

1. God so understood the importance of rest and rejuvenation for our optimal functioning that He referred to His prescribed weekly day of rest from the very beginning of scripture right to the end. This rest day, the Sabbath, is a gift to us. It rejuvenates our mind, body, and spirit as we disconnect from our work, so we can bring our best selves back to our ventures once the week begins again. For information on passages of scripture that reference the importance, benefits, and blessings of the Sabbath, head over to the "Resources" section under Chapter 11 at: **melanemullings.com**.

2. Nature is either in balance or is constantly striving toward it. We can see evidence of this in the human body as well, which constantly moves toward a state of equilibrium or homeostasis. From optimal conditions for enzyme action (the way our body catalyzes internal chemical reactions) to thermoregulation (how our bodies regulate our internal temperature), our bodies, like nature, constantly seek balance[14]. The activities we engage in on our road to success should also reflect an understanding of this concept of balance as well.

   a. As you spend time in nature, what lessons are you seeing in action that relate to balance that can help you build your venture?

3. How do you currently invest in yourself to achieve balance in your life? List the ways.

4. After reading this chapter, what can you add to that list?

5. What are three ways you can balance your diet going forward?

6. What professional development activities or continuing education initiatives—courses, workshops, seminars, conferences, skill-based training sessions—will you invest in, in your next fiscal year to help you grow as an entrepreneur or business owner? List at least three.

7. What is a cause you feel passionate about that you can donate 10% of your personal AND professional income to?

LEMONADE CHALLENGE

Increase your water intake for the next three weeks. If you're unsure of the amount to drink each day that is advisable for your current health status, start with one and a half glasses a day and increase from there based on how you feel, along with guidance from your physician. Journal the benefits you notice in the following categories at the end of your three weeks:

- Focus and overall mental acuity
- Energy level
- Bowel regularity
- Clarity of your skin
- Weight regularity

12

LEARNING FROM THREE IS KEY

*"One of life's realities is that major improvements take time;
they don't happen overnight…
If you make a commitment to learning something new every day,
getting just a little bit better every day, then eventually
over time, you will reach your goals."*

—JACK CANFIELD

Entrepreneurship can be a lonely road. In the beginning, there'll be seasons that will require you to hunker down and traverse your journey alone (or with a select few), which can leave you and your team feeling isolated from the outside world. Prior to my breakthrough, I became isolated, living in a perpetual state of low-grade anxiety over my lack of progress. I regularly felt judged and misunderstood by those close to me, many of whom questioned why I was subjecting myself to all the proverbial blood, sweat, and tears of entrepreneurship anyway. It was as though the whole world was turning around me, but I was frozen within the confines of my mind, and my business.

The truth is you are not alone, though, and I wasn't alone either! Even though there are times during the entrepreneurial journey that will require you to work alone to focus on specific tasks and execute them effectively, there are other entrepreneurs and business owners worldwide dealing with the same realities as you! Drawing strength and wisdom from a carefully curated group will be like injecting a burst of power into your business, and in our increasingly interconnected world, there's no need to suffer in silence. The process of learning from three specific sources will help you: build the foundation for a sustainably successful business, connect meaningfully with those around you, and grow into the leader your lemon experiences have prepared you to be.

NO MAN (OR WOMAN) IS AN ISLAND

There are countless others just like you that have made the decision to allow their lemon experiences to propel them headfirst into the waters of entrepreneurship. There's also a treasure trove of information out there to get you to your goal, and people who have succeeded in building a business that are willing to share their success strategies with you.

Yes, your purpose is unique to you, and if that purpose includes the delivery of a product or service, much of what has brought you to this point in your life—your lemon experience(s) and your skills—has uniquely prepared you for your venture. Keep in mind, though, that others have paved the way and have left success clues that can serve as a guide to help you achieve your goals, and protect you from self-inflicted business wounds or your own unnecessary, internal sequestration. Without guidance, we can unnecessarily inflict wounds on our business in the form of mistakes that can cost us time and money to remedy, if they can be remedied at all. Other times, we can get so caught up in creating success from our venture that we start to isolate ourselves from the outside world. In my case, instituting balance in my life was instrumental in rescuing me from isolation and stagnation. Utilizing three sources of help, readily available to you, will also help to set you up for success and prevent you from wasting time, money, and resources; help that can divert you from potential pitfalls as you progress forward.

How you learn is as important to your success as the learning itself. If you invest in learning from the following three specific sources during your entrepreneurial journey, you will reap exponential benefits in the form of personal growth and the growth of your venture at a rate faster than if you were to go at it alone:

Source #1 - Professional Development Initiatives

As the person blessed with the purpose-driven direction for your venture, you are your greatest asset. As you travel along your entrepreneurial journey, remember all the knowledge you eagerly absorbed to ready yourself for your breakthrough. Remind yourself of all the ways you consistently and intentionally carved out a portion of your time to grow your knowledge base. Continue now, putting the time in to invest *in yourself* to grow. You're worth it!

Life moves quickly. Market trends and technology are ever-changing. The entrepreneur or business owner who can build on their success over time and grow understands the importance of continuous learning. Immersing yourself in the trends within your industry, continuing to hone your craft, reading books and industry publications, attending workshops, conferences, and courses are all valuable success strategies to help keep you sharp and able to operate effectively in your role. Be intentional about investing in yourself as a business leader, and take the time to continue learning and improving.

I found it useful to subscribe to industry publications in my space and carved out time in my schedule on a regular basis to read about the trends impacting my industry. I also attended annual general meetings for the professional associations I belonged to, which gave me an in-depth understanding of the real-time issues at play within my industry that directly impacted my business. Over the years, the continuing education initiatives I participated in directly helped me improve my sales skills, business communication skills, and competence in my area of business expertise, which has now rendered me a subject-matter expert on the nursing shortage and the most effective strategies to address this critical issue for the future.

In addition to all the courses I completed and personal development and business books I read, I found that all the motivational conferences I attended across North America (specifically, the Essence *"Women Who Are Shaping The World"* conference, and the Tony Robbins events) were invaluable to my growth and development as an entrepreneur. The industry groups I joined and networking opportunities I participated in were extremely valuable as well. They connected me with other like-minded entrepreneurs and business owners, which expanded my professional network, and helped rescue me from my periods of isolation.

On a personal note, a life-long friendship was born out of my time regularly attending a women's entrepreneurial success breakfast group. Over ten years ago, I met a woman in that group who has become one of my most trusted business advisors and dearest friends. A bridesmaid at my wedding, she and I continue to enjoy supporting and encouraging each other personally and professionally. Had I not taken the time to invest in my growth as a business owner, I would have missed out on this incredible, unexpected friendship.

IN ORDER TO GIVE YOUR BEST TO YOUR BUSINESS, YOU'LL NEED TO BE FULLY equipped with knowledge and skills on how to deliver your product or service with excellence, and how to grow yourself into a leader that can handle the success you're envisioning. Additionally, if you've hired employees, it's important to equip them with the skills they need as well, to help them continue bringing their "A-game" to your business.

It is best practice to provide opportunities for your team to grow and improve. For many in the workforce today, opportunities for professional growth and possibilities for advancement within the organization are among the top attributes of an employer they consider when seeking employment. Set the tone within your organization around the value you place on continuing education *for yourself* by publicizing some of the professional development initiatives you've completed, and ask your team to communicate their ideas for courses and training that they're interested in that could help them thrive in their positions as well. If you don't provide continuing education initiatives or communicate the value you place on their growth and opportunities for advancement within your organization, void of any other strong draw to stay, they will likely leave your organization at some point for another that does. Become a best-practice organization by clearly communicating to your team your commitment to invest in their growth and development. Lead by example and demonstrate that not only do you want to see continual growth and excellence from them, but you openly strive to improve yourself as well.

Source #2 - Professional Advisors

To accomplish your goal, you'll need to draw from people you trust to instruct, motivate, and invest time in you—people who are willing and able to help propel you to success. You won't achieve the full culmination of the success you were created to be without a carefully curated success team, and biblical principles[1] and a vast amount of business literature expand on the veracity of this claim. I've personally benefited from several individuals who continue to bless me with their experience and expertise to this day. Individuals on your success team may come and go, but ensuring that you consistently draw from a carefully curated group is key.

Mentors can be useful sources of information as you build your business. While I was in the second year of my Bachelor of Science degree, my childhood dentist, a family friend and mentor of sorts, offered me a chance to job shadow him while at work for a day, which saved me a mountain of student loan debt and a boatload of future regret following a moment of serious consideration of a career in dentistry. After shadowing and discussing the job with him, I quickly learned that dentistry wasn't for me. Had I chosen that route, I would have detoured far away from my journey toward my purpose.

An effective mentor will provide you unbiased, direct counsel and constructive criticism, which is crucial for your growth and development. Having people in your corner who've accomplished the goals you aspire toward, who are willing to tell you the truth and invest quality time in you, are worth their weight in gold.

But though they're valuable, mentorship relationships have their limitations. My early business mentors are giants in their respective industries who provided me invaluable nuggets of wisdom that helped shape the way I operated my business. However, when the results I was generating weren't reflective of the time invested by either party, it resulted in mutual frustration. Since the relationship wasn't entirely reciprocal—I was the one primarily benefiting from it—I started to feel guilt and internal pressure to produce results more quickly to keep them engaged. I was blessed to have secured their support in the early years of my business, but as their time was limited, I eventually realized that more specialized support was warranted.

An effective business management consultant is a source of "experienced wisdom" you can draw from, as they can provide you with consistent and direct assistance to address your specific business challenges while supporting you as you work to accomplish your goals. Think of us as a physician at your local urgent care clinic. You may have family members or friends in the medical field who can provide you advice on your maladies; however, they'll be leery of doing so comprehensively if they don't have a full understanding of your situation. And they likely won't give you direct advice to prevent potential future liability either.

After gaining a full understanding of your business challenges, an effective business management consultant, like a physician, can provide you with a diagnosis of your "business maladies" and determine if they are a good fit to help you. Physicians specialize in different facets of medicine. Similarly, your entrepreneurial journey requires the services of a specialized business consultant who understands the particular nuances of your challenges as a purpose-driven entrepreneur or business owner. One that will commit to helping see you through the formative process of not only your venture's development but also your own.

Help is available to propel you to business success! When you're ready to roll up your sleeves and take actionable advice to improve your business, contact a business management consultant to help you successfully navigate your business journey. Prior to securing outside help, it's prudent to vigilantly vet those you welcome into your space. Conduct your due diligence by thoroughly researching them to gain an understanding of their area of expertise and how they can help you address the particular challenges within your business. *Select one that has experience successfully operating a purpose-driven venture themselves*, one that suits your specific needs, and also one that meshes with your personality; you have to like them too! Your comfort level with your business management consultant will determine your willingness to: open up and communicate your challenges clearly and honestly, listen to their advice, then take appropriate action. A good rapport with your consultant will help ensure you can draw the best from their expertise and your engagement with them, which can save you an inordinate amount of time, money, and effort as you grow your business.

"Iron sharpens iron, and one man sharpens another."[2]
—Proverbs 27:17

Since no man (or woman) is an island, it's important to take advantage of the opportunity to learn from people with valuable knowledge, experience, resources and, most importantly, the time and effort they are willing to extend to you. Through my consulting practice and group coaching sessions I've facilitated, I've had the opportunity to help struggling entrepreneurs and business owners by sharing pivotal experiences from my own entrepreneurial journey that have helped them avoid unnecessary pitfalls and gain a better understanding of the purpose-driven journey to the lemonade of their success! I've provided them with practical advice, powerful tools, customized strategies, world-class support, and an understanding of spiritual principles that help them avoid costly mistakes and grow their ventures. I've been blessed with the opportunity to help my clients transform their businesses, but their personal transformations have been the most rewarding for me. Do your research and find a business management consultant that has not only achieved success in a purpose-driven business venture themselves but also shares your values and perspective. Don't wait to invest in the growth of your business. Be intentional about getting the help that you need. Now.

Source #3 - Feedback

Feedback provides you with a treasure trove of information that can be utilized to improve your product or service and is a necessary source of information to glean from to grow your business effectively. The clothing company Zara—one of the world's largest apparel retailers—provides a great example of the power of feedback to shape business operations and the enormous success that can be generated from doing so. At Zara's corporate headquarters, they read through thousands of consumer feedback comments, relying on their customers to help create their clothing lines. It's a user-generated approach to fast fashion, which they claim is one of their keys to success.[3]

Customer complaints are a 'learning' experience... and the FIRST thing you need to learn is how to use the office shredding machine.

However, opening yourself up to receive feedback is an absolute exercise in vulnerability and humility. In this time of bad online reviews and social media trolls, it takes a healthy dose of internal strength to open yourself up to potentially negative feedback. Vulnerability absolutely requires courage and strength, but it is your superpower as a business owner! In order to secure honest, constructive, actionable feedback that can help you improve on your product or service, however, you'll first need to build trust with your audience so they feel safe to provide you the comprehensive feedback you need. And the most effective way to build trust is to be open, vulnerable, and transparent yourself.

Brené Brown—author of five #1 *New York Times* bestsellers, famous for her work on vulnerability—had *Forbes* reflect on her perspective on vulnerability in the workplace in this way:

"Vulnerability, as a resource in leadership and within the workplace, can impact the entire culture and creativity of a team. It can increase output, it can create a place for courage and is a strength that should be harnessed.
*...one of Brené's points, **vulnerability and leadership go hand in hand.**"*[4]

Vulnerability in the workplace is important because a willingness to open up and share your own experiences makes you more likable and approachable. Sharing as a business leader by communicating how you overcame your own challenges and discussing areas you are working to improve to bring your best foot forward yourself helps others understand your values, decisions, and perspectives. This can translate into their willingness to support you and follow your lead. In some cases, your vulnerability can resonate with people so strongly that they take it upon themselves to help propel you to achieve your business goals as well.

In my experience with all my entrepreneurial endeavors, I've learned the power of vulnerability in leading with my story—my lemon experiences—and how they've propelled me to achieve my business goals. Doing so has proven instrumental in building trust with those I seek to solidify business relationships with.

I FIRST LEARNED OF THE POWER OF THIS CONCEPT FROM SERIAL ENTREPRE-neur, investor, and prolific TV personality of CNBC's *The Profit*, Marcus Lemonis, who stated: "The key for me in building…relationships with business owners is by starting by unveiling myself first, and uncovering my mistakes and my frailties and my weaknesses."[5] He goes on to state that: "…the only reason that I talk about the rough patches in my life isn't to have people feel sorry for me… it's to try to create relatability between people. So that they can be comfortable uncovering theirs."[5] This strategy has reaped dividends for myself, Marcus, and countless others on our rise to success. While helping over one hundred small businesses through his work on *The Profit* and all his other business endeavors and investments, Marcus' net worth as of 2021 has been estimated at $500 million.[6] Not bad for someone that leads with vulnerability!

Vulnerability is simply the key to better leadership.

In order to build solid business relationships that will stand the test of time, those that interact with you and your business will need to develop a sense of trust, which is effectively built on vulnerability and transparency. And *that starts with you*, the leader. When clients and customers see you as a real person, you build the coveted "know, like, and trust" factor that is so important to creating customer loyalty in today's market; if your market has an understanding of you (*know*), if they resonate with you and your story (*like*) and come to *trust* you, the more likely they will readily purchase your product or service and become a loyal customer. And if you add "an exceptional product or service offering" to the "know, like and trust" list, the greater likelihood you'll secure a brand ambassador for the long haul!

Under normal circumstances, trust is a precursor to opening up. But you must be able to be vulnerable with others first to help them build trust in you and your business. Exercise resolve to open up and be vulnerable, to secure honest, comprehensive, and actionable feedback from clients, customers, and your team. Your openness will help them see you as *a real person* and increase your likability factor, which will help them feel safe to provide you with honest feedback to help you reach your goals. Their honest opinions on your programs, products, and services—as we reviewed from the Zara example—will provide you with the most direct and immediate information that you can use to improve your business.

ALL FEEDBACK IS USEFUL, EVEN THE NEGATIVE. ENTRENCHED IN THE VITriol of an extremely negative comment or review will most likely lie a nugget of truth you can learn from. Search for it. When you remind yourself of Who sent you and the "why" of your venture, and you continue your inner work with a belief in your ability to accomplish your goals, you will develop a strength that can stand up to attacks.

The issue lies not in the negative feedback itself, but rather in the permission we grant the negativity to infect our *perception* of ourselves and/or our venture. Receive the feedback, extract the truth from it, then release it. This isn't easy, but actively soliciting feedback and learning to evaluate it *is* necessary for you to build a solid foundation for your business.

When soliciting feedback for your company:

Be direct.

Set your intention for the feedback by listing the reasoning for why you're seeking your audience's input: to improve on your product(s) and/or service(s). Informing your audience that their feedback will help you improve will, in many cases, disarm people that seek to do harm.

Decide how you'd like to receive the feedback.

If you don't have a social media strategy or people on your team delegated to curate and monitor your social media presence, it may not prove useful to solicit feedback online. If you're delivering a service, consider emailing your clients a survey to glean an understanding of their experience after you deliver it. Soliciting feedback demonstrates your vested interest in the development of your business, commitment to open communication, and a desire to continue earning their business beyond the first interaction.

Consider *offering an incentive* when you ask customers for feedback: a percentage off their next order or one free item, for example. Remember to institute balance in your business interactions wherever possible.

Follow up quickly.

Whatever route you choose, ensure that you solicit feedback in a manner that you can follow up and reply to quickly. If you're a solopreneur and are not particularly proficient with computer platforms, you may want to choose an online option through a third party to solicit your feedback. If you don't have the time to sort through reply letters in the mail or by fax, it probably isn't prudent for you to mail or fax out your survey. Consider the means of soliciting your feedback and the manner in which you can quickly reply to it before asking.

Respond with thanks.

As a consumer, I find it frustrating when I take the time to extend feedback only to receive radio silence from the requesting party. Reply to your audience quickly, acknowledging your appreciation for their willingness to take the time to honor your request. They've just provided you with much-needed information that may have the potential to save you time and money in the future. Continuing to interact with and thank your audience for their input (clients, customers, team, vendors, etc.) on a consistent basis will help your business in the long run since you'll be increasing customer loyalty and engagement through the process.

THE SUCCESS OF YOUR VENTURE WILL BE DETERMINED BY THE INVESTMENTS you make in yourself and your business and the investments made by others. No matter how intelligent, disciplined, spiritual, and focused you are, you'll need to continue sharpening yourself by preparing for every potential business experience, drawing on the expertise of those ahead of you, and by taking action on the feedback you've solicited.

Jim Rohn—prolific motivational speaker, entrepreneur, author, and mentor to some of the world's most successful people in their areas of influence (including Tim Robbins)—was famously quoted as saying, "Don't let your learning lead to knowledge. Let your learning lead to action." The fact that this book is in your hands is proof-positive of your willingness to invest in yourself and learn a new strategy to achieve success. The application of knowledge is key, though. Although no one will be able to serve the world from your perspective, there's no need to go at it alone, and doing so is not advisable if you want to drastically decrease the amount of time it will take to accomplish your business goals. Others have created successful ventures in your space, and learning from the masters, along with your team, clients, and customer base, will provide you with invaluable information to help you create the business of your dreams.

Put yourself in the position to consistently learn from these three sources—professional development initiatives, professional advisors, and feedback—and with consistency and intentionality, take action on the knowledge you receive. And before you know it, you'll be taking a sip of the lemonade of your success!

FOR DEEPER REFLECTION...

Strategy #12: Continuously Learn from Three Key Sources

1. Entrepreneurship is indeed a lonely journey, so intentionally connecting with others that can relate to the challenges you're enduring is key. What are three ways you can intentionally connect with others within your industry this quarter as you seek to build your venture?

2. Create two lists. With the knowledge you have now, list the names of courses, workshops, seminars, or conferences that you'd like to attend in your current or next fiscal year to help **build you** into the owner you know you can be and that your purpose-driven venture deserves. Create another list of professional development initiatives you'd like to engage in over the same period of time **to grow your business** as well.

   a. Are there any free options for these initiatives above? List them.

   b. Are you willing to budget for these initiatives going forward?

   c. MasterClass, an e-learning platform, grants subscribers access to industry leaders and celebrities who have achieved success in their areas of expertise. I've learned so much from the plethora of classes available, and I cannot stress enough the importance of seeking knowledge from others who have accomplished what you're striving to achieve. Consider an online resource such as MasterClass, as it could prove useful as a source of one of your yearly professional development initiatives.

3. Who are your current professional advisors? List them.

   a. Are you satisfied with the level of assistance you've received from them so far to help you grow personally and/or professionally? Why or why not?

4. Seek honest feedback from friends by asking the following:

   • Are you willing to provide me with constructive feedback that I can use <u>to improve on my product or service</u>? (Remember: It's very important to clearly articulate your reasoning behind why you're asking before asking)

- What do you think are my strengths and weaknesses?

- How do you see me limiting myself?

- What are some areas where you see I can improve as an entrepreneur or business owner?

- How do you experience me and my business?

5. List three methods you'd like to implement going forward to secure feedback from your clients, your team, consultants, or consumers.
   a. What method of thanks will you extend to each separate group to demonstrate your appreciation for their feedback?

13

GIVE BACK & GET MORE

"When you have a need, sow a seed."

—ANONYMOUS

OVER THE YEARS, I'VE BEEN BLESSED TO HAVE HAD THE OPPORTUNITY to connect with some of the most successful women in my industry. Award winners, chart-toppers, and billion-dollar giants in business, each one inspired me to achieve greatness and provided me with a tangible example of what success looks like when hard work, discipline, competence, and belief are coupled with heart, strength, and a drive toward excellence. Beyond all the priceless nuggets of wisdom they shared, it was their willingness to give or spend their limited time to connect with me that was most impressive, and their example was instrumental in the transformation of my business.

In the early years of building my venture, having become so overwhelmed by the challenges of sporadic business, I decided to take a chance and sought out specialized help. I was granted an audience by a powerfully influential business leader who took the time to teach me the importance of *being* a walking example of higher principles, rather than simply absorbing all I could to attain my business goals and material accomplishments. My experience with her set me on a course to become a fuller version of myself and helped me develop more of a service mindset, not only personally but professionally as well. This lesson was essential for my future success. How might you ask? Diving into my experience with her will reveal why it was so transformative to my understanding of the importance of giving back personally and professionally, and how much you stand to receive back when you do.

There could have been no greater teacher of this principle. She'd reached the pinnacle of success in her career, and here she was, at a business meeting, teaching me the value of giving back in the most unexpected place…

"We cannot seek achievement for ourselves and forget about the progress and prosperity for our community. Our ambitions must be broad enough to include the aspirations and needs of others. For their sakes and for our own."

—Cesar Chavez

I met her through my first mentor. The sentiment was that this individual might have access to more connections that could help me navigate specific issues in my business, as she was a highly respected executive that had deep connections with key individuals in my industry. After receiving her contact information from my mentor and the gentle admonition to seriously value this golden opportunity to connect with her, I was naturally nervous and enthusiastically prepared for our meeting.

During our meeting, I was blown away and beyond impressed, but not for the reasons you might expect. She was completely unassuming: humble, vibrant, passionate, and open. Above all, I was surprised at where she asked me to meet her, and the topic she was most keenly interested in discussing.

She had just returned from a volunteer mission trip that included a stop in Israel and was emanating exuberant joy! She requested I meet her at our local homeless shelter, where she was serving as an executive board member. For much of our afternoon together, I was completely transfixed by her willingness to freely discuss her passionate relationship with God with me, a stranger who had requested a business meeting! As we walked around the shelter grounds, she excitedly informed me of the ways the organization was tangibly meeting the needs of our local homeless population. Out of what seemed like nowhere, she uttered words that have impacted me to this day:

*"**I** might be the only Bible someone reads today."*

As a Christian, she wanted to be an example of Christ in the world at all times, in her personal life and in the business arena as well. The effect of this perspective on her own life was palpable, beyond her discussing the sense of fulfillment she'd experienced through her various volunteer projects worldwide.

I was in complete shock that this successful business leader, *Order of Canada* recipient, and winner of multiple business awards, would not only take the time to connect with me but would use her limited time to volunteer. On top of that, it amazed me that she was willing to speak about her dynamic relationship with God during a business meeting!

Eventually, we ended up transitioning to a restaurant for a business lunch, giving me the opportunity to discuss my burning business questions with her. Full transparency, I don't remember the industry contacts she provided me that day or the many nuggets of wisdom she shared. It was her passion for volunteerism as an executive, and her willingness to share her belief in God *through her life* that impacted me so profoundly, which helped transform how I began to operate personally and professionally going forward.

Shortly thereafter, I began volunteering with the same organization and, for the next six years, I organized and led a group of seventy volunteers from my church that regularly served the homeless population with basic services to the shelter that included the distribution of food and clothing and computer lab monitoring. We held weekly Bible studies, and for a time, we performed a monthly musical concert at the main shelter location as well. My experience with that executive not only impacted me but also significantly influenced the lives of hundreds of others for the next several years as well.

And all of this took place prior to my breakthrough.

This experience with my mentor's mentor taught me one very valuable principle of success that was transformative to my life and business: When you find yourself at a precipice of need to receive something urgently, personally or professionally, it is far more important to be ready and willing to first, give.

WHY GIVE BACK WHEN *YOU* NEED THE HELP MORE THAN EVER!

The time I took away from my business to volunteer and give back enriched my understanding of the human experience and blessed me with a greater sense of compassion, which was necessary for me to deliver my service to my audience more effectively. By volunteering, I was practicing for success in a manner congruent with my purpose—to serve, albeit now in a capacity different from the delivery of my business service. During this time, clearly, I was still engaged in my intellectual, daily business preparation for success (reading business and personal development books, developing my service packages and standard operating procedures, reaching out to clients, completing ongoing market analysis and courses, and so on) that had previously monopolized my time. But volunteering, quite honestly, blessed me so much more than the time I was sacrificing to do so; I was giving back, but I was getting more!

One of the ways I benefited from volunteering during that time was that it rescued me from my frustration with my lack of accomplishment, bouts of depression, and the times when I would doubt my worth and abilities as a leader to usher my company to a place of sustained profitability. On the surface, it may seem counterintuitive to invest in anything beyond your balance activities and business operations while you're growing since that further divvies up your waking hours. But I've experienced the overflowing benefits of giving back consistently through devoting my time, talents, and resources to something meaningful, and I strongly advocate for it! Doing so will help you continue building a solid foundation for your business while opening up both a world of opportunities for your personal and professional growth and resources from your Higher Power that will flow in abundance to you as never before.

"Give, and it will be given to you.
Good measure, pressed down, shaken together, running over
will be put into your lap. For with the measure you use,
it will be measured back to you."[1]

—Luke 6:38

I have lived the truth of this passage.

When I made the decision to consistently give my time and talents to volunteering and diligently tithe my gross income, my business experienced *exponential* growth almost immediately. Individuals that had previously proved difficult started speaking on my behalf in meetings. Issues that had previously seemed impossible to resolve dissipated into thin air. I experienced a myriad of miracles on a regular basis after committing to the practice of giving back consistently, which directly helped to solidify my business on stable ground, setting it up for growth and success.

I was helping others, but this practice also had a profound impact on me as well. Moving out of the center of my seemingly constant, business-challenging, emotionally-taxing universe to help others was absolutely instrumental in allowing me to gain perspective on what's really important. As we discussed in Chapter 2, your purpose encompasses the delivery of your "good work" to the world. Whether it's a product or service, your business offering is meant to *serve* the world in some way. It truly is better to give than to receive,[2] and learning to serve in *more than one capacity* will actually strengthen your ability to be effective in your business and will draw others to you.

LAW OF NATURE

As we've reviewed in the "For Deeper Reflection" section of Chapter 11, nature is either in balance or is seeking equilibrium. Taking a cue from nature, when you receive, make it a practice to give! This will bring you even closer to a balanced state in all aspects of your life.

If you benefit from the kindness of others, express your thanks! Yearly, I've made it a practice to send out an intricate, quality Christmas card and/or gift to my vendors, clients, staff, and other outside professionals I work with. Particularly, on *Administrative Professionals Day*, I send a gift or a card to the executive assistants I have the pleasure of working with as well. The years of sporadic business directly taught me to intentionally value *each* client and member of my success team. Sending a token of thanks is the very least I can do to show appreciation for their participation in my success story.

Operating in balance personally and professionally dictates that we release to the ebb and flow of life that we see in nature to achieve balance:

spend/save, up/down and now, get/give. And I would even take it a step further and encourage you to give *before* you get as, in my experience, giving of my time, talents, and resources **prior** to my breakthrough helped to develop me as an entrepreneur. I strongly believe in this practice of giving before you get, in accordance with God's admonition in Luke 6:38. Learning to give before getting was directly instrumental in unlocking blessings in my life, personally and professionally, and I encourage you to give it a try.

THE POWER OF CONSUMER GRATITUDE

Another way to give includes the acknowledgment of exceptional customer service. Those that operate their businesses with excellence are worth our appreciation and thanks, at the very least, for respecting us enough to provide a quality customer experience.

There are so many large and small organizations operating with excellence that deserve kudos. I think of a local specialty grocery store in my hometown, Sunterra Market, which provides a unique European-style shopping experience. Each year, they send out a birthday card with a coupon for a slice of cake and a coffee to their member customers to thank us for our business—such a thoughtful gesture! Their stated purpose of nourishing their customers with affordable, fresh, wholesome food is evident all over the market, but it is their commitment to providing a first-class service experience that consistently impresses me the most.

I also think of the global beauty retailer Sephora. They refund products weeks after purchase, and their staff are committed to spending an inordinate amount of time educating their customers on product offerings, making them a leader in global prestige retail.

If you're still on the fence about giving back, know that expressing your thanks to a business in the form of a positive written review, verbal thanks, or a token of appreciation has a *definite* positive impact on those on the inside. As a former registered nurse—one of the most thankless professions—I can personally attest to the encouraging and energizing value of thanks received from patients, their loved ones, and even other staff.

While building my first entrepreneurial venture, I kept a file of all the thank you cards and emails I received—items I would draw from my *come-back closet* (as discussed in Chapter 7)—that effectively encouraged me to press forward during some of the darkest days of my business journey. Don't underestimate the power of gratitude! We often speak of the power of the consumer dollar to shape company policy, product offerings, and community involvement. But, looking at the other side of the coin, consider the power of *your appreciation* extended to others and the positive effect it can have on a business. Then, commit to using it consistently.

As you build your venture, you, too, will greatly benefit from the expressions of thanks from your customers, clients, vendors, and team during your dark days, and I guarantee you will benefit from their expressions of thanks in more ways than one. In anticipation of the gratitude you stand to receive, commit to *first*, give thanks to all those who enrich your life and business with their products and service offerings.

Strive to *live* thankfully! It will change your perspective on your own situation, refresh the lives of those around you, and set you up to receive exponential blessings in the future. You can't help but be changed when you are living thankfully. When your giving flows from a thankful heart, God can't help but honor you and shift circumstances in your favor. Live thankfully, and you will, in time, reap exponential benefits in your life and business.

HOW YOU CAN GIVE BACK AND GET MORE

It's been said that "money is like manure. If you spread it around, it does a lot of good, but if you pile it up in one place, it stinks like hell."[3] When you block the cycle of giving/getting, you stunt your progress and the progress of your venture. Your business is of service to the world, yes, but also, the voluntary gift of your time, talents, and resources to other causes releases vast amounts of benefits to you in more ways than one, which we will now explore. God has promised abundant rewards and blessings to those who operate with an understanding of this principle,[4] and I have personally experienced the benefits to my business when I decided to become intentional and systematic about doing so.

The organized and systematic way in which you operate your business should be reflected in how you structure and plan your giving initiatives as well. Determining the manner in which you plan to systematically give back now will help you divvy up portions of your schedule to ensure you allot time and resources to do so effectively. As we are intentional about creating the conditions by which we expect to get paid for our product(s) or service(s), it is important to bring an aspect of that same specificity to how we plan to give. Consider the following as you think of ways to give of your time, talents, and resources going forward:

Time

We all have the ability to change our society through volunteerism. Whether you extend two hours of your time once a quarter, or one hour per week, volunteering your time for people and causes aligned with your purpose is imperative to achieving impactful success.

Volunteering allows you to learn about different demographics and develop empathy, problem-solving skills, and teamwork: all necessary to operate your business effectively. Remember, your purpose is not a vocation—like a doctor or a lawyer. It encompasses the impact you'll have as a result of your good work of service, ideally operating *through* your chosen vocation. Volunteer work is just as meaningful as paid work, and success isn't achieved solely through your work at the office or in your business. Serving others positively impacts everyone around you and helps you develop into an effective, purposeful leader.

If you're still not convinced of the power of giving back of your time and the many blessings you stand to gain by doing so, consider the following statistics on the benefits of volunteering:

1. *Volunteerism improves health. Of those that volunteer[5]:*

   - 96 percent say that it enriches their sense of purpose in life
   - 94 percent say that it improves their mood
   - 78 percent say it lowers their stress levels
   - 25 percent say that it helps them manage a chronic illness

2. Volunteering reduces the risk of depression and anxiety.[6]

3. Volunteering increases self-confidence and helps you stay physically healthy; people who volunteer have lower mortality rates than those who don't.[7]

What an overflow of blessings to your physical, social, mental, and relational health for those who take the time to volunteer! As discussed in Chapter 1, the entrepreneurial journey is rife with situations that can challenge one's health. Choosing to carve out time to volunteer can indirectly help you through the above-mentioned benefits or directly by helping you address some of the very issues you're facing as you grow your venture. How can it help you directly? Think of it this way: Volunteering is a great way to network, which can lead to business opportunities.

Successful, wealthy people know the power of volunteering. Those serving beside you may also have their own businesses or know of others who can help you secure funding, provide their expertise, or even provide you resources to help you grow your business! Opening yourself up to giving back from a humble, altruistic place will pay you back in dividends and from directions you might never expect.

Additionally, volunteering can help you hone skills as a leader that are directly beneficial to your business. In my case, volunteering provided me the opportunity to hone my skills—in leadership, management, effective public speaking, creativity, negotiation, team management, and more—in an inconsequential environment that proved integral to my success.

As volunteer coordinator for my group of volunteers that served the homeless shelter, I learned how to manage conflict in a group setting, build teams effectively, and so much more—all invaluable skills to my development as a successful business leader. It is far more difficult to manage a group of people who are sacrificing their free time than it is to manage employees, believe me! This opportunity was invaluable, and it directly prepared me to operate an impactful business. Volunteering has since become a staple aspect of my life, helping me maintain balance and an opportunity to consistently and intentionally give back for everything I've been given.

Talents

At this point in your entrepreneurial journey, you're well aware of your strengths and talents. Consider sharing them with others as a means of giving back. When you're feeling frustrated or discouraged in your business, step away and think of tangible ways to help someone else.

Are you a gifted artist?

Consider making a card for a struggling family member navigating a difficult time.

Are you a specifically gifted educator?

Consider offering your talent to help tutor disadvantaged youth at a local organization.

Are you skilled at cutting hair?

Consider volunteering at a local community organization that services the homeless, who are in need of this type of service.

The way you extend your talent is less relevant than your commitment and willingness to actually use it in the service of others. Find a way to serve from a place of thankfulness for your talents. It is truly one of the beautiful compensations of this life that when we give of ourselves and help others, we indirectly help ourselves.[8] And the vast benefits that flow to us after, in many ways, are usually far greater than the initial investment of our giving.

Resources

As discussed in Chapter 11, the practice of giving back financially is a success principle adopted by many of the world's most successful people. In 2020, Mackenzie Scott, one of the richest women in the world, gave away close to six billion dollars from her Amazon fortune to several philanthropic causes.[9] At the time of writing, chairman and CEO of Berkshire Hathaway, Warren Buffet, is worth more than ninety-six billion dollars,[10] and through his Giving Pledge, he's committed to giving more than ninety-nine percent of his wealth to philanthropy during his lifetime or at his death.[11] He's also asked hundreds of rich Americans to pledge at least fifty percent of their wealth to charity as well.

Giving is not only for the wealthy or for those with an abundance of free time or many skills. The call to give is placed on each of us from our Higher Power, and it completes a necessary cycle that brings us closer to a state of balance. As it relates to your venture, adopting this intention of giving *from your business* is best practice, and it is also instrumental to your ability to create an impactful and sustainably profitable business.

THE POWER OF CSR INITIATIVES

Think of a cause that resonates with you and your venture and develop a Corporate Social Responsibility (CSR) initiative around it for your business. CSR is the idea that a business has a responsibility to the society that exists around it,[12] which is precisely the case for your purpose-driven venture. According to Harvard Business School Online, businesses "are often guided by a concept known as the triple bottom line, which dictates that a business should be committed to measuring its social and environmental impact, *along* with its profits. The adage 'profit, people, planet' is often used to summarize the driving force behind the triple bottom line."[12]

When we operate our businesses with an intention beyond just profit, in turn, they become more attractive to our market. Consumers in today's marketplace have a keen understanding of the power of their consumer dollar and are far more likely to support products and services that align with their values or those that are intentional about their social and/or environmental footprint. You can stand out from the crowd of your competitors by the quality of your product(s) and service(s), yes, but also by becoming intentional about creating impact and giving back as a business. This "people planet" aspect of the triple bottom line theory that expands business success metrics beyond just profits has gained traction within the business community in recent years. More large and small organizations realize that the measure and impact of their business giving is also a determinant of their success.

Indirectly, your company's commitment to giving impacts, to some degree, the sustainability of your venture as well. When your company gives back, and you communicate your commitment to doing so in your marketing, your business becomes more attractive to your stakeholders, which serves to positively impact your bottom line[13]; more people buy—consumers—and potentially then, more people buy-in to your product(s) or service(s)—other stakeholders. So, if you're wanting to solidify your company's presence in your market space, which all of us that start a business do, giving back is another way to accomplish this, one that can help build a solid foundation for your venture to help it stand the test of time.

BEING A SOCIALLY RESPONSIBLE COMPANY NOT ONLY IMPACTS THE PROFITability and sustainability of your business in your market, but internally, corporate social responsibility initiatives can boost employee morale and lead to greater productivity within your organization as well. Those entering the workforce today, in part, stay engaged with organizations that invest in creating positive social impact. If your business has grown and you've hired staff, employee retention is pivotal to your success. As we've discussed in Chapter 6, getting the right people seated in the right positions on your success plane is key, and when you've done all that heavy lifting to hire great people and invest in their professional growth and development, it's important to create a culture within your organization that engages them to stay. When organizations successfully engage their workforce, amazing things occur, and they enjoy[14]:

- 30 percent better customer satisfaction scores
- 26 percent less employee turnover
- 21 percent greater profitability for the business
- 20 percent fewer employee sick days

When you give back as a business, truly, you get more! The potential for increased profitability for your business, sustainability, productivity, employee retention, customer satisfaction, and less employee turnover with fewer sick days—beyond the internal gratification that you are making a societal impact—these benefits of giving back through a CSR initiative provide you more than enough reason to give it a try in your business. Become a leader in social impact, and the internal and external benefits you'll reap *will invariably* flow to you from more than one direction, in abundance.

A BUSINESS APPLICATION

Online eyeglass retailer Warby Parker is a great example of a company with an effective CSR initiative. I prefer buying my glasses in person, but Warby Parker doesn't have a physical location near me. Despite that, I've bought all of my glasses from them because of their impressive CSR initiative to give away a pair for every pair purchased.

Their marketing is clear about their support of a non-profit that provides glasses and training to low-income entrepreneurs in developing countries. And, beyond the fact that they have fabulous glasses, are eco-friendly, provide exceptional customer service, and have a modern, user-friendly online platform, their CSR initiative is what has made the most impact on me as a consumer. And because of it, I've become one of their most avid brand ambassadors within my sphere of influence.

In today's market, your target audience will likely be influenced by the presence or absence of your CSR initiative(s) as well. Set an example of your personal giving by creating a thoughtful, purpose-driven CSR initiative that is congruent with your organization's values. Ten percent of the proceeds of this book will be donated to a cause that supports entrepreneurs that are immigrant women, as well as to *Alex's Lemonade Stand Foundation*, an organization that works to end childhood cancer. I've also donated a minimum of ten percent of my profits over the years to various, rigorously vetted causes near and dear to my heart—from clean water initiatives overseas, work/study and school lunch programs for students in an Indigenous school, to summer camps for disadvantaged kids and various health, natural disaster, and church initiatives around the world. My giving has created an impact that I may never see, but knowing I've contributed to creating positive change around the world has been beyond rewarding in every way. Whatever cause or type of initiative you choose, commit to being intentional, consistent, and systematic in your corporate and personal giving, and you, too, will reap benefits in more ways than one, guaranteed.

"My father always taught me that when you help other people, then God will give you double. And that's what has really happened to me. When I have helped other people who are in need, God has helped me more."
—Cristiano Ronaldo

Cristiano Rolando—arguably the best soccer player in the world and, at the time of writing, the third-highest paid athlete in sports—and many other successful, wealthy people have vouched for the truth of this claim that when you give back, you truly do get more! Yet, despite the benefits you stand to gain from giving back, that shouldn't be your primary reason for doing so. Those of us who've experienced an abundance of benefits from giving back do so from a place of thanks and in recognition for what we've already received. In my own life, I've come to understand that giving that flows from a humble, altruistic motivation will, as promised by God, set in motion abundant blessings in return.

You can't help but be transformed when you give back consistent-ly. Once you do, your character transformation will become evident to all those around you. And when your clients, customers, business associates, and team notice the change in you and your business, profitability, sustain-ability and the lemonade of your success are just around the corner!

Assess your life. Recognize that even now, in more ways than one, you've been the recipient of someone else's thanks or willingness to give back.

You're currently reading mine!

Now, what will be the impact of your thanks, in advance, for what you stand to gain from your successful business?

FOR DEEPER REFLECTION...

Strategy #13: Give Back

God has made powerful promises to those who live thankfully and give their time, talents, and resources. Head over to **melanemullings.com** under the "Resources" section for Chapter 13 to review these passages of scriptures.

1. What are three ways you're a living representation to the people around you of the most important values that guide your life? List the three values and how you represent them.

2. What are some ways you can practice giving back in your everyday life? Consider some of these options as tangible means of giving back:

    - The next time you receive a gift of clothing, set aside a garment from your closet to give away to charity.

    - Head to your local fire department or hospital emergency department to drop off a thank you card with a message of appreciation for their presence within your community. This is a powerful method of expressing thanks and giving back.

    - Rake/mow a lawn or shovel snow for a neighbor.

    - Provide bottled water to people walking by on a hot day.

    - Purchase a bulk order of twenty-dollar, gift credit cards and drop them off at your local women's shelter.

    - Regularly donate 10% of your personal AND business income to a cause that resonates with you.

3. List three businesses that you appreciate within your community.
    a. Why do you appreciate them?

    b. What can you do to tangibly show your appreciation to each of them this week?

4. Think of a cause that resonates with your product or service offering or the market you're servicing. Commit to developing a CSR initiative around this cause for your business by:
    a. Deciding on the manner in which you will give of your company's time (volunteering), how you can draw from the talents of your staff to support the cause (talents), and how much you will donate your resources (money).

    b. Deciding on the length of time you plan to extend your time and talents: bi-weekly, once/month, once/quarter?

    c. Communicate your CSR initiative in your marketing (website, contracts with clients, vendors, investors, etc.).

** *If you've hired a team, be sure to involve them in the process of choosing the CSR initiative for your organization and how you will roll it out in your organization.*

Launch your CSR initiative when you're ready, and when you feel you and your team can consistently and effectively commit to the cause.

5. When choosing an organization to donate to, be sure to rigorously research or vet them to ensure they're a reputable organization, and that a high percentage of your donation will be allocated directly to their cause versus to their operational costs, marketing, etc. To avoid cons, you can research your chosen charity through sites such as Charity Navigator, GuideStar, or the Better Business Bureau.

    Compare causes. This will allow you to donate your money with confidence, and help organizations in desperate need that are using raised funds in the most responsible manner.

LEMONADE CHALLENGE

#1: Think of three things you're thankful for. For the next seven weeks, think of three new things each day. Express thanks to your Higher Power each day for these blessings. At the end of week three, journal what you've noticed within yourself and your perspective. Repeat this at the end of the seven weeks as well. Review both entries, compare results, and reflect on how this practice has impacted your business as well.

#2: Prior to your next fiscal quarter, decide on one organization to donate 10% of the money you're paying yourself, one way in which you can donate your talents, and one organization you can volunteer at (the last two might be one and the same). Research or vet the organizations thoroughly. For the next two fiscal quarters of your company, plan to give back in all three areas personally. Journal the effect you notice in yourself personally at the end of the 180 days, then journal how giving back has impacted you professionally. Share your results with your team, professional advisor, and those within your sphere of influence.

14

BECOME A MAGNET FOR MORE BUSINESS

"Work hard in silence, let success be your noise."

—FRANK OCEAN

During my years in business, I've lived through the rise and fall of several companies led by entrepreneurs and business owners within my network. When they were on the rise, I would've given my right arm to draw from their confidence and perceived competence. When they fell, I realized that things weren't so great when I was comparing myself and my journey to theirs. Insecurity and imposter syndrome will have you believing others are more capable, worthy, or prepared than you are—and that they're on a faster trajectory to success. However, it's important to remember that things aren't always as they seem, and learning to accept and respect *your own pace* to greatness is key.

In my years in business, I've had the pleasure of interacting with a plethora of people from varying backgrounds who've accomplished differing levels of success. I've found that the leaders who achieve sustainable success almost always possess three distinct character traits that seem to magnetically draw business to them, and also key people—the competent, loyal, purpose-driven type who are eager to invest either their time, talents, or resources to steer the business toward success. If you too become intentional about developing and modeling these three character traits, you'll become a magnet for more business, which will help you build a solid foundation for your venture.

"A leader is best when people barely know he (or she) exists, when his (or her) work is done, his (or her) aim is fulfilled, they will say: we did it ourselves."

—Laozi

It is a societal misconception that successful companies always have powerful, gregarious leaders with big personalities at the helm. However, there are a plethora of real-world examples that reflect exactly the opposite.

GOOD IS THE ENEMY OF GREAT

This first line of Jim Collins' book, *Good to Great*, powerfully illustrates two of our magnetic attributes. Collins reflects on his findings from a five-year study of 1,435 "good," established companies, in which he evaluated those that made the leap from good to great. He examined the performance of the good companies over a forty-year period and found that, of the 1,435, *only eleven* became great and were able to sustain their greatness for at least fifteen years.

The leaders of these "great" companies were described as self-effacing, quiet, reserved, mild-mannered, understated, and even shy. They possessed a paradoxical blend of *extreme personal humility* and *intense professional will*.[1] Examples given were: Darwin Smith, past chief executive of paper-based consumer product company, Kimberly-Clark and Coleman Mockler, past CEO of personal-care product company Gillette. On the surface, it would seem strange for the leader of a successful company to be described in this way; however, Collins's research indicates that leaders that possess extreme personal humility and intense professional will magnetically attract key people and, in many cases, they also attract more business as well.

Prideful leaders can be extremely difficult to interact or conduct business with, as pride has an all-encompassing, corrosive effect that can be challenging to manage. **Humility**, defined as having a modest perception of your own sense of importance,[2] is one of the most important attributes you can possess as a business leader. Its effects are far-reaching; from directly impacting your team's effectiveness to the bottom line of your company, humility is magnetic. It has the power to draw people to work with and for you and invest in the success of your venture.

In a 2015 study examining CEO humility and its relation to firm outcomes, researchers found that "when a more humble CEO leads a firm, its top management team are more likely to collaborate, share information, jointly make decisions, and possess a shared vision." They go on to state that "CEO humility has important implications for firm processes and *outcomes*."[3] When a humble leader leads a company, their teams feel more open to connecting with one another more meaningfully, which can lead to a greater willingness to share ideas—even dissenting ones—more openly. Humble leaders truly want the best for their companies, and this sentiment, received by their staff, will help encourage a collective willingness to make the company the best it can be. This simple leadership trait will continue to help you build a solid foundation for your business. And a business that is built on a leader that is humble has a greater likelihood of enduring the test of time.

How? Because humble leaders recognize their own shortcomings and seek honest input from their team. They admit mistakes and create an environment of honesty, open dialogue, and respect. They're accountable, gracious, and authentic. They prioritize achieving success for the business rather than personal aggrandizement, which will help propel the company forward and draw key people to invest and support it. Humility will help you acknowledge your own weaknesses; once you've done so, you can more effectively hire staff to fill in the gap left by your weaknesses, resulting in a stronger team. When you are purpose-driven with a sound character that includes humility, it shows; your customers, clients, and team members alike will be drawn to help you achieve your goals and will cheer you on along the way.

Real-world examples of humble, successful leaders[2] include:

David Green

Known for giving much of his wealth to charity, the *Hobby Lobby* founder has said he wants to be remembered more for his good works and influence than his business empire, and he's keeping true to his word. He even flies economy class when he travels.

Mark Rutte

Despite his title, the Dutch prime minister rides his bike to work every day, and he also offers his time to teach in a school once a week. As a result of working for and with his community, he has an incredible *influence* on his nation. He's also not afraid to take credit for embarrassing moments either. When visiting the Dutch Ministry of Health, he spilled a cup of coffee and mopped it up himself!

Warren Buffet

Warren Buffet, one of the richest and most philanthropic people in the world, is also impressively humble. Despite being a multi-billionaire, he drives a $45,000 Cadillac and at the time of writing, lives in a house he purchased for $31,500 in 1958.

Humility is magnetic; it's especially impressive to witness in people who have every reason to be prideful. However, to be humble, you don't have to be a millionaire who donates swaths of your fortune to charity, or be self-effacing or self-deprecating. As prolific writer C.S. Lewis beautifully articulated, humility is not thinking less of yourself; it's thinking of yourself less.[4]

HUMILITY ISN'T AS VALUED IN POPULAR CULTURE AS IT SHOULD BE, BUT IT will garner you unimaginable opportunities, an audience with influential people, and the commitment and loyalty of the coveted—like-minded, competent individuals who are eager to invest either their time, talents, or resources in your success. Humble leaders are simply a cut above the rest and humility is crucial to sustaining purpose-driven success. Leaders who embody humility and develop a culture around it within their organizations draw their companies to higher heights and profoundly impact and influence those around them.

Humility naturally develops from a place of self-awareness and a keen recognition of your shortcomings and weaknesses. In my case, I was fully aware that I alone could *never* have built my business to become a success; after all, I didn't initially possess the experience, expertise, or confidence traditionally deemed necessary to start or operate a successful business. Realizing that God's blessings on my tireless efforts made all the difference in my success story is what led me to operate with a greater sense of humility, out of acknowledgment of my own shortcomings, and also out of thanks for the success I'm blessed to enjoy. If you consistently acknowledge the truth of who you are and the truth of your circumstances while still giving thanks for all of your blessings, your humble spirit will inevitably be revealed. Notice the change in you and celebrate it!

A PRACTICAL EXAMPLE

In elementary school, I had the privilege of playing saxophone in my school band. During one of our special, evening performances, I was especially nervous; I was about to play a short duet alongside the first chair, and I wasn't feeling particularly confident about my preparation, especially due to the large size of the audience in attendance. However, beside me, that day sat an older gentleman, a special, guest-of-honor performer I initially dismissed in the midst of my anxiety. Before the performance started, and probably sensing my fears from my constant fidgeting, he began talking with me about inconsequential topics, which I now understand were intended to take my mind away from my moment of perceived impending doom. I remember his gentle, calm, encouraging demeanor and his seemingly genuine interest in my responses to his questions. I don't recall how my saxophone duet progressed that evening, but permanently imprinted on my mind was the moment I learned by a whisper in the midst of the performance, the identity of the guest performer sitting beside me; he was Dr. Gimbel, one of the most influential and accomplished ophthalmologists of the 20th century[5] and a major donor to my school. He was the star of the show, but instead of basking in the attention his presence garnered, he took the time to calm a nervous little girl.

Despite being wealthy, successful, and accomplished, Dr. Gimbel personified humility in an experience that has impacted me to this day. After that performance, I vowed *when* I reach my heights, like Dr. Gimbel, I would humbly interact with everyone around me as well.

Think of your own experiences. If you've ever come across someone successful yet humble, they've likely impacted you. Strive to embody humility, and you will find that your road to success will be paved with opportunities to create impact beyond your wildest imaginings.

"Show me a man who excels in his work.
He will walk among kings and not ordinary people."[6]
—Proverbs 22:29

During his examination of the eleven companies that made the transition from good to great, Jim Collins reveals that the leaders of the great organizations embodied "a ferocious resolve, an almost stoic determination to do whatever needed to be done to make the company great."[7] One of the "great" CEOs was described as having an inner intensity, a dedication to making anything he touched the best it could possibly be—not just because of what he would get, but because he simply could not imagine doing it any other way.[7] I term this attribute **a drive toward excellence**, and it is the second most attractive and magnetic business quality.

Mediocrity can be achieved quickly, but it takes time to *become* exceptional and develop the ability to operate your organization with excellence. This shouldn't be confused with drive alone, since there are many people who are driven to operate their businesses in an unscrupulous manner for nefarious gains. However, when excellence is the goal, leaders tend to draw from their values. Furthermore, purpose-driven leaders who have endured lemon experiences usually have an innate need to pay tribute to the journey that brought them to entrepreneurship in the first place; operating in excellence sets them apart from the rest and garners notice.

Think of brands or companies that operate with a drive toward excellence. What do they do that makes you think of them that way? Do they communicate effectively? Are they accountable and honest? Are you impressed with their service offering or their respect for you as a consumer? Your answers to those questions will directly help YOU build a solid foundation for your business and propel you to create a business that is committed to developing an excellent product or delivering a service offering with excellence.

Excellence drives brand loyalty. Excellence also builds your confidence in your product or service offering, rendering you more effective at communicating your value to your target audience. Excellence magnetically draws people to purchase, join, invest, or follow you. A relentless drive toward excellence is imperative to experiencing a sense of accomplishment from your purpose-driven venture. You haven't endured your lemon experiences and built a business to create impact from them to now cut corners in your product or service offering!

Relentlessly pursue excellence as you build every facet of your business. It may take more time, a considerable amount of effort and sacrifice to experience the benefits of operating your venture with excellence, but success that leads to peace is built upon giving your best. And when you operate your venture with the very best of you, your purpose, and all your business has to offer, your drive toward excellence will magnetically draw others to you, resulting in success that leads to peace in the end.

NOT ENOUGH CAN BE SAID OF OUR LAST ATTRIBUTE, WITHOUT WHICH your journey to success will likely prove difficult and without it, you'll also be seriously compromised in your ability to maintain success with any semblance of peace.

In a survey conducted by Robert Half Management Resources, a global human resource consulting firm, one thousand employees and more than two thousand corporate leaders were asked about the top three most important attributes in a leader. Both groups rated **integrity** as *the most essential* leadership trait.[8]

The results came as no surprise to the executive director of Robert Half Management Resources, Tim Hurd. "People want to work for those who are ethical," he explained. "They know that if their leader acts with integrity, that leader will treat them right and do what's best for the business."[8]

Invariably your level of integrity will either draw or repel others to or from you. It can also inspire others to operate with integrity as well. Leaders with integrity are trustworthy and can instill a sense of calm, resulting in increased productivity among their teams. When your team knows they can trust the "one at the top" to operate in a manner that is in their best interest and that of the company, it frees them up from expending time and energy looking out for themselves and protecting their interests, and can also encourage them to interact with their co-workers with integrity, modeling your example as well.

In many cases, a leader with integrity will, by extension, draw the best out of their teams. This quality alone can encourage your employees to put their best foot forward to support the collective goals and follow your lead. Tim Hurd continued that "companies with strong, ethical management teams enhance their ability *to attract* investors, customers and talented professionals," and added that "ethical behavior starts at the top and allows companies to create a culture that values integrity."[8] Acting with integrity will magnetically draw others to buy, support, invest, work for, and follow you, and potentially even champion your causes within their sphere of influence. Emanating this crucial trait on a consistent basis is integral to building a solid foundation for your business, as it helps you create effective and productive teams, garner internal and external support necessary to propel you to success, encourages the modeling of that same behavior, and helps to create an engaging environment where your employees can thrive and put their best foot forward to help you build your business.

"The supreme quality for leadership is unquestionably integrity. Without it, no real success is possible, no matter whether it is on a section gang, a football field, in an army, or in an office."

—Dwight D. Eisenhower

According to the Oxford Language dictionary, integrity is defined as "the quality of being honest, having strong moral principles, and the state of being whole and undivided"[9] and "situated at the intersection of consistent actions and strong values."[10] In other words, it's a quality of people who do the right thing at all times, even when no one is looking, and especially when it is difficult to do so.[10] Whole, morally upright, and honest, even in the face of challenging circumstances—that's what a sound leader operating from a place of integrity looks like.

We can never be at peace when we're operating outside of integrity or honesty, as discussed in Chapter 1. Operating in this state unchecked—living a lie—renders us unable to operate in any manner other than deception, which is dangerous not only to our personal state of being, but also to our purpose-driven venture as well. Every interaction, business or personal, that operates outside of integrity will eventually begin to overflow from a place of deception, and such an individual or business is compromised and will never be at peace.

This may explain people or organizations that seem to be constantly plagued by conflict or consternation. The process of living a lie is rooted in the deception *within ourselves* and eventually permeates into the way we deal with others. When we can't trust ourselves, we operate in an untrustworthy manner with others. In business, this tends to show up in simple things first: telling untruths in a meeting, cheating your consumers ever so slightly on the amount of promised product, or cutting corners to increase productivity or profitability. A lack of integrity is dangerous, and deception is corrosive to your personal well-being and that of your venture. When you strive to operate from a place of integrity within yourself *first*, as discussed in Chapter 1, the person you become will invariably impact the viability of your venture.

True leadership is measured by influence, which is earned over time by consistently demonstrating core values and character. One of the surest ways to secure influence is to demonstrate your integrity. People will eventually discern the depth of your character, even if they don't completely share your moral compass. As previously discussed, trust is built when words match actions over time. Leaders who consistently demonstrate integrity, especially when doing so is unpopular or compromising, are invaluable to their organizations. Operating with integrity communicates to everyone around them that they are trustworthy, which can build credibility and inspire others to act in the same manner.

So, HOW CAN YOU DEVELOP AND MODEL INTEGRITY, THIS CRUCIAL TRAIT that directly impacts your ability to create a sustainably successful business, and one that more than two thousand corporate leaders rated as the most essential leadership trait? You can strengthen your level of integrity by considering the following[8,10,11]:

Be Honest and Treat People Well

Don't exaggerate your successes, and be quick to praise others' contributions. Treat everyone well and fairly, regardless of a person's standing in or outside of your organization. A spiritual admonition that helps ground me in an understanding of this concept is "do unto others as you would have them do unto you."[12] Following this simple "golden rule" will have you operating your businesses with integrity and excellence at every turn.

Hold Yourself Accountable

Ask yourself: *Am I accountable for my behavior, the decisions I make, and the results my business is generating? Am I setting a good example for my direct reports?* Hold yourself accountable to your peers, team, clients, and consumers alike, recognizing that by doing so, you will build integrity and set yourself up to achieve sustainable success.

Find Out How Others View You

It's one thing to ponder how others perceive you but quite another to know for sure. Secure feedback by talking with your team, with business associates outside of your company, and with friends about what you do well and what you can do better. This feedback from others is invaluable, as we covered in Chapter 12, and you can use it to help strengthen your level of integrity, which will help you operate from a place of truth and improve on the areas you're lacking.

Don't Be Afraid to Be Vulnerable

Ask yourself: *Do I regularly accept responsibility when I make mistakes, or do I try to hide them or make excuses?* When you make a mistake, say so, and do all you can to fix it. Go above and beyond in cleaning up your messes. The people around you don't expect you to be perfect, and you can end up alienating them if you're unable to admit your faults when things go wrong. Being vulnerable, with humility and integrity, opens the door to build the coveted "know, like, and trust" factor discussed in Chapter 12. Your target market is much more likely to purchase from and stay loyal to companies they know, like, and trust. And when you lead by setting a good example, others within your organization will follow suit, resulting in a company worthy of your purpose and poised for sustainable success.

Keep Your Word, Even When It Hurts

Ask yourself: *Do I follow through on my commitments and keep my promises? Do I conduct myself in a manner that builds trust with my direct reports and with everyone who comes in contact with my business?* Developing integrity starts with how you treat *yourself.* If you struggle to keep your word to yourself, it will be difficult to do so with others, which you'll need to achieve sustainable success. Building trust involves keeping your word over time, even about the little things and even when it hurts.

Keeping your word to yourself will teach you the value of evaluating requests before making commitments to others. When you make a mistake or inadvertently break a commitment, own it, make the situation right, and move on. Nothing is worth shattering your reputation, and little can erode it more quickly than broken commitments. In business, the last impression is the lasting impression,[13] so leave all of your interactions demonstrating high integrity, and watch your company grow and thrive over time.

THE THREE MAGNETIC CHARACTER TRAITS—HUMILITY, DRIVE TOWARD excellence, and integrity—can be developed through self-reflection, strengthening your emotional intelligence, commitment, and working with a specialized business management consultant. If you allow them, your lemon experiences can also teach you about all three as well.

From the CEO to the disadvantaged among us, on one level or another, we all struggle with feelings of doubt, fear, insecurity, and other negative emotions. As such, pride should find no place among any of us. Those of us who have achieved purpose-driven, impactful, sustainable success as a result of our lemon experiences are cognizant that this success is, in part, a result of pain. The humble realization of who you are, how you achieved success, and what your purpose is will propel you to operate with excellence and integrity, bringing justice to the very challenges that set you on your journey. If you truly want to attract a loyal contingent of brand ambassadors, supporters, and consumers, strive to become your ideal self. If you operate your business as a humble leader with integrity who continues to be driven toward excellence, and your venture is built upon the same qualities, your influence will indeed reverberate throughout your industry and beyond.

FOR DEEPER REFLECTION...

Strategy #14: Operate with Humility, a Drive toward Excellence, and Integrity

1. Review the chapter and write down the ways discussed in which humility, a drive toward excellence, and integrity can render you a magnet for more business.

2. Think of three examples of individuals you know personally or individuals within your business network that you would describe as humble.
   a. How does this trait influence how they operate their life or business?

   b. How do you perceive this trait impacting those around them, personally and/or professionally? How does it impact you?

3. What are three ways in which you can demonstrate greater humility when connecting with your team?
   a. Your clients?

4. What are three ways in which you can demonstrate a drive toward excellence in your next quarter?
   a. Your next fiscal year?

5. Would your team, consultants, customers, clients, or market describe you as a leader with integrity? Why or why not?
   a. Humility? Why or why not?

   b. A leader with a drive toward excellence? Why or why not?

LEMONADE CHALLENGE

Create a plan for your next quarter to demonstrate a higher level of integrity as you operate your business. Write down the five strategies listed in the chapter to strengthen your level of integrity, and create an action plan on how you can demonstrate each during your workweek.

Ask yourself: What can I do to treat my team, clients, or customers well this week? When I make a mistake, what can I do to remind myself to be honest about what happened, hold myself accountable, and be vulnerable and open about my mistakes? Ask yourself questions about the five areas listed, and place a reminder in your calendar at the end of your week to encourage you to review how you demonstrated professional integrity during the week. Journal your progress weekly. At the end of the quarter, review your journal entries and reflect on your progress. Share it with your professional advisor and celebrate your growth as a business leader!

15

THE #1 INDICATOR FOR SUCCESS IN BUSINESS

"Many of the world's most talented and ambitious people fail to achieve their potential simply because they haven't mastered the art of effective communication."

—MICHAEL LEBOEUF

GROWING UP, I WAS RARELY GIVEN THE OPPORTUNITY TO SPEAK IN family settings. As the youngest of four siblings, I was forced to develop my listening skills quickly, and during conversations, I struggled to get a word in edgewise. When I would finally speak, however, my thoughts were frequently jumbled and littered with frustrated emotion, since I knew that I would only be granted seconds before everyone started paying attention to something or someone else. This frustration permeated through my formative years and many thereafter, eventually rendering me deathly afraid of situations involving public speaking.

When I started my business, I knew that my shyness, insecurities, and fear of public speaking would be debilitating to the sustainability of my venture, and that improvement would be necessary to attain any modicum of success. Despite understanding this intellectually, it was only after years of sporadic business and a steady fall deeper into debt that I finally decided to take the leap to learn how to communicate effectively—particularly from the perspective or in the "business language" of my clients.

Truthfully, business wasn't the only arena of my life that suffered from my inability to communicate effectively; relationships, past and present, had become strained as well. Constant frustration from repeating myself in meetings, answering the same client or RN candidate's questions, and feeling the need to address miscommunications on a relatively consistent basis all eventually propelled me to revisit my inner work. I *had* to tell myself the truth and acknowledge that the problem was me and my inability to communicate effectively. I realized that the health and viability of my venture were at stake, and if I didn't improve quickly, I could lose it all.

FOR CONSUMERS TO REPEATEDLY ENGAGE WITH YOUR BUSINESS, THEY WILL need to feel heard, understood, respected, and validated. Timely responses to their inquiries and communications are a must if you're striving to operate your business with excellence. For your team to be willing to adopt your vision or respect your leadership, they will need to clearly understand the "why" of your venture and why you are deserving of their trust.

Similarly, for consumers to buy your product or utilize your service, you'll need to effectively relay why doing so is a worthy investment. In many cases, you're only granted minutes or even seconds to convey your intended message to your target audience before any level of "buy-in" decision is made. From your team to consumers to potential investors and target market, learning to effectively communicate in business is one of the single most important skills you'll need to master as an entrepreneur or business owner, and is the #1 indicator for sustainable success in business.

THE RELATIONSHIP BETWEEN COMMUNICATION AND SUCCESS IN BUSINESS

To communicate effectively, it's important to have a thorough understanding of your target audience. All the information you relay in business communications should be applicable to your target audience specifically, and easy for them to understand and act on.

In too many instances, early-stage entrepreneurs and business owners feel they have the remedy to all their consumer's ailments; they believe their job is to "hard sell" their remedy and convince their target market that they need it at all costs. As a successful entrepreneur, you will solve your consumer's problems at a profit from the perspective of your purpose but, to secure their business at the outset, you'll need to effectively persuade them that you, your service, or your product are a worthy investment. The most effective way to accomplish this? Speak in the language of their pain.

AS WE REVIEWED IN CHAPTER 1, PEOPLE WON'T CHANGE THEIR BEHAVIOR unless or until their circumstances cause them significant enough pain. Unless there is a demand for your product or service—it addresses a specific need in your target market by making their life easier or better, or it is more cost-effective than another option—the likelihood they'll choose to patronize your business is relatively low. This coincides with the statistic that forty-two percent of businesses fail due to a lack of demand for their product or service.[1] If your target market's pain is a slow bleed—staying with their current option is not costing them much in terms of time or money, or they don't perceive the value of your product or service—they're unlikely to choose the remedy of your business. But if their pain is a gaping wound, costing them significant time and money, and you've effectively communicated that your offering can save them one or both, you'll gain their attention and an opportunity to secure their business.

If you directly address a demand in your market or your customers' needs with a great product or amazing service, if you *communicate effectively* with them and deliver seamlessly, reliably, and with exceptional service, you won't just gain a loyal customer—you'll gain a willing brand ambassador for your business that will help drive future sales. For free! And that's just one aspect of the power of communication to your business success story. Collectively, without effective internal and external communication, all your other efforts will eventually fall flat.

COMMUNICATING IN THE LANGUAGE OF YOUR TARGET MARKET REQUIRES you to identify their pain point and demonstrate an understanding of its impact on their spending behavior. This is where a deep dive into market analysis comes in. It's important that you understand not only your market, including trends and best practices, but also the *perspectives* of your target market: their motivations, needs, and concerns, if any, about their current state and product option(s). This is precisely why feedback from focus groups, stakeholders, and even family or friends is extremely helpful. Effectively communicating with your target market will provide you with key information on how to develop, present, or market your offering for desired results.

I'm a prime example of this concept. In years past, if you were to hold up a glass of water and implore me to drink at least thirty ounces or close to one liter a day simply because it's good for me, the likelihood I would have listened was next to nil. However, if you were to inform me that drinking water was likely to help increase my focus and comprehension during my workday, improve the clarity of my skin, and help with regulating my weight,[2] I would've grabbed it from you immediately and drunk it eagerly because you would have been speaking to areas of my pain at the time.

It wasn't until *I understood* the information on the value of drinking adequate water daily that I made the decision to consume it on a regular basis. Now, I am a self-described "water aficionado," regularly consuming fifty to seventy ounces, or 1.5–2 liters of water a day. You'd be hard-pressed to find me without a water bottle on me because I now *understand* the vast array of health benefits that can be ours simply by drinking adequate amounts of water each day.

When you effectively communicate with your audience in the language of their motivations, needs, perspectives and, ultimately, their pain, you position your business to adequately address and transform their current circumstances, giving you a greater chance of success at securing their business, and loyalty for the long haul.

Especially when dealing with clients or consumers, it's important to become intentional about learning to communicate in not only the language of their pain, but also in the business language of their competency. For example, if you've been granted a meeting with the CFO of a potential client organization, come prepared to speak the CFO's language; communicate from a perspective they will understand and resonate with—how your offering will impact or improve the organization's financial performance, and so on. If you're discussing your product with an athlete, be ready to relay how it will maximize their performance and/or help them condition their body more effectively. Spend time learning the language of your target audience prior to communicating with them and recognize that when you do, you'll likely experience greater success in your interactions with them, rendering you closer to achieving your business goals.

A BUSINESS APPLICATION

This may all sound daunting, and, in all honesty, it can be! A specialized business management consultant can help you develop your business communication skills. We can reveal areas for improvement that will help you avoid costly mistakes, while guiding you along to secure increased business and improve your bottom line.

One of my first consulting clients experienced challenges communicating in several aspects of her business, which directly affected her ability to secure more clientele. Insecurities, fears, and a lack of confidence seemed to paralyze her in meetings, and she even struggled to communicate effectively with me during our sessions. One of the ways I helped involved joining her on a videoconference with one of her potential vendors. At the start of the call, she introduced me as her business management consultant and conveyed to the vendor that I would be weighing in on the conversation to help guide her decision-making. My input during the call allowed her the opportunity to listen to me navigate the negotiation. It also provided her a real-world example of how to speak in the language, and from the perspective of the listener, with a tone that disarmed the intensity of the moment;

which in this case, involved negotiating the parameters and pricing of a proposed service package. This call also provided her a deeper understanding of the importance of curating one's thoughts prior to communicating, a topic we'll explore later in the chapter. The interaction ended with a result better than we had hoped, and a real-world example of the power of communication to achieve stated business goals.

Over the months of our consulting relationship, I witnessed her confidence grow; she learned how to communicate her thoughts, needs, requests, and concerns more effectively both with me and in her business interactions. Through consistent guidance and specialized support, she blossomed in her communications, transforming her, personally and professionally, for the better.

You may be as smart as a whip, possess all the capital one could hope to amass, and hold more degrees than a thermometer. But even with the greatest product or service offering in your market, your venture is in jeopardy if you lack effective communication skills. To remedy this, acknowledge the need for your skill development in this area, seek help, gain an understanding of the components of effective communication, and use them consistently and intentionally to help you achieve your business goals.

THE ANATOMY OF EFFECTIVE COMMUNICATION

University of Wisconsin professors Scott Cutlip and Allen Center defined a set of principles known as the *seven Cs*[3]—seven characteristics of effective communication. They are completeness, conciseness, consideration, concreteness, courtesy, clarity, and correctness. Collectively, they are the backbone upon which effective communication is built. Utilizing each of the seven in your communications will provide you with a great template upon which you can strengthen your communication skills.

Completeness

Effective communications are complete, providing the receiver with all the information needed to process the message and take action.

Conciseness

The content of your message should be succinct and allow the receiver to focus and quickly glean key points. Conciseness helps speed up information processing and encourages improved understanding of your message.

Consideration

Consider the ways in which a receiving party might perceive your message. Communicating from a place of understanding and empathy will help strengthen the relationship between you and your receiver, increasing the likelihood that they'll understand your intended message. When you're cognizant of the receiver's motivations, needs, context, and culture, you can specifically tailor your message to their perspective.

Concreteness

Your message should be concrete and supported by facts, which enhances credibility. It should also be specific, tangible, and vivid. Concrete messages mitigate the risk of misunderstanding, foster trust, and encourage constructive criticism.

Courtesy

Courtesy, like consideration, respects the receiver—their culture, values, and beliefs—and ensures that messages are conveyed in a polite and unbiased manner.

Clarity

Most communication pitfalls originate from a lack of clarity. The clearer your message, the easier the receiver will decode it according to your original intent. Clear communications that utilize exact terminology that both parties can understand reduce ambiguities and confusion.

Correctness

A sure way to increase the credibility and effectiveness of your communications is to use correct grammar and syntax. Egregious errors or the use of slang in business settings affect the clarity of your message, trigger ambiguity, and raise doubts. Such errors might also have a negative impact on others' perceptions of you, which could damage your credibility.

THE FOUR PILLARS OF COMMUNICATION

The ultimate goal of communication is to understand and to be understood. This concept of understanding is of paramount importance in the business context. If you're unable to effectively convey the benefits of your product or service to your target market, your venture will invariably suffer. If your market does not clearly understand how, or if your product or service can address their pain or need, the likelihood that your venture will stand the test of time is next to nil.

I define effective communication as the ability to speak, write, listen, and present oneself in a manner that clearly reveals the intent of a message. Each of the four pillars of communication—speaking, writing, listening, and non-verbal presentation—should clearly reflect your intended message to achieve the results you're seeking from your interactions.

Continued ineffectiveness in conveying a message using any one of the four pillars can be detrimental to your business, so let's review each of them in greater detail to help you gain a clear understanding of how you can build the overall strength and effectiveness of your communications.

Speaking

One of the most powerful methods I used to improve my communications skills in business involved becoming aware of the necessity to think before speaking. Frequently, when I listened in conversations with clients or in meetings, thoughts would race through my mind like a whirlwind, and I would then say what I was thinking. This, combined with my insecurity, fear of public speaking, anxiety, and imposter syndrome, resulted in disastrous communication, which undoubtedly played a role in my slow climb to success. Learning to slow down in my communications, as well as process and structure my thoughts in my mind before speaking, marked a turnaround in my journey to develop my communication skills, which led to more successful business interactions thereafter.

If your receiver is confused by your communications and cannot follow your train of thought or idea while listening to you speak, your conversations will eventually fall flat. This is completely counterproductive to achieving your goals for the interaction! If you struggle to communicate effectively, start constructing your ideas in your mind first before releasing them out into the world. This practice drastically helped me improve my communication in business settings and directly led to compounding achievements of my business goals. Whether it be one-on-one communications with your team, clients, vendors, or customers, or in presentations delivered to small or large groups, carefully crafting your thoughts in your mind first will help you deliver effective messages, which will set you on the road to becoming a proficient speaker.

How you communicate is of equal importance to the message you relay. Content and tone are extremely important, so in all your interactions, strive to speak with:

1. <u>Empathy</u> - Consider the circumstances and perspective of your receiver and relate to them from a place of understanding from this vantage point.

2. <u>Authenticity</u> - Present yourself as you really are and not who you believe your receiver wants you to be.

3. <u>Integrity</u> - Be honest, keep your word even when it hurts and don't be afraid to be vulnerable when you speak. As discussed in Chapters 12 and 14, doing so will magnetically draw others to you and render you a more effective business leader.

4. <u>Humility</u> - As mentioned in Chapter 14, humble leaders are more effective at building solid teams for future success. People are typically drawn to those who communicate with humility, void of big words and lofty ideas. Remember, one of the goals of communication is to be understood. Consider your audience and communicate with humility on their level for maximum impact.

5. <u>Confidence in tone and presentation</u> - One of the sure ways to secure buy-in from your receiver is by communicating with confidence, and we'll discuss this in greater detail in the next section.

Communicating with empathy, authenticity, integrity, humility, and confidence will greatly impact the success of your communications and, by extension, the success of your business.

COMMUNICATION TIPS FROM A FORMER FBI HOSTAGE NEGOTIATOR

To achieve your business goals, it's important to foster a collaborative spirit with the people who interact with your business, internally and externally. One of the surest ways to accomplish this is to encourage connection, and the simplest manner to do so is through the tone of your voice.

Former FBI hostage negotiator and CEO of The Black Swan Group, Chris Voss, beautifully articulates the importance of tone in negotiations in his lesson, *The Art of Negotiation*,[4] on the online MasterClass platform. If we nail the right tone in negotiations, he says, we can build the all-powerful trust-based influence (from the know, like, and trust factor previously discussed in Chapter 12) and close the gap between parties to solidify a great deal. According to Voss, the three main tones of voice are: the assertive voice, the playful/accommodating voice, and the late-night FM DJ voice.

The assertive voice delivers a message like a punch; it's always counterproductive, as it leaves a negative residue in negotiations, so don't use it! The playful/accommodating voice delivers messages gently and playfully. This should be your go-to voice in negotiations; Voss encourages its use eighty percent of the time. When the other party is upset or anxious, however, that's when you should use the late-night FM DJ voice: a straightforward, soothing voice with a downward tilt, which serves to diffuse tension. I've found that when you add confidence to each, the benefits compound.

The tone of your voice during even the most challenging of situations has the ability to diffuse tension, foster connection, and even solidify deals. You are your business, and the tone you set as a leader, verbally and otherwise, will reverberate throughout your entire organization and beyond.

You might not ever find yourself in a high-stakes negotiation situation, but your communications with your target market should still take into consideration Chris Voss's strategies to foster collaboration, connection, and buy-in. It is true that in the end, people don't remember as much of what you say, but more how you make them feel,[5] so strive to leave your target audience with a positive impression of you and your business with the confident and effective way in which you speak. Leverage the power of your tone of voice in all your business communications, and you will eventually enjoy the positive impact on your bottom line.

Writing

Emails, business communiqués, social media posts, and marketing materials are all examples of how you can use the written word to represent your business. Branding is an extremely important aspect of your business, so ensure all of your written materials reflect the "seven Cs" we reviewed earlier in the chapter to maximize their effectiveness. Also, all of your marketing materials should be congruent in tone, messaging, and design; layout, typography, and colors all have a direct impact on how your message is received as well.

"I know it's misspelled, but market research
shows that cute sells."

No, cute does not sell for the long haul! You can get away with mistakes here and there, sure, but your business communications are ultimately a reflection of you, so it's important to be mindful about putting your best foot forward in memorialized documents that ultimately represent you and your brand.

As the leader of your venture, your written word in every form carries incredible weight with your target audience, as it should! As a nursing student, I distinctly recall my professors and clinical instructors instilling the fear of God into me and my classmates on the importance of accurately documenting information in the patient's record. Essentially, we were taught to document as though everything we wrote could be read in a court of law.

Ever since, my practice of writing with complete accountability has stayed with me throughout my years in business, saving me during negotiations, meetings, and conflict situations. When you write your business communications with no fear of them being read internally or externally, that is freedom! The resulting peace of mind will allow you to function in your business with confidence, knowing that you can defend your well-curated communications with ease. It takes time to develop the skill of writing with the seven Cs in mind, but investing in developing this skill will help both you and your business as you grow toward sustainable success.

THE TRUTH ABOUT YOUR WRITTEN WORD

Another perspective to consider is the professional nature of your writing. Tell yourself the truth: Is it at a level representative of your title, your experience, or your best? Remember, your venture is purpose-driven. To do your lemon experience(s) justice and to use your talents to the best of your ability, endeavor to consistently and intentionally operate with excellence in every area of your business. In part, this can be accomplished through effective communication, especially as it relates to your business writing.

I've had the misfortune of cultivating a positive image of an executive in my mind after meeting them on several occasions, only to be woefully disappointed later by their inability to effectively draft a professional email or document. As mentioned, the inability to properly communicate using the "seven Cs" of correctness can damage your credibility. Don't be a disappointment to your target market; it will likely cost you. Ensure that your written communications are spell-checked, properly formatted, and grammatically correct prior to their release. You want them to be representative of your very best at all times.

Much to my chagrin, I still take an inordinate amount of time to draft my business communications. They are certainly not perfect, but I strive to give my best since I'm aware that I'm representing not only my brand but also, by extension, God through my purpose-driven ventures. We all make mistakes. None of us who have achieved success can claim arrival at any level of self-actualization. We don't get it right every time, and we're all on a journey of learning and self-improvement. It's important to place priority on your writing and strive to improve, though, recognizing that once your business communications and marketing materials are released to the public, they are a permanent reflection of you and your brand.

So, continue to tell yourself the truth. If you need to develop your skills in this area, invest in yourself and take a business writing course. There are many in-person or online options to choose from, free and for a fee, and there are software options you can use to help improve your writing as well. The importance of effective written communication and its impact on your business cannot be overstated. Developing your business writing skills will take time, but the investment will certainly pay off.

---

*"We have two ears and one mouth so that we can
listen twice as much as we speak."*

—Epictetus

Listening

Listening is one of the most important components of communication, but it's, unfortunately, one of the most widely undervalued, under-utilized skills among many new entrepreneurs and business owners. I can personally attest to the results, or lack thereof, I experienced as an early entrepreneur due to my inability to effectively listen to my target market and use key information they were readily communicating to adjust my service offerings accordingly.

If you're similarly oblivious to the power of effective active listening, you, too, will miss important cues from your target market, which are essential for the development of your business. Again, people want to be heard and *feel* heard when it comes to the delivery of your product or service. So, developing keen listening skills is key if you want to be responsive to your market and financially benefit from their needs.

One of the most consequential experiences of my leukemia hospitalization, which incidentally led me to a career in nursing, was a pervasive feeling of invisibility. I regularly felt unheard and unseen as my overworked nurses scurried around my room to deliver the necessities of my nursing care. It appeared that my nurses had no interest in or time to sit down and listen to my concerns, hold my hand, or reassure me, a seventeen-year-old navigating through an exceedingly challenging season. (Of course, I later learned while an RN that the compromised emotional care I experienced was due to a shortage of nurses across the region at the time.) Regardless of the reason, though, feeling unheard and unseen during such a critical moment in my life had an incredibly debilitating effect on me for years after I was released from the hospital. If the nurses had practiced active listening, I wouldn't have felt such acute after-effects.

Active listening is an important skill for medical staff to master so they can provide quality care to patients, but it's also important for you, too, to ensure your target audience remains engaged with your business. Too few business owners and entrepreneurs demonstrate an understanding of this key component of communication—as evidenced by their inability to adapt to market changes, adjust their consumer engagement, or even direct changes to their product or service offerings. I was one of these business owners in the early days, but thankfully, through the advice I received from one of my mentors, I learned to listen to my market keenly and pivot strategically, which was instrumental in building a solid foundation for my business.

Your consumers will always communicate with you; either directly in reviews or on social media, for example, or indirectly through your bottom line. Strive to listen more effectively, absorb what you hear and see objectively, and act on the information accordingly in the development of your product or delivery of your service. Proficiency in active listening is crucial to the growth, profitability, and sustainability of your venture.

PEOPLE WON'T LISTEN UNTIL THEY'VE BEEN LISTENED TO

This is a well-known concept within nursing circles. As an emergency room RN, this practice of granting the patient a window of opportunity to empty or communicate their thoughts and concerns was key for me to glean necessary information quickly to ensure the delivery of quality patient care. The most effective health practitioners I worked with during my nursing career were masters at this skill, even when caring for patients with life-threatening ailments required access to time-sensitive information quickly. Think of it this way: If a patient has a pet alone at home, has lost their job due to their hospitalization, or is dealing with family issues, it's unreasonable to assume they'll be emotionally or intellectually present to accurately relay information required of them, or absorb any information relayed, for instance, during a moment of teaching on how to use their new blood sugar monitor. As it is in nursing circles, so it is in business. If a member of your team, a client, or a consumer has concerns or questions racing through their mind, the likelihood they'll have the bandwidth to listen to what you have to communicate is extremely low—especially if they're not experiencing enough urgency or pain to propel them to do so. Allowing the people in your target market the opportunity to empty *first* builds connection, demonstrates you care, and allows them to open up and eventually listen to your messaging.

A real-world example would involve calling a client to discuss an issue, but taking time to first ask how they are doing; in essence, engaging in a brief conversation with genuine interest first before broaching the subject of your issue. Another example would involve listening to a team member voice their concerns, especially when they are unrelated to the work at hand, and offering them genuine support in their time of need before discussing work-related issues.

Implementing this particular strategy of listening first definitely requires an intention toward balance; *if you need to talk, first be prepared to listen*. Not only is it simply just courteous—one of our "seven Cs"—when you practice active listening consistently, your business relationships will blossom, and trust will begin to solidify, creating a stronger organization and opening the door for new opportunities that you may have thought were previously impossible. During my entrepreneurial career, there have been several instances when keenly listening to a client led to securing new business. Active listening also helped me improve my service offering, and helped me learn new ways to deliver my service more effectively. All those opportunities came simply by actively listening to the musings of my clients!

Because so few business owners or entrepreneurs engage in active listening from a place of authenticity and genuine care for their audience, your willingness to do so will set you apart from the pack and position you to reap significant, and at times unexpected, benefits from your communications.

THE GUIDING VOICE ABOVE ALL OTHERS

Developing proficiency in listening also involves your willingness and ability to effectively discern promptings from your Higher Power. During your purpose-driven entrepreneurial journey, expect to receive guidance in many forms from your Higher Power, including, but certainly not limited to: impressions on your conscience, messages spoken into your mind, clarity on business concepts while walking through nature, words spoken through a friend, a sermon, or a business colleague, and even dreams. I regularly received guidance through reading God's Word, the Bible, and one of the three reasons I decided to jump into the waters of entrepreneurship with no business education or experience was the admonition I received from God: *Quit your job, move back to Calgary, and start the business.* The two others were faith in His promise in Matthew 21:22 and belief that God would keep His Word. Had I not previously become accustomed to listening to God and accurately discerning His voice, I would never have trusted his prompting to change the course of my life so drastically and give up my comfortable lifestyle for the arduous road of entrepreneurship.

"And your ears will hear a voice behind you saying,
'This is the way, walk in it,' when you turn to the right or when
you turn to the left."[6]

—Isaiah 30:21

Think of it this way: If you're in a closed room and you hear a loved one speak audibly yet softly from another room, how can you be sure it's them? You would know by the strength of your relationship that it's your loved one speaking to you. Similarly with God, as you continue to connect with Him through prayer and reading of scripture, you, too, will come to know Him, recognize His voice, and understand how He speaks *to you* in particular. Some people experience Him speaking to them through nature, some through sermons. Others hear Him through a friend. And we all can hear Him speaking through his Word if we're open to the process of discovery.

God isn't lost. He tells us that if we seek Him, we'll find Him—if we search for Him with all our heart.[7] On *numerous* occasions, I experienced God's guidance for my business through His Word and, when I acted upon the guidance immediately, it saved me from disastrous business decisions and encouraged me to stay the course when I was on the precipice of giving up. His promptings to connect with several important people resulted in bountiful successes for me as well. Learning to effectively discern the voice of your Higher Power and then commit to taking action on what you hear will invariably strengthen, empower, bless, and encourage you to press forward on your purpose-driven journey to experience the lemonade of your success!

Non-Verbal Presentation

It has been said that, in communication, only seven percent of a message is received from the literal content or words spoken in the message. Thirty-five percent is received from the tone of voice, and fifty-five percent comes from body language; this is collectively known as the 7-38-55 rule.[8] In other words, *ninety-three percent of what we communicate is non-verbal!* This is astounding and underscores the importance of being mindful in your communications, recognizing that the tone of your voice and your body language carry significantly more weight than what you actually say.

We've already covered the power of your tone of voice earlier in the chapter. Since fifty-five percent of communication is non-verbal, it becomes crucial for you to understand and harness the power of this fourth pillar of communication—non-verbal presentation or body language—and leverage it for your success.

The most influential reason I chose the RN career path was to help ensure that the horrific emotional experience I'd endured during my hospitalizations wouldn't become the norm for other patients. Due to my direct experience as an RN myself, however, I eventually realized that the care a nurse can provide to four patients is very different from the care they can give when they have eleven. But, as a patient receiving compromised emotional care, no amount of justification could make up for the experience.

In the rush to do all of the necessary medical tasks for my care during their shift, engaging with me meaningfully didn't appear to be a priority for most of my nurses. To me, there appeared to be a lack of awareness of their body language. Rarely did they sit with me—a frightened yet faithful and, at times, confused young patient—to ask how I was feeling and navigating the entire cancer experience. Rarely did they even look at me when completing their assessments while scurrying around the room to hang my chemotherapy medication, change my central line dressings and complete all the other necessary technicalities of my care. While I'm extremely thankful for their service to me as a patient, their inability to effectively communicate with me through the use of their body had a huge impact on me. The same is the case in business. The way you use your body can significantly impact how, or if, your intended message is received.

As you become more aware of how your body language will enhance the reception of your spoken messages, you'll gain more confidence in using it to your advantage. Face your clients directly when speaking to them, demonstrate interest by nodding while your sender is speaking, use appropriate facial expressions that match your verbal messages, become more aware of your posture, presence, and positioning in relation to your sender, notice if you have any particular distracting mannerisms, and pay attention to the presence or absence of fidgeting. Show emotion along with your body language that matches the message you're communicating to convey your empathy, care, and concern.

Again, people will remember *more* about how you or your business left them feeling than solely the content of your messages, so the next time you communicate with a team member, client, vendor, or investor, pay close attention to your body language. Ensure that there is congruence between your body language and spoken words, and watch your audience closely to evaluate their reactions to your communication style.

When your body language doesn't match your message, it results in a disconnect that leads to confusion or even a misunderstanding of the message spoken, completely counterproductive to achieving your goals for the interaction. Again, the main goal of communication is to understand and be understood. If your body language is conveying an entirely different message from your words and tone of voice, you run the risk of botching the communication entirely, which compromises your ability to effectively achieve your business goals and grow your venture. Become intentional about removing all obstacles that might lead to doubt, misunderstanding, or confusion in your messages and pay attention to the way your body language influences your communications.

DEVELOPING YOUR COMPETENCY IN ALL FOUR PILLARS OF COMMUNICATION will help ensure you place yourself and your business in the best position to win! Again, if you struggle to bring all the components together on a consistent basis in your business, there are several free or for-a-fee online and in-person resources you can secure to help you develop your business communication skills. A specialized business management consultant can also provide you training, advice, and actionable strategies you can implement to develop in the particular areas you're struggling with, helping you balance all four pillars in your business communications. There are components of communication that are more consequential than others, but strengthening your communication skills in all four areas places you in the best position to reap a bounty of benefits of this #1 indicator of business success.

One of the reasons it's crucial to strengthen your communication skills now, is to help you prepare to effectively communicate in times of stress and conflict. Failure to do so can cost you time, money, potentially your reputation, and increased business if the challenging seasons are not navigated effectively. As discussed in Chapter 5, invariably, there will be seasons in the life cycle of your successful business when you'll be forced to navigate internal and external conflict as the leader. Your inner work of forgiveness will help push you through to the last stage of conflict resolution, which is necessary to move forward in a positive direction thereafter. A closer look reveals that your outer, tangible work of communicating effectively, using a balanced approach of all the four pillars, is what provides you the necessary mechanics to progress through conflicts successfully, to get you to the point where forgiveness propels you toward full resolution. Your ability to communicate effectively in seasons of conflict will determine whether the foundation you've built for your venture will survive the storms of your entrepreneurial journey. Undoubtedly, leveraging the power of the "seven Cs" along with the other aspects of communication are crucial in times of conflict. But there are three advanced tools you can use while progressing through conflict seasons that are a game-changer that will also help ensure you rise from conflicts successfully.

EFFECTIVELY COMMUNICATING IN SEASONS OF CONFLICT

In the final episode of the epic, twenty-five-year run of her daytime talk show, Oprah Winfrey, one of the most prolific interviewers of our time, reflected that after interviewing nearly 30,000 people on her show, she discovered a commonality among all of us: We all desire to be seen, to be heard, and to feel like what we say matters.[9] In conflict conversations, however, there's a tendency to defend and protect one's position rather than fostering discovery and a need to understand the other's point of view.

Communicating in seasons of conflict can be jarring for leaders. Such times call for a greater need for clarity and calm. In the early years of building my business, I found communication during moments of conflict especially challenging, as I was afraid that my opinions would not be heard or that I had a limited time to deliver them, a direct trigger from past childhood experiences. This fear and frustration caused me to deliver confusing messages with low confidence, which was reflective of my insecurity, underscoring the importance of the need for me to heal and grow through the completion of my inner work.

Thankfully, while navigating the devastating emotional toll from a relationship breakup, I was introduced to a concept called the Imago Dialogue,[10] conceived by world-renowned therapist and bestselling author Dr. Harville Hendrix and his wife, Dr. Helen Hunt. It completely shifted my understanding of communication in conflict, which drastically improved relationships in my personal life. Unexpectedly, it improved my business communications, too, positively impacting my bottom line almost instantaneously.

The Imago Dialogue encourages the responsibility of both the sender and the receiver during communication—to openly listen and effectively speak with the intent to understand and be understood—and outlines three distinct tools you can use to help you progress through both sides of conflict conversations successfully:

1. Mirroring

2. Validation

3. Empathy

Use of these three during conflict communications serves to strengthen the connection between the sender and the receiver, helping to ensure *understanding*, which is important in building the trust-based influence we discussed in Chapter 12. And the ability to understand, especially in conflict, is the highest level of communication.

In the first step of the Imago Dialogue, **mirroring**, the sender provides the receiver time to absorb their message and the opportunity to communicate their reaction. The receiver, then, paraphrases what they heard from the sender without judgment, passive-aggression, or criticism. This mirroring is repeated until the sender feels the receiver has fully heard their concerns and what the receiver has heard from the sender is fully correct. This complete "sender emptying" fosters a connection between the two parties, which will help them successfully progress through the remaining steps.

In business, your clients, consumers, and team members will, at some point, have grievances to communicate. However passionately they do so, remaining calm and mirroring effectively while they release their frustrations will allow you to clearly understand their perspective, which will, in turn, provide you with valuable feedback on how to progress forward.

When your target audience feels heard, they are more likely to stay engaged, allowing you to build a connection and, ultimately, more business. You may have instances where your listening ear allows your clients to empty themselves of grievances that may not even have anything to do with you or your business! I've been on the receiving end of many such conversations. Through it all, I've come to learn that by simply listening and mirroring, especially in times of conflict, you can effectively build connection and trust, which is extremely helpful in resolving conflicts, which has the potential to positively affect your bottom line.

THE SECOND STAGE, **VALIDATION**, ENCOURAGES THE RECEIVER OF A MESsage to validate the sender's point of view. This isn't the same as agreement! Validation simply communicates the receiver's understanding of the sender's perspective.

Validation is extremely crucial to effective communication in business. If the innate need to feel heard is left unmet, it can threaten to stymie your entire effort to effectively address conflict and build a connection with your target audience.

Dr. Hendrix believes validation is vital to building a connection. It's not always the simplest of tasks for the receiver, especially when you feel slighted or "in the right." However, if you draw from your emotional intelligence and recognize what you stand to gain from this simple strategy—increased productivity in your teams, a positive work environment, more effective working relationships, opportunities for growth, increased business, and so on—you'll gain the strength to implement the strategy of validation on a consistent basis, and can then watch the nature of your conflicts shift positively right before your eyes.

LASTLY, PRACTICE **EMPATHY** AND COMMIT TO TAKING ACTION ON THE concerns that your sender communicates. If done with precision, empathizing with your audience will invariably distinguish you from other businesses in your market.

When you fail to communicate empathy to your target market, your business can take a hit instantly. Unfortunately, too many businesses miss the mark in communicating empathy, ranging from appearing insensitive in their advertising to dismissive of the needs of their workforce. However, there are companies that are getting it right,[11] and they demonstrate how communicating empathy can set you apart from the rest:

- When an **Airbnb** customer claimed he was being denied a stay with a host based on the color of his skin, the company responded immediately with a zero-tolerance policy on racial discrimination. The policy states that all Airbnb patrons are to "treat all fellow members of [the Airbnb] community, regardless of race, religion, national origin, disability, sex, gender identity, sexual orientation or age, with respect, and without judgment or bias." At the time of writing, the company is implementing this policy by comping the stay of *any* Airbnb user who feels they are being discriminated against, either in another Airbnb location or a hotel.

- In addition to donating over half a million dollars' worth of shoes to frontline healthcare workers during the COVID-19 pandemic, sustainable shoe and clothing company **Allbirds** took a step further by creating a culture of empathy among their own customer base. The shoe company's "We're Better Together" program allowed its consumers to donate sixty dollars toward a new pair of shoes for a healthcare worker in need.

- With an understanding of the increasing number of dual-income households, multibillion-dollar streaming entertainment service company **Netflix** provides paid parental leave to both mothers and fathers on their payroll. Salaried employees at Netflix can take up to twelve months off after the birth or adoption of a child. The company even shares first-hand employee experiences about their parental leave policy on their jobs page.

From the consultant that offers you sporadic services to the client that blesses you with repeat business, everyone is worthy of your empathy, validation of their point of view, and willingness to mirror their concerns when communicated. The more you place a human face on your business interactions and communications, the more adept you'll become at fostering connection, trust, and loyalty with your target audience.

"The art of communication is the language of leadership."
—James Humes

In his book, *Don't Drop the Mic*, New York Times bestselling author, world-renowned minister, filmmaker, and philanthropist T.D. Jakes writes, "Many have been the pallbearers of their dreams simply because they didn't understand that enhancing their communication skills could be the conduit to reaching those dreams. The ability to speak can aid in helping people, serving the disenfranchised, increasing sales, reaching the masses, stopping wars, and gaining untold, boundless advancement, simply by commanding and channeling the constructive, creative force of language. The more adept we become at using all available resources to convey our message, the greater our impact."[12] Well said!

ATTAINING SUSTAINABLE SUCCESS FOR YOUR BUSINESS WILL REQUIRE EF- fective communication in all four quadrants. Your inner and outer work will make it easier for you to do so with confidence and conviction. Weaving all the strategies of your inner and outer work (now including the components of effective communication) through all your business interactions provides you a conduit through which you can build a strong foundation for your business, able to weather the storms and all of the iterations of change you will inevitably encounter on your journey to the lemonade of your success.

So, as you prepare for an important meeting, draft an email to a vendor, develop your marketing materials, address conflicts within your team, or engage in any internal or external business communication, remember your inner and outer work. Keep your "why" and your vision in the forefront of your mind. Tell yourself the truth about your communication shortcomings, acknowledge your weaknesses, and humbly invest in your skill development in this pivotal area. Through my consulting practice, I assist entrepreneurs and business owners in the development of their business communication skills, which can save them time and money from cleaning up unnecessary mistakes, all the while helping them build a solid foundation for sustainable success.

Forgive yourself and anyone who may have wronged you, and never use your communications as an opportunity to vent or exact revenge. Draw from your inner fight and stay focused and intentional about implementing components of effective communication, even in conflict. Demonstrate balance in all four components of communication and also be balanced in your approach to situations in your business. For example, be firm and direct in your communications when warranted while extending compassion and understanding as needed. Be patient with your growth and development; missteps will happen, and all of us are on our own journeys toward complete communication proficiency. Give back at every turn; communicate appreciation to your team and vendors for a job well done, and be sure to communicate thanks to your clients for patronizing your business. Incorporate your CSR initiatives into your communications as appropriate and prepare for and believe in your success! Effective communication, along with the other strategies of your inner and outer work, will get you there.

REGARDLESS OF HOW STELLAR YOUR PRODUCT IS, HOW AMAZING YOUR team is, how competent you are, or how much funding you've acquired, you'll invariably compromise your venture if you don't communicate effectively. As you press forward with consistency and intentionality in the completion of your inner and outer work, I believe, by God's grace, you're bound to accomplish your goal of growing a sustainably successful, impactful business.

FOR DEEPER REFLECTION...

Strategy #15: Communicate Effectively at Every Turn

1. Think of past business interactions that did not progress well or according to plan. Was ineffective communication a contributing factor?
   a. What could you have done differently?

   b. What components of this chapter can you implement to help you navigate the same type of situation more effectively in the future?

2. From your market analysis, what is the area or areas of your target market's pain? List them.
   a. Is your product or service offering adequately addressing this pain/is there a tangible demand for what you are offering?

   b. How do you know?

3. Are you comfortable with public speaking?
   a. What can you do to strengthen your public speaking skills?

4. List three things your target audience, internal with your team or external in your market, have communicated to you in the last fiscal year through direct or indirect feedback (reviews, client and/or team conversations, social media comments, impact on your bottom line, etc.)?
   a. What action(s) have you taken in your business based on what you've learned from their feedback?

5. What has your Higher Power communicated to you during the life of your business?
   a. How have you taken action based on what you heard?

6. What are some ways you can listen more effectively going forward in your business?

7. From the chapter, what are the seven ways you can improve on your non-verbal communication skills?
    a. Think of three others you can implement while communicating in your business. List them.

LEMONADE CHALLENGES

#1: Write down the seven Cs of effective communication and place them where you can readily see them in your workspace. Before connecting with your clients, team, vendors, professional advisors, and all others you interact with during your workday over the next 12 weeks, make it a point to glance at the list. At the end of each week, journal how you see yourself progressing in your ability to communicate effectively. Repeat this practice of journaling until the end of your next quarter. View all the entries and celebrate your progress with a friend and your professional advisor(s).

#2: The next time you face a conflict situation in your business, and until the end of your next quarter, add the three advanced tools of mirroring, validation, and empathy to your strategy of balancing all four quadrants of effective communication. Journal how doing so impacted your ability to resolve the conflict and move you toward the last stage, forgiveness. Review your journal entries regularly and decide on the areas where you did well during the interactions, and areas where you need to improve to strengthen your ability to effectively communicate in conflicts going forward. Discuss your findings with your professional advisor.

PART THREE

You Worked It!

16

IT'S ALL GOOD,
EVEN WHEN IT ISN'T

*"All things work together for good to those who love God,
and are called according to His purpose."[1]*

—ROMANS 8:28

ART, SOUR, BITTER, EVEN STINGING—WHEN EATEN ALONE, LEMONS are unpalatable for most. At their worst, our greatest challenges are paralyzing but, with a change in perspective, the lemon experiences of our lives can be the very keys that open the door to our greatest blessings.

When you surrender yourself and your entrepreneurial journey to your Higher Power in faith, all the lemon experiences of your life—the painful, the unfair, the heartbreaking, and the debilitating—will ultimately work out for the best in the end. Your purpose-driven entrepreneurial journey toward success will be arduous and will likely appear divergent from the path traveled by other entrepreneurs. However, the impact of your good work on the world will render it worth all the challenges, in the end refreshing you with a sense of accomplishment and peace that no amount of money can buy.

Before reading this book, you may have felt stagnant. Perhaps you felt like one of Ralph Waldo Emerson's "mass of men" that are living lives of quiet desperation. Maybe you tried to garner success in the past using a traditional, academic "how-to-start-a successful-business" approach, but none of your efforts yielded the results you anticipated. Perhaps working a "nine-to-five" was unfulfilling or left you feeling burned out, and you had a nagging suspicion that you were on the wrong track, or needed to course-correct your current one. If you're like me, you may have spent many a night sick with frustration, fear, doubt, and despair—directionless, knowing there had to be more to life than what you've been experiencing. There is hope! I encourage you to *make the choice* to intentionally implement your inner and outer work strategies consistently, with the belief that if you've discerned your purpose accurately from Chapter 2, you will eventually experience the lemonade of your success!

BUT IT'S JUST NOT GOOD RIGHT NOW!

You may be in the throes of a challenging season in your business now, and despite implementing the principles of your inner and outer work, you still haven't experienced your breakthrough.

I can completely relate!

It took *years* of applying core strategies of my inner and outer work consistently before I experienced my breakthrough. But after I began to systematically and consistently apply principles of both my inner and outer work to every aspect of my life, in time, I eventually experienced combustible success.

Rome wasn't built in a day, and neither will you or your successful business. It will take time, along with consistent and intentional effort, before you'll experience combustible, sustainable success. Building your "business house" effectively—so it can have maximum impact, stand the test of time, and release to you all the benefits that come with living your purpose—is not a quick or easy process, despite how it may seem in the lives of other successful people.

In order to build a solid foundation for your business house, you'll need to have a clear and detailed vision of what you want your house to look like in the end, with a design that's drafted according to regulations or specifications for the particular type of house you're building. You'll need to have completed robust market research allowing you to build effectively and determine the most effective way to execute your vision, so you can enjoy the benefits you desire from your home. Building your business house effectively will require a continual investment of your time, effort, and resources and will also require you to make a significant amount of sacrifices. And in many cases, building the house of your dreams in the best manner will end up taking longer than you anticipated, and will draw more from you than expected so you'll need to practice active patience to make it through.

You'll need to hire the right contractors that are qualified for your type of project, and that will take proper vetting. Sometimes you'll get it wrong; those you've hired may break your heart and wreak havoc on you or your project, but you'll have to make the decision to let them go in the best interest of the dream home you're building. Building your house the best it can be will be worth the sacrifice of letting them go in order to find someone else more suitable for the job.

You'll have to believe in your project, and have faith that you'll make it through, even when everyone else on your team may become doubtful, and you'll need to be able to communicate hope, and an understanding of your vision with crystal-clear clarity, to ensure the vision you have in your mind and have researched and sacrificed for is executed with excellence. It will become important that you hire a qualified and experienced construction project manager on your team that has built a successful purpose-driven "business house" themselves before. Since they have direct experience with your type of project, they're particularly qualified to oversee the overall construction of your business house. They can steer you away from pitfalls, save you time, money, and effort, and show you how to pivot and progress forward effectively to execute your dream in the best manner possible.

In essence, implementing the aspects of your inner and outer work together will help you create a successful business with a solid foundation. And it is precisely the most challenging life experiences, past or present, that possess the seeds within them to propel you to purpose-driven success.

THE THINGS IN LIFE THAT PUT US IN THE POSITION TO HAVE THE GREATest impact that, in the end, bless us with abundant joy, peace, fulfillment, and success all come at a price. Quick and easy success is fleeting and unsustainable. Building a solid foundation for your business takes time, and includes the consistent and intentional implementation of the strategies of your inner and outer work, especially during the moments when it just doesn't seem like things will ever come together.

There are seasons during your business journey that will leave you feeling hopeless and wanting to give up. You may feel that it's taking too long to turn the corner to sustained profitability, and you're doubtful that you have what it takes to usher your business to success. ***Know this***: The sheer act of your determination to read this book and complete the *For Deeper Reflections* and the *Lemonade Challenges*, your consistent willingness and commitment to work on you (inner work) and build your business house effectively (outer work) while surrendering it all to your Higher Power (spiritual anchoring), will inevitably pay off in the end.

So, don't give up! The presence or absence of results in the early stages of your venture will not determine its viability in the end. Again, it was *years* before my efforts yielded success, and others who have achieved great feats in business have had to endure incredibly challenging experiences and lengthy seasons of waiting before accomplishing their goals too!

Remember Thomas Edison made *ten thousand attempts* before achieving success with his light-bulb invention, which surely must have been frustrating and filled with days of feeling like a failure and wanting to give up. Colonel Sanders of Kentucky Fried Chicken fame would likely be able to relate as well, after suffering a series of major career defeats, until finally selling his business to a group of investors at seventy-three years old. It's natural to feel like challenging seasons and negative conditions in your business will never change while you're diligently and consistently doing your part to execute your business operations effectively. For most of us, patience does not come naturally, especially when we're continually sacrificing so much for so long without seeing results. In these instances, it really is all good, though, even when it isn't in your business, and nature provides a powerful example of this concept that can give you hope, and encourage you to keep pressing forward to success.

NATURE WEIGHS IN

A poignant example from nature beautifully illustrates the point that it's all good, even when it isn't. Consider that within the earth lies a layer separating our habitable environment from its molten core, an area known as the mantle, the region where diamonds extracted from the earth are made. Carbon, the fourth most abundant element in the universe[2] on its face, ***appears insignificant and of little value***. However, when carbon situated in the mantle is exposed to extreme heat (> 2000°F/1093°C) and pressure exceeding 725,000 lbs. per square inch[3] over time, the glamorous symbol of opulence we enjoy as the diamond is revealed.

If extreme pressure, heat and time are necessary to turn carbon, a common resource, into a valuable commodity, you too will likely need to endure seasons of wait and pressure—internal and external—to achieve a state of sustained profitability for your business as well. Think of yourself and your venture as a diamond in the making! Diligently complete the components of your inner and outer work, and your transformation will eventually come, even if right now, it doesn't *feel* as though it will.

FROM NATURE'S DIAMOND EXAMPLE, IT'S ALSO IMPORTANT TO NOTE THAT diamonds developed in the earth are only revealed *after eruption* through "deep source volcanoes" that are three times as deep as typical volcanoes.[2] High levels of magnesium and carbon dioxide force the magma from these volcanoes to the surface, which results in a violent eruption. Diamonds included in the magma are typically elevated to the surface through an associated substance called kimberlite, through which they can be readily mined. So, we see here that nature once again provides a powerful perspective on one of our key concepts: that right now, you have deep within you the raw materials of what it takes to propel you to success—your purpose, which was generated from your lemon experiences and your inherent skills. Even before carbon completes the process to become a diamond, it's all good simply as the piece of carbon because *it's transforming,* and it's situated in the right place in the earth's core for development. It simply needs external pressure, heat, and time to develop, then with some help (a volcano) to propel or erupt it to the surface, its greatness is revealed!

So, before carbon situated within the earth's core actually becomes a diamond, it's still all good as carbon! You, too, are in the process of transformation. The "heat" of life or your lemon experiences are a component of the process that will reveal your ultimate greatness and impact on the world. Exercising patience amidst the pressure of the entrepreneurial journey, and the heat of your challenges is uncomfortable for sure, but they're all a required aspect of the journey to the beauty of your transformation.

RIGHT NOW, EVERYTHING IN YOUR LIFE AND BUSINESS REALLY IS ALL GOOD, even if it isn't because you're in the process of transformation to get you to your goal of living your purpose, and achieving success that leads to peace through it. Even when it doesn't *feel* as though your preparation will ever yield fruit, trust that everything will be okay; you are in transition and in the process of *becoming* successful from your purpose-driven venture. Know that when you build your venture with a strong foundation in the direction of your purpose, through the completion of your inner and outer work with spiritual anchoring to your Higher Power, your results will manifest eventually.

"Starting out to make money is the greatest mistake in life.
Do what you feel you have a flair for doing,
and if you are good enough at it, the money will come."

—Greer Garson

Nothing you've experienced will be wasted when you are on your purpose-driven journey. As I look back on my life, every job, every degree, and every lemon experience has prepared me to effectively operate in the direction of the fullness of my life's purpose now. Once I made the decision to trust and surrender my venture to God and intentionally complete my inner and outer work, all things in my life and business were eventually made beautiful in God's time.[4] I firmly believe that consistently progressing through the components of your inner and outer work will eventually yield the fruits of your efforts too. Enjoy them all! You've earned the harvest.

MY UNCONVENTIONAL JOURNEY IN BUSINESS WAS LITTERED WITH EXPERI-ences you won't learn in a business class. I've lived these truths, made many sacrifices and mistakes in discovering them, and have witnessed the transformation of my consulting clients as they've applied them. I've endured multiple lemon experiences from cancer, disappointments, heartbreak, debt, depression, and a debilitating car accident. After surviving it all intact, and by applying principles of my inner and outer work along with spiritual anchoring, I was able to transform from a terrified, insecure registered nurse at the beginning of my entrepreneurial journey to a successful, impactful, purpose-driven entrepreneur. Ultimately, my personal transformation has been the greatest success of all. Your transformation will render all the obstacles endured along your way obsolete, yet necessary to bring you to the place where you can now operate your purpose-driven venture authentically, effectively, and eventually, successfully.

As you progress through life, continually squeeze your life lemons dry and recognize the power in these experiences to propel you to success that leads to peace. As you progress through your entrepreneurial journey to success, fill your glass and share your offering with the world! Your batch of lemonade is unique to you and your purpose, and the world needs a sip of your specific "good work." I've poured out my lemonade batch to you, and in the words of Jesus in Luke 10:37, go and do likewise.

FOR DEEPER REFLECTION...

Strategy #16: Recognize That Even Now, It's All Good!

1. List one thing in your **personal** life that is currently a source of stress for you.
    a. With the components of this chapter in mind, how can you look at that situation from a different perspective going forward?

2. List one aspect of your **business** that is currently a source of stress for you.
    a. With the components of this chapter in mind, how can you look at it from a different perspective going forward?

3. Since reading this book and applying the principles, what seven aspects of your life and/or business have changed? List them.

4. Which goals from your goals list have you accomplished since starting this book? List them.
    a. Now that you've arrived at the last chapter of the book, how has your perspective changed on the likelihood of achieving the rest of your goals?

LEMONADE CHALLENGE

#1: Write down one good thing about your life and one good thing about your business every morning for one month. It can be an aspect of your life and business from the "thank you" list you created for the Lemonade Challenge in Chapter 13. Each morning, write down one new item for both categories (personal and professional life) and review it again before bed. At the end of the thirty days, reflect on your new perspective on your life and business, and discuss your findings with your professional advisor(s).

17

CELEBRATE!

"The more you praise and celebrate your life, the more there is in life to celebrate."

—OPRAH

CONGRATULATIONS! RAISE YOUR GLASS OF LEMONADE, DANCE, RELISH in your journey of transformation, acknowledge your achievements thus far, and celebrate!

You've made it; whether your goal of achieving purpose-driven, impactful, sustainable success has been realized yet or not, you're already successful! The process of becoming *is* the success; it allows for the eventual manifestation of your goals and will determine your ability to sustain a state of sustained profitability and continue in the growth of your business for the long haul.

The material things that can accompany success—financial freedom, accolades, and influence—are simply by-products of what can be achieved through *who you become* in the process of attaining it. This is precisely why people can start a venture from the ground up, attain success, lose it all, pick themselves up, start again, and achieve even higher heights than before. During the formative years of your entrepreneurial journey, the person you become will determine your ability to navigate peaks and valleys effectively. The realization that success is a journey rather than a destination will propel you to celebrate your successes along the way, helping to catapult you to the season when your goals will eventually manifest.

THE DANGER OF DWELLING

There are two primary methods by which we retain information and remember memories: by repetition or impact. Since our failures or challenging life experiences are, in many cases, significantly impactful, we tend to remember them more readily than our successes. This poses a sizable challenge when we aspire toward a set of goals.

The experiences at the forefront of our minds expand. Meaning that the consuming thoughts that circulate in our minds consistently, or that are imprinted there, enlarge, whether positive or negative. If you're constantly thinking about how your business is never going to make it, or other negative thoughts concerning you or your business, eventually those thoughts, having sunk deep into your subconscious, will impact the way you show up in your business. If, however, your perspective is one of hope, faith, belief in yourself, your purpose, and your Higher Power—even in the midst of challenging circumstances—your positive mindset will expand, placing yourself in a better position to win! The narrative curated in our subconscious directly affects our ability to attain success and, if we're not careful, our natural propensity to dwell on our mistakes and failures will weigh us down, slow our progress, and stymie our success.

In the early years of building my business, I made the mistake of focusing on one specific end goal, despite having several I was striving to accomplish. I erroneously defined my ultimate success as my ability to achieve this one particular goal, and until I achieved it, I discounted all my other accomplishments. This fueled my constant state of frustration with my progress, which made it difficult for me to maintain a positive state of mind. Changing my perspective one day ended up freeing me to fully believe in the inevitability of my comprehensive success story, trust the process of its manifestation in my life, and recognize the power in celebrating successes along the way.

A PRACTICAL EXAMPLE

While cleaning out my wallet one day, I stumbled across one of my business cards. On it, I had written my breakthrough goal, as encouraged by the book, *The Success Principles*[1]. At this point, I was several years into my business and was in the midst of yet another challenging season. But, after reading the back of the business card, I became transfixed at what I had written on it in the early years of my business, which equipped me with another source of fuel to help propel me to experience combustible success.

This breakthrough goal—a goal I believed when starting my business would mark my arrival—I had already accomplished three years prior!

I was paralyzed with shock. When I regained my composure, I sat and reflected on the experience. I learned a key lesson that day: *revisit your goals list often and celebrate the successes you're achieving along the way!* Doing so will help you find confidence and courage, which are necessary for you to build momentum. *When* you achieve your goals and take the time to celebrate yourself for a job well done, this simple acknowledgment helps you to believe that more success and the accomplishment of bigger goals is possible as well!

All of your successes—large and small—warrant a personal pat on the back. One of the exercises I guide my consulting clients through is a systematic recognition of their successes at the end of each week. Watching their productivity transform from week to week through completing the aspects of their inner and outer work, which includes the simple act of acknowledging their *own* successes, is so gratifying and empowering for both of us to hear! Articulating your progress and celebrating your successes is a powerful tool that, over time, will strengthen your self-esteem, impact your willingness to take more risks, and reveal that you are, indeed, making strides toward accomplishing your business goals.

So celebrate your transformation! Celebrate the people that help you along the way. Celebrate your hard work and sacrifices that have resulted in your accomplishments daily, monthly, and quarterly. Even though it may not look or feel like it, you *are* making progress!

Remember: You are your greatest asset. Your personal investment in yourself is paramount. You've reached the end of this book, and that alone is a testament to your commitment to your outer work, as discussed in Chapter 12! Continue the process of pouring into yourself and your development, honor and remember the sacrifices you've made, look back at the items in your comeback closet, and celebrate your hard work. Your personal transformation and your commitment to living your life's purpose make you successful; a diamond in the rough. So regardless of the status of your "carbon state" right now, celebrate!

YOU'VE WORKED HARD, NOW PLAY HARD!

Mother Teresa was famously quoted as saying, "There is more hunger for love and appreciation in this world than for bread."[2] The ideal work environment is one where leaders value their employees' contributions, appreciate them, and implement strategies to acknowledge their accomplishments.

The importance lies not in the complexity of the effort to reward or "play" but rather in the leader's intention to communicate appreciation to their teams in a thought-driven, consistent manner. When you develop a culture of celebration within your organization, it becomes attractive to your team, which can become a key recruiting tool to draw others.

We're all looking for acknowledgment in one form or another. When we're acknowledged for our actions, we are more likely to repeat those actions. When you and your team work hard and accomplish your objectives, balance dictates that playing hard is also in order! As your budget allows, take your team on a fun team-building activity, or be intentional about appreciating them in another thought-driven manner. And be sure to treat yourself too! Celebrate your successes along the way, and you'll have more reasons to celebrate as you continue forward.

DON'T CRY OVER SPILLED MILK

Things will go wrong. Your rise to success may take longer than expected. You will make mistakes, and some of those mistakes will likely cost you money. These are the realities of the entrepreneurial journey, and the more you're prepared for it, the easier it will be to navigate these experiences.

During my early years in business, I spent an inordinate amount of time embroiled in the paradoxical state of bemoaning the slow speed of my rise to success while still believing in the blessings I knew I was uniquely prepared and positioned to receive. The perspective gained from your lemon experience(s), your talents, and the continual progression through your inner and outer work will uniquely position you to speak to your target audience from a place of authenticity, which is devoid in many businesses today. When you hear the "nos," make mistakes, or become discouraged, revisit your inner and outer work and navigate your challenging seasons by putting your preparation into practice. The storms will invariably come, but don't allow yourself to be rattled.

Play in the spilled milk that your challenges create!

Learn from them, rise from them, and move forward. The reality is that there are more successes to celebrate than spilled milk to clean up. But since we are hardwired to focus on our mistakes, it's important that we become intentional about consistently acknowledging the positives.

CHANCES ARE YOU PICKED UP THIS BOOK FOR A NEW PERSPECTIVE ON HOW to attain success in business. You've tried to apply conventional business wisdom, and it hasn't yielded the results you anticipated. You may be feeling overwhelmed and as though there's no way anything positive can come of all your investments of time, energy, money, or belief at this point. Know that almost anyone can be taught how to run a business; the vast number of graduates from business schools worldwide each year are a testament to this.

But one of the main differences between running *a* business and running a sustainably profitable, purpose-driven, impactful business is *the leader*, and who you are as the leader of your organization is of far greater importance than the technical knowledge you bring to the role.

As an entrepreneur or business owner operating from a position of wholeness and healing within yourself, you are freer to extend the necessary energy needed to bring your best self to your business, having squeezed dry all the lemon experiences you've endured along your way. Who you are, right now, really is enough!

I LEAVE YOU WITH THIS, MY LIFE MOTTO: *GO BOLDLY, DARE GREATLY, LOVE passionately, and live intentionally!* Go forward with gusto, courage, passion, and intentionality as you squeeze your challenging life experiences to create your successful business! Live thankfully, live intentionally, and strive to live your life in and on purpose. And use the strategies in this book while celebrating yourself and your successes along the way.

I hope to meet you at a conference, corporate event, or one of my speaking engagements one day and hear how you achieved success through the completion of your inner and outer work as you spiritually anchored it all to your Higher Power. And through your personal and professional transformation and success, you'll undoubtedly empower others to step out in the direction of their life's purpose and refresh their corner of the world as well.

"If your actions create a legacy that inspires others to dream more, learn more, do more and become more, then you are an excellent leader."
—Dolly Parton

A legacy that inspires others to be their best is the epitome of your success. Your legacy—the ultimate measure of your impact—is the residue you leave on the world after you've touched it with your good work of service. Every person that watches your journey that will now muster up the courage and strength to believe they, too, can heal from their lemon experiences, gain an understanding of their life's purpose, and turn it into a successful business will all become a part of your legacy. Each person you meaningfully touch through your business, each person you serve through your good work of service, each brand ambassador you create, each and every person you positively impact during your purpose-driven business journey has the potential to result in the exponential and compounding impact that can reach places you cannot imagine possible.

And that is the essence of true leadership, the ultimate point of your purpose-driven venture and your entire transformation journey. You are a conduit through which a flow of positive, authentic influence can create change in the world. And that is why I encourage you to squeeze your challenging life experiences and create your successful business! Beyond the material accoutrements of success, beyond the sense of accomplishment, even beyond the sense of fulfillment and peace that accompanies living the fullness of your life's purpose—there is no other component of success greater than your impact, and even now, you're placing your imprint on your corner of the world, so celebrate! Know that your continual progression through your inner work and outer work while spiritually anchoring the entire process in faith will help you build a solid foundation for your business, creating a compounding impact in your sphere of influence, and beyond.

So celebrate! Continue to solve the problems of your target market at a profit from the perspective of your purpose and drink from the lemonade of your success! Whether your success has fully manifested yet or not, it already exists in the large scheme of things, so live, give thanks in advance, and celebrate! Know that the impact of your good work of service on the world will render everything you've endured to this point worth it all in the end.

Much love and blessings, and know I'm rooting for your success!

Help Me
SPREAD THE WORD!

Are you ready to change lives?

I'm on a mission to encourage, empower, and equip an army of entrepreneurs and business owners. With the right tools, we can positively impact the world through our sustainably successful, purpose-driven businesses. And you can help! If *Lemonade!* has helped you, tell your friends, coworkers, family members, and leaders within your sphere of influence. Let's create change in the business landscape together!

melanemullings.com

ACKNOWLEDGMENTS

THE BIBLE TELLS US THAT IN EVERYTHING WE ARE TO GIVE THANKS, for this is the will of God for us. My entire journey from surviving leukemia to the release of this book would not have been possible without the many people who invested an inordinate amount of their time, talents, resources, and/or prayers to support me. I love and appreciate you all, and thank God for this public opportunity to 'give my flowers away' to those of you who are still alive to receive them.

First, to my late university professor, Dr. Bill Van Scheik, who was the first (in an academic setting) to really see me, value me, and invest in me. To your surviving loved ones: Dr. Van Scheik's impact on my life and career has been profound. May you know how much he was valued and appreciated.

I extend my deepest gratitude and thanks to my success team: Susan Cassidy, Derek Costea, Ken Leigh-Smith, Glen Stanley-Turner, Arnold Pena, Kester DaCosta, Raj Auluck, Tony Johnson & Kevan Mickkelsen, Steve Demy, Al Graca, Robert Reid, Ben Berhe, Anthony Black, Mervis Higgins, Basil Saunders, Myrtle Melnik, Craig Gillespie, Christina Denysek, Geoff Zaparinuk, Robyn Smith, Catarina Oey, Gerald Chipeur, Peter Williamson, Mario Dickerson, Lisa Richter, Terry Zimaro & Nadine Weller, Erin Garneau, Kaylene Brueckman, Steve Fylypchuk, Julia Herscovitch, Shana Cain, Svetlana Ratnikova, Karolina Turek, Stan Jensen and Maggie McLaughlin. Thank you so much for the integral part you played in my arrival to this point.

Many, many thanks to Rhett Power, Pastor Balvin Braham, Christian Hosoi, and Danette Kubanda for offering your quotes in support of this book. And to Janice Bryant-Howroyd and Shannon Bowen-Smed: my heart overflows with thanks for not only your contribution to this book, but for the indelible impact you've had on my life and business. I will forever be grateful.

Special thanks to Jack Canfield, whose influence on my life, personally and professionally has been so all-encompassing since I read *The Success Principles* in 2008. Words cannot adequately express my sincere thanks for your willingness to bless my book with your Foreword, and for all the advice, feedback and encouragement you extended to me at key points during this project. I appreciate you more than you could ever know.

MANY THANKS TO EVERYONE THAT MADE THIS ENTIRE BOOK PROJECT POSsible. From my team of beta readers, designers, and illustrators, to my distribution specialist, image consultant, media coaches, and all around cheerleaders; this book, and all the marketing and distribution efforts that have been associated with it, is a reflection of your feedback, support and input. Thank you BookHive, Tanya & Chris Stevenson, Alyse DaCosta, Tracey Myers, Kingston Kodan, Romando Carey, Rochelle-Ann Thomas, Janice Seto, ayasuarjaya, ijlal101, oneshoterick, PickFu, and the customer service team at 99designs. Thank you also to Cristina Smith for introducing me to Constellation Book Services, through whom I connected with my "lifesaver" Maggie McLaughlin. My heartfelt thanks to each of you for all the effort and time you extended on my behalf.

To my editor Olivia Peluso, proofreader Ana Joldes, cover designer Miroslav Jolic, and interior designer Olivier Darbonville—thank you for going above and beyond for me! All of you are masters at your craft, and I'm so thankful to have had the opportunity to benefit from your expertise on this project.

To the entire team at Bradley Communications Corp., especially Joe McAllister, Laura Harrison, Geoffrey Berwind, Mary Giuseffe, and Danette Kubanda; your placement in my life, and the timing, was undoubtedly divine. Thank you for challenging me to grow as an author and for encouraging me to own my story, all the while equipping me with actionable strategies to effectively share it with confidence, authenticity, and joy.

And to Steve Harrison: you are one of the most powerful examples of a humble, passionate, level 5 leader I've known. Your commitment to excellence is palpable! Thank you for allowing God to use you and your business, Bradley Communications, in such a mighty way in my life, and for being such a great example of a Christian in business. I'll never forget your prayer for me, and for your willingness to champion my cause when I needed help. I pray that God will continue to richly bless you and enlargen your territory of influence beyond your wildest imaginings.

To those who have occupied various seats on my success plane over the years—Crystal, Joanne, Rommel, Tanya, Howard, Elliot, Uncle Al, Zebad, Hannan, Nancy, Tehz, Adeola, Veda, Stevie B, Treslyn, Fiona, Stacey, Dana, Gidget, Ken, Pria, Rachael, Heidi, Chris, Kelly, Mitch, Dianna, Naima, Tommy, Edwin, Zoran, Kaley, Camille, Amanda, Leisa, Griffin, Sis. Carolene, Evelyn & Joe, Sis. Horrell, Muli, Symone, Verna, Mary & David, Uncle Headley & Aunt Cynthia, Aunt June, Auntie Min, Aunt Mavis, cousin Michelle & Natasha, and Zee & Zolani—thank you for helping me enjoy the essence and beauty of life! Each of you is a thread weaved into the fabric of who I've become, and I am eternally grateful for your placement in my life.

And a special thank you to Paulette Anilus. You've worn many hats in my life beyond RN mentor, but it was the two pieces of life-changing advice you shared with me after I graduated with my nursing degree that impacted my life and career the most. Thank you for your friendship and sincere care for my parents and I. You are deeply loved and appreciated by all of us!

Thank you to all those who propelled me forward during some of the darkest days of my first entrepreneurial journey: Bruce McFarlane, Chiaka McNaughton, Sade Abiola, Pastor John Adams, David Chimwaso, and Pastor Terrence Horrell. Whether you knew it or not, your placement in my life was purposeful, and provided me more evidence of God's care and concern for me when I needed it most. I will forever be grateful for each of you.

And to my therapist, Patrick. Thank you for your timely, wise guidance, and for listening to my musings—reasonable and unreasonable—with kindness, patience and compassion. You are definitely a cut above the rest, and I acknowledge and appreciate the difference you've made in my life.

To my past and present prayer warriors: Grandma, Sis. Grant, Bro. & Sis. Tolloch, Sis. McNeish, Sis. Barbara, Desiree, Anett, and Lisso—thank you for the many times you petitioned the Throne of Grace on my behalf. You are living proof that when we humbly kneel before God, we can stand up to anyone and triumph over anything!

To my R.O.D. 'sistas': Nadia and Tanya. What can I say? Over the years we've known each other, you've seen me at my best and my worst. Thank you for loving me, laughing with me and sticking with me through it all. I love you and appreciate you.

A special thank you to who I affectionately refer to as "Ms. Multimillionaire", Tacita Lewars. Thank you for introducing me to the book, *The Success Principles*, and for being my partner in the trenches during the early days of my entrepreneurial journey. Our prayer sessions, weekly book club meetings, "success lunches", "walk as if" experiences, and the many conferences and networking events we attended together those first few years were pivotal to my personal and professional growth as an entrepreneur. I'm at a loss for words to adequately express my love and appreciation for you. May the blessings of God overtake you in every area of your life, and may He continue to use you in a mighty way to bless others.

And thank you to Mereta Bailey for being a living example, within my cultural community, of the power of humility, patience, a drive toward excellence, radical faith, and kindness. Thank you for demonstrating that the principles outlined in this book transcend age, culture or any other constraints we tend to place on success.

To my besties, Teisha and Lesley: Thank you for the hours and hours you extended your loving and supportive listening ears to me, for always championing my causes, and for rejoicing with me on my hilltops and grieving with me in the valleys. You both are my 'Jonathan and Nathan'! Thank you for always going above and beyond for me, and for being a shining example of what it means to be a friend.

To my sisters: Marie Mullings, Marian (Andrea) Dickerson and Sharon Marglin. From childhood, each of you in your own way inspired and equipped me to live the fullness of my life's purpose. Your presence in my life gifted me with the confidence to believe that no matter what, I would always have love and support to fall back on. My success has your fingerprints all over it! Thank you for filling my life to this day with such amazing memories! I love and appreciate you all with the same childlike awe I had when we were kids, and am so blessed to call you my big sisters!

To my Pops, Milton Mullings: Thank you for your love and care for our family and for your example of humility, altruistic concern for others, work ethic, and a drive toward excellence. Thank you also for helping me understand the power of humor and it's relationship to enjoying a fulfilling life! For all the insightful talks, for giving in to my many reasonable and unreasonable requests, and for teaching me the importance of knowing and living Biblical principles, thank you, and know I love you and appreciate you "nuff nuff"!

And to my Mom, Fay Mullings: Far beyond all the many gestures of love and concern you continually extend to me, it's been the quiet moments of unshakeable faith, strength and support I witnessed from you that have impacted me so profoundly. When you sat silent with me on the floor of my bedroom while I inconsolably cried after my first breakup, when you bathed my emaciated body in the hospital night after night when I was at my lowest during my battle with leukemia while singing, 'What A Friend We Have in Jesus', to your driving to my condo in blizzard, winter weather to stay and comfort me during one of the lowest points of my first entrepreneurial journey—these experiences and so much more fill my heart with overflowing love and appreciation for you! Thank you for always being present, for believing in me when I didn't believe in myself, and for being the most powerful example in my life of drive, discipline and focus while working toward the accomplishment of a goal.

And above all, to my Papa, my Father in Heaven: Thank you teaching me what faith looks like, for remembering me, and for saving me from all my challenging life experiences. Thank you for your comforting, strengthening, merciful, restorative, peaceful and propelling presence that continues to minister to me. Had you not rescued me during the many times I came close to sabotaging my arrival to this moment, I certainly would not have made it. I love and appreciate you beyond all others, and pray that my offering of this book is a blessing to many, and brings glory, honor and praise to your name.

AND TO ALL OF YOU READING THIS, I PRAY THAT YOU'LL BE BLESSED AND enriched with the abundance of God's storehouse, and may you be empowered to enjoy the lemonade of your success that flows from a life of purpose, love, faith, perseverance and peace.

NOTES

1. TELL YOURSELF THE TRUTH, QUICKLY

1. David Brown, "Every Entrepreneur Should Prioritize This Risk in 2018." Inc. Magazine, accessed November 9, 2020, https://www.inc.com/david-brown/32-percent-of-entrepreneurs-struggle-with-mental-health-prioritize-your-personal-health-in-2018.html

2. Selina Troesch, "Born In the Crucible of Recession." Risky Business, last modified August 27, 2020, https://medium.com/touchdownvc/born-in-the-crucible-of-recession-35babf23a550.

3. Stephen Mugo Weru, "10 Successful Businesses That Were Started During Economic Downturns." Benzinga, last modified May 4, 2020, https://www.benzinga.com/general/education/20/05/15944325/10-successful-businesses-that-were-started-during-economic-downturns.

4. Graham Isador, "12 Surprising Entrepreneur Statistics To Know In 2021." NorthOne, accessed October 14, 2021, https://www.northone.com/blog/small-business/entrepreneur-statistics

5. Neil Patel, "90% Of Startups Fail: Here's What You Need To Know About The 10%." Forbes Magazine, last modified January 16, 2015, https://www.forbes.com/sites/neilpatel/2015/01/16/90-of-startups-will-fail-heres-what-you-need-to-know-about-the-10/?sh=28543d736679

6. The Holy Bible, New Living Translation (Tyndale House Publishers: 2007), "Asa", 685.

2. TWO QUESTIONS THAT WILL CHANGE YOUR LIFE...AND BUSINESS

1. Graham Isador, "12 Surprising Entrepreneur Statistics To Know In 2021." NorthOne, accessed October 14, 2021, https://www.northone.com/blog/small-business/entrepreneur-statistics

2. "Rick Warren." Simon & Schuster, retrieved November 11, 2020, https://www.simonandschuster.com/authors/Rick-Warren/39904606

3. "The Henry D. Thoreau Mis-Quotation Page." The Walden Woods project, accessed November 11, 2020, https://www.walden.org/what-we-do/library/thoreau/mis-quotations/

4. Mallory Simon, "75,000 Americans At Risk Of Dying From Overdose Or Suicide Due To Coronavirus Despair, Group Warns." CNN Health, last modified May 8, 2020, https://www.cnn.com/2020/05/08/health/coronavirus-deaths-of-despair/index.html

5. Caroline Redmond, "11 Of History's Most Famous Suicides, From Artists To Politicians." ATI, last modified July 21, 2020, https://allthatsinteresting.com/famous-suicides

6. The Holy Bible, New King James Version (Nashville: Thomas Nelson Publishers, 1982), Ephesians 2:10.

7. "Albert Einstein quotes." Goodreads, accessed November 11, 2020, https://www.goodreads.com/quotes/4455-energy-cannot-be-created-or-destroyed-it-can-only-be

8. "Laws Of Thermodynamics." Accessed November 11, 2020, https://www2.estrellamountain.edu/faculty/farabee/biobk/biobookener1.html

9. Kenya Evelyn, "Amanda Gorman Books Top Bestselling Lists After Soul-stirring Inaugural Poem." The Guardian, last modified January 22, 2021 https://www.theguardian.com/us-news/2021/jan/21/amanda-gorman-star-rises-inaugural-poem

10. "The Hill We Climb." Penguin Random House, retrieved May 14, 2021 https://www.penguinrandomhouse.com/books/689867/the-hill-we-climb-by-amanda-gorman-foreword-by-oprah-winfrey/

11. Barack Obama (@BarackObama). Twitter post, January 20, 2021, https://twitter.com/BarackObama/status/1351995663475728386?ref_src=twsrc%5Etfw%7Ctwcamp%5Etweetembed%7Ctwterm%5E1351995663475728386%7Ctwgr%5E%7Ctwcon%5Es1_&ref_url=https%3A%2F%2Fwww.theguardian.com%2Fus-news%2F2021%2Fjan%2F21%2Famanda-gorman-star-rises-inaugural-poem

12. Marcus Buckingham and Donald O. Clifton, *Now Discover Your Strengths* (New York: The Free Press, 2001), 5.

13. "CNN Heroes." Wikipedia, last modified August 14, 2021 https://en.wikipedia.org/wiki/CNN_Heroes

14. Allie Torgan, "He Spent 15 Years In Prison For A Crime He Didn't Commit. Now he's on a mission to help others." CNN, last modified June 6, 2019, https://www.cnn.com/2019/06/06/us/cnnheroes-richard-miles-miles-of-freedom

15. "Former Bartender Turns Wine Into Water." CNN, last modified December 18, 2013, https://www.cnn.com/2013/12/06/world/cnnheroes-hendley-wine-to-water

16. "CNN Heroes: Millie Bobby Brown Honors Young Wonder Cavanaugh Bell." CNN, accessed May 3, 2021, https://www.cnn.com/videos/tv/2020/12/14/millie-bobby-brown-cavanaugh-bell-young-wonder-cnnheroes.cnn.

17. "Burn-out An "Occupational Phenomenon": International Classification of Diseases." World Health Organization, accessed October 6, 2021, https://www.who.int/news/item/28-05-2019-burn-out-an-occupational-phenomenon-international-classification-of-diseases

18. Cassie Werber, "Burnout Is Making Us Worse At Our Jobs, According To The WHO." Quartz at Work, last modified May 27, 2019, https://qz.com/work/1629015/burnout-is-a-medical-condition-says-the-world-health-organization/

19. "How to Tell When Your Stress Level is Becoming Harmful." National Alliance of Mental Illness, last modified September 16, 2020, https://www.nami.org/Blogs/NAMI-Frontline-Wellness/2020/How-to-Tell-When-Your-Stress-Level-is-Becoming-Harmful

20. Burnout is an indicator you are either off track, or that it is time to progress forward to the next stage, toward completion of your overarching life's purpose. Such burnout is not to be confused with burnout associated with a medical condition or mental illness. Burnout can be associated with prolonged stress from emotional, physical and or mental exhaustion. The burnout referenced in this section is as a result of operating in a capacity that is outside of one's purpose.

3. THE POWER OF PERSPECTIVE

1. "Seeing Color." Arizona State University, accessed May 4, 2021, https://askabiologist.asu.edu/rods-and-cones

2. "How Do We See Color?" Pantone, accessed May 4, 2021, https://www.pantone.com/articles/color-fundamentals/how-do-we-see-color

3. "Curious Kids: Do Different People See The Same Colours?" The Conversation, accessed May 4, 2021, https://theconversation.com/curious-kids-do-different-people-see-the-same-colours-107972.

4. Jack Canfield, *The Success Principles* (New York: HarperCollins, 2005), 242.

5. "New Study Reveals Just How Many Thoughts We Have Each Day." Newshub., last modified September 14, 2021, https://www.newshub.co.nz/home/lifestyle/2020/07/new-study-reveals-just-how-many-thoughts-we-have-each-day.html

6. Jack Canfield, *The Success Principles* (New York: HarperCollins, 2005), 229, 231.

7. Jack Canfield, *The Success Principles* (New York: HarperCollins, 2005), 75-80.

8. The Holy Bible, New King James Version (Nashville: Thomas Nelson Publishers, 1982), Proverbs 23:7.

9. Saul McLeod, "Cognitive Dissonance." SimplyPsychology, last modified February 5, 2018, https://www.simplypsychology.org/cognitive-dissonance.html

10. Kendra Cherry, "What Is Cognitive Dissonance?" Verywellmind, last modified July 2, 2020, https://www.verywellmind.com/what-is-cognitive-dissonance-2795012

11. Jack Canfield, *The Success Principles* (New York: HarperCollins, 2005), 85-87.

12. Jack Canfield, *The Success Principles* (New York: HarperCollins, 2005), 57.

Jack Canfield, *The Success Principles* (New York: HarperCollins, 2005), 30.

13. "6 Famous People Say Visualization Will Work For You!" Problem Solving 4 Life, last modified March 27, 2018, https://problemsolving4life.com/6-famous-people-prove-visualization-works/

14. "This Visualization Technique Helped Me Build a $100M Business." Inc. Magazine, accessed May 4, 2021 https://www.inc.com/empact/this-visualization-technique-helped-me-build-a-100m-business.html

15. Shamseer Mambra, "15 Brave Organisations Fighting To Save Our Oceans." Marine Insight, last modified August 26, 2021, https://www.marineinsight.com/environment/15-brave-organisations-fighting-save-oceans/

16. Raymond Edman, JollyNotes.Com, accessed May 3, 2021, https://www.jollynotes.com/joyful-living/never-doubt-in-the-dark-what-god-told-you-in-the-light/.

17. "The Power Of Focus." Internet Business Guide, accessed May 5, 2021, https://www.hochstadt.com/the-power-of-focus

18. Steve Glaveski,"10 Quick Tips for Avoiding Distractions at Work." Harvard Business Review, last modified December 18, 2019 https://hbr.org/2019/12/10-quick-tips-for-avoiding-distractions-at-work

4. YOUR STABILIZING CORE

1. The Holy Bible, New American Standard Bible, (Lockman Foundation: 1971), Matthew 21:22.

2. Karen Kemmis, PT, DPT, MS, GCS, CDE, FAADE, "Core Strength & Balance." SUNY Upstate Medical University, accessed October 8, 2021, https://www.upstate.edu/hospital/pdf/healthlink/core-strength-03232017.pdf

3. "Bone Marrow Aspiration Needles." Argon Medical Devices, accessed May 9, 2021 https://www.argonmedical.com/products/bone-marrow-aspiration-needles

4. The Holy Bible, English Standard Version, (Crossway: 2001), Philippians 1:6.

5. "Theodore Roosevelt's The Man in the Arena Speech 100th Anniversary." LeadershipNow, last modified April 23, 2010, https://www.leadershipnow.com/leadingblog/2010/04/theodore_roosevelts_the_man_in.html

6. "A story of what's possible – In 1990 Jim Carrey, A Broke, Unknown 28-year-old Comic In LA, Decided To Write A Check To Himself: For $10 million." GeniusU, accessed May 19, 2016, https://app.geniusu.com/articles/3871392

7. Jack Canfield, *The Success Principles* (New York: HarperCollins, 2005), 57.

8. "Married at First Sight – Journey Through The Lens Of A Viewer S:3 E:10." Reality With Bee, accessed May 9. 2021, https://realitywithbee.com/2016/02/married-at-first-sight-journey-through-the-lens-of-a-viewer-s3-e10/

5. THE MOST IMPORTANT STEP IN CONFLICT RESOLUTION

1. Jack Canfield, *The Success Principles* (New York: HarperCollins, 2005), 208, 212.

2. Jack Canfield, *The Success Principles* (New York: HarperCollins, 2005), 209.

3. Jack Canfield, *The Success Principles* (New York: HarperCollins, 2005), 212.

4. Forgiveness & reconciliation bible texts. For clarity, review each in the New Living Translation: Matthew 18: 15-17, Luke 17: 3,4, Colossians 3:13, Matthew 5: 23,24.

5. Jack Canfield, *The Success Principles* (New York: HarperCollins, 2005), 216.

6. Kathi Norman, "Forgiveness: How it Manifests in our Health, Well-being, and Longevity." Penn Libraries, accessed May 12, 2021, https://repository.upenn.edu/cgi/viewcontent.cgi?article=1124&context=mapp_capstone

7. Ashley Abramson, "Holding a Grudge Can Make You Sick." Elemental, last modified November 20, 2019, https://elemental.medium.com/holding-a-grudge-can-make-you-sick-5179ed066e11

8. "Adrenaline." You And Your Hormones, accessed May 12, 2021, https://www.yourhormones.info/hormones/adrenaline/

9. Travis Bradberry & Jean Greaves, *Emotional Intelligence 2.0* (Talent Smart: 2009),102-103.

10. "Stress Management For The Health of It." National Ag Safety Database, accessed May 12, 2021, https://nasdonline.org/1445/d001245/stress-management-for-the-health-of-it.html

11. Nicolle Monico, "The 12 Steps of Alcoholics Anonymous (AA)." American Addiction Centers, last modified October 4, 2021, https://www.alcohol.org/alcoholics-anonymous/

12. The Holy Bible, New King James Version (Nashville: Thomas Nelson Publishers, 1982), 2 Corinthians 13:11.

6. YOUR PLANE HAS ASSIGNED SEATING

1. The Holy Bible, New Living Translation (Tyndale House Publishers: 2007), Proverbs 4:23.

2. "Lisa Nichols." Motivating the Masses, accessed June 21, 2021, https://motivatingthemasses.com/about/lisa-nichols/

3. "3 Brutal Truths About Becoming Successful You Must Hear – Lisa Nichols." Fearless Motivation, accessed December 1, 2020, https://www.fearlessmotivation.com/2018/07/12/brutal-truths-becoming-successful-lisa-nichols/

4. Dharius Daniels, *Relational Intelligence* (Grand Rapids: Zondervan, 2020), 21-74.

5. The Holy Bible, English Standard Version, (Crossway: 2001), Proverbs 18:24.

6. The Holy Bible, English Standard Version, (Crossway: 2001), John 15:13.

7. The Holy Bible, English Standard Version, (Crossway: 2001), Proverbs 17:17

8. Bill McGee, "Bumped For Balance? How Airplane Weight Can Affect Your Flight." USA Today, last modified March 24, 2019, https://www.usatoday.com/story/travel/columnist/mcgee/2019/03/23/airplane-weight-balance-bumped-luggage/3248734002/

7. FIND YOUR INNER FIGHT & WIN

1. Madeline Berg, "From Poor As Hell To Billionaire: How Tyler Perry Changed Show Business Forever." Forbes, last modified September1, 2020, https://www.forbes.com/sites/maddieberg/2020/09/01/from-poor-as-hell-to-billionaire-how-tyler-perry-changed-show-business-forever/?sh=3ec017ce34b5

2. Erin Scottberg, "9 Famous People Who Will Inspire You to Never Give Up." themuse, accessed May 17, 2021, https://www.themuse.com/advice/9-famous-people-who-will-inspire-you-to-never-give-up

3. Gillian Zoe Segal, "This Self-Made Billionaire Failed The LSAT Twice, Then Sold Fax Machines For 7 Years Before Hitting Big—Here's How She Got There." CNBC, last modified April 3, 2019, https://www.cnbc.com/2019/04/03/self-made-billionaire-spanx-founder-sara-blakely-sold-fax-machines-before-making-it-big.html

4. Julie Ellis, "Never Giving Up: 9 Successful Entrepreneurs Who Failed at Least Once." Business.com, last modified January 19, 2016, https://www.business.com/articles/never-giving-up-9-entrepreneurs-and-millionaires-who-failed-at-least-once/

5. Matt Valentine, "9 Incredibly Successful Entrepreneurs Who All Failed Big Before Winning Big." Goalcast, February 22, 2018, https://www.goalcast.com/2018/02/22/successful-entrepreneurs-who-failed-big/

6. "Goliath." Brittanica, accessed August 23, 2021, https://www.britannica.com/biography/Goliath-biblical-figure

7. The Holy Bible, New Living Translation (Tyndale House Publishers: 2007), 1 Samuel 17: 12-51.

8. Richard Mansfield, "How Tall Was Goliath? 1 Samuel 17:4 in the LXX & DSS." Accordance Bible Software, accessed May 17, 2021, https://www.accordancebible.com/goliath-lxx/

9. The Holy Bible, New Living Translation (Tyndale House Publishers: 2007), Genesis 15: 18-21, 26:3, 28:13, Deuteronomy 1: 7,8.

10. "Peyton Manning Takes Over and The Internet Explodes." Mile High Sports, accessed January 3, 2016, https://milehighsports.com/peyton-manning-takes-over-and-the-internet-explodes/

11. Discussed at length in Chapter 11; *Maintaining Balance In Extreme Times*

12. I write entries to myself in my prayer-walk journal, chronicling challenging experiences I'm navigating, how I feel about them and how they are impacting me, in real-time. I typically write several entries during the challenging season all the way to the resolution of the issue. Reviewing the entries at a later date has been instrumental in blessing me with strength, courage, faith and peace when dealing with new challenges, as I look back on how each past situation started, progressed and eventually resolved for my greatest good.

8. GET READY FOR THE ONSLAUGHT!

1. "The Flywheel Effect." Jim Collins, accessed May 19, 2021, https://www.jimcollins.com/concepts/the-flywheel.html

2. Martin Hoffman, "Get an MBA If You Want to Get Ahead in Business. Skip It If You Want Your Business to Get Ahead." Entrepreneur Magazine, last modified April 20, 2018, https://www.entrepreneur.com/article/311212

3. Mike Juang, "A Secret Many Small Business Owners Share With Mark Zuckerberg." CNBC, last modified July 19, 2017, https://www.cnbc.com/2017/07/19/survey-shows-majority-of-business-owners-lack-college-degree.html

4. Texts on abundance texts from The Holy Bible, English Standard Version, (Crossway: 2001), Proverbs 10:22 and Matthew 14: 17-20.

5. The Holy Bible, English Standard Version, (Crossway: 2001), Psalm 37: 4,5.

6. Paraphrased from The Holy Bible, New Living Translation (Tyndale House Publishers: 2007), Zechariah 4:10.

9. PRACTICE ACTIVE PATIENCE

1. Fatou Darboe, "Mailchimp's $525 Million Email Empire & the 17 Years of Patience." CRM.org, last modified June 10, 2020, https://crm.org/articles/mailchimps-525-million-email-empire-the-17-years-of-patience

2. Dan Western, "7 Success Lessons From Colonel Sanders." Wealthy Gorilla, accessed May 25, 2021, https://wealthygorilla.com/7-success-lessons-colonel-sanders/

3. Eugene Cheng, "10 Most Successful Entrepreneurs (And What to Learn from Them)." Lifehack, accessed May 25, 2021, https://www.lifehack.org/286158/8-signs-incredibly-successful-entrepreneurs

4. "Alibaba Net Worth 2011-2021 | BABA." Macrotrends, accessed May 25, 2021, https://www.macrotrends.net/stocks/charts/BABA/alibaba/net-worth

5. "Nature vs Nurture: How Do Baby Birds Learn How To Fly?." BU, last modified October 9, 2012 http://blogs.bu.edu/bioaerial2012/2012/10/09/nature-vs-nurture-how-do-baby-birds-learn-how-to-fly/

6. "Friedrich Nietzsche quote." BrainyQuote, accessed May 25, 2021 https://www.brainyquote.com/quotes/friedrich_nietzsche_103819 May 25

7. "Why You Need a Strong Core For Running." Runkeeper, accessed May 26, 2021, https://runkeeper.com/cms/training/why-you-need-a-strong-core-for-running/

8. "Core Exercises: Why You Should Strengthen Your Core Muscles." Mayo Clinic, accessed May 26, 2021, https://www.mayoclinic.org/healthy-lifestyle/fitness/in-depth/core-exercises/art-20044751

9. Sherry Dineen, "Play In The Rain For Better Health." Motivation Alliance, accessed May 27, 2021, https://

www.motivationalliance.org/play-in-the-rain-for-better-health/

10. Denise Mann, "Negative Ions Create Positive Vibes." WebMD, last modified May 6, 2002, https://www.webmd.com/balance/features/negative-ions-create-positive-vibes

11. Debra Fulghum Bruce, PhD, "Exercise and Depression." WebMD, last modified February 18, 2020, https://www.webmd.com/depression/guide/exercise-depression

12. The Holy Bible, English Standard Version, (Crossway: 2001), Ecclesiastes 3:11.

13. Charles Stanley, *Waiting on God* (New York: Howard Books, 2015), 23.

10. STAY HUNGRY EVEN WHEN YOU FEEL FULL

1. The Holy Bible, English Standard Version, (Crossway: 2001), Proverbs 16:26.

2. Graham Isador, "12 Surprising Entrepreneur Statistics To Know In 2021." NorthOne, accessed October 14, 2021, https://www.northone.com/blog/small-business/entrepreneur-statistics

3. Chris Loh, "What Happened To Canadian Airlines?" Simple Flying, last modified October 31, 2020, https://simpleflying.com/what-happened-to-canadian-airlines/

4. "Awards." WestJet 25, accessed May 28, 2021, https://www.westjet.com/en-ca/about-us/history/awards

11. MAINTAIN BALANCE

1. "Breathing Boost Oxygen Can Make You Smarter!" Boost Oxygen, accessed May 30, 2021, https://boostoxygen.life/news/breathing-boost-oxygen-can-make-you-smarter

2. "The Benefits Of Resting And How To Unplug In A Busy World." Forbes, last modified January 15, 2021, https://www.forbes.com/sites/womensmedia/2021/01/15/the-benefits-of-resting-and-how-to-unplug-in-a-busy-world/?sh=51f423a21338

3. Rhett Power, "A Day of Rest: 12 Scientific Reasons It Works - Most Major Religions Call For A Day Of Rest… Science Agrees." Inc. Magazine, accessed May 31, 2021 https://www.inc.com/rhett-power/a-day-of-rest-12-scientific-reasons-it-works.html

4. Jack Canfield, *The Success Principles* (New York: HarperCollins, 2005), 282-284.

5. Helen Sanders, "How Exercise Improves Productivity and Your Brain Function." Burke Britton Financial Partners, last modified October 15, 2018, https://www.bbfp.com.au/latest-articles/how-exercise-improves-productivity-and-your-brain-function

6. J.C. Coulson , J. McKenna & M. Field, "Exercising At Work and Self-Reported Work Performance." *International Journal of Workplace Health Management* 11, no. 3 (September 2008) https://www.emerald.com/insight/content/doi/10.1108/17538350810926534/full/html

7. Amy Magill, "What Is The Relationship Between Food and Mood?" Mental Health First Aid from the National Council For Mental Wellbeing, last modified March 13, 2018, https://www.mentalhealthfirstaid.org/external/2018/03/relationship-food-mood/

8. "How Much Water Should You Drink?." Harvard Health Publishing, last modified March 25, 2020, https://www.health.harvard.edu/staying-healthy/how-much-water-should-you-drink

9. Mallika Marshall, MD, "The Big Benefits Of Plain Water." Harvard Health Publishing, last modified May 26, 2016, https://www.health.harvard.edu/blog/big-benefits-plain-water-201605269675

10. "Malachi 3:10, Revised Standard Version." Bible Gateway, accessed December 13, 2021, https://www.biblegateway.com/passage/?search=Malachi%203%3A10&version=RSV

11. Texts regarding tithing from The Holy Bible, English Standard Version, (Crossway: 2001), Genesis 28: 20-22, Leviticus 27:30, Hebrews 7:1,2

12. Jack Canfield, *The Success Principles* (New York: HarperCollins, 2005), 413.

13. Jim Collins, *Good to Great* (New York: HarperCollins, 2001), 12.

14. "Why Do We Need To Maintain A Constant Internal Environment? - OCR 21C." BBC, accessed May 30, 2021, https://www.bbc.co.uk/bitesize/guides/zp29y4j/revision/2

12. LEARNING FROM THREE IS KEY

1. Bible texts on the importance of having a success team. The Holy Bible, English Standard Version, (Crossway: 2001), Proverbs 11:14, Proverbs 15:22, Proverbs 12:15, Proverbs 19:20

2. The Holy Bible, English Standard Version, (Crossway: 2001), Proverbs 27:17.

3. Thompson, Derek, "Zara's Big Idea: What the World's Top Fashion Retailer Tells Us About Innovation," Atlantic, last modified November 13, 2012, https://www.theatlantic.com/business/archive/2012/11/zaras-big-idea-what-the-worlds-top-fashion-retailer-tells-us-about-innovation/265126/

4. "Leverage The Power Of Vulnerability At Work." Iyarn, last modified May 13, 2020, https://iyarn.com/blog/apply-vulnerability-at-work-brene-brown/

5. Marguerite Ward, "Marcus Lemonis: Why Vulnerability Is Important in Business." CNBC, last modified March 10, 2017, https://www.cnbc.com/2016/10/25/marcus-lemonis-why-vulnerability-is-important-in-business.html

6. "Marcus Lemonis Net Worth." Wealthy Gorilla, accessed October 21, 2021, https://wealthygorilla.com/marcus-lemonis-net-worth/

13. GIVE BACK & GET MORE

1. The Holy Bible, English Standard Version, (Crossway: 2001), Luke 6:38.

2. The Holy Bible, English Standard Version, (Crossway: 2001), Acts 20:35.

3. Jack Canfield, *The Success Principles* (New York: HarperCollins, 2005), 416.

4. Bible texts referencing God's promises to those who give back from The Holy Bible, New Living Translation (Tyndale House Publishers: 2007), Proverbs 11: 24 & 25, Luke 6:38, Proverbs 19:17, Proverbs 28:27, Psalm 41: 1-3, Galatians 6:9.

5. Tatiana Morand, "The Ultimate Volunteer Appreciation Guide - Why Do We Volunteer?" Last modified September 25, 2020, https://www.wildapricot.com/blog/volunteer-appreciation-guide#why-do-we-volunteer

6. "The 6 Health Benefits Of Volunteering." Mayo Clinic Health, accessed January 13, 2021, https://www.mayoclinichealthsystem.org/hometown-health/speaking-of-health/helping-people-changing-lives-the-6-health-benefits-of-volunteering

7. "Volunteering and Its Surprising Benefits." HelpGuide, accessed January 13, 2021, https://www.helpguide.org/articles/healthy-living/volunteering-and-its-surprising-benefits.htm

8. Paraphrased from Ralph Waldo Emerson's quote. Forbes Quotes, accessed October 22, 2021, https://www.forbes.com/quotes/7810/

9. "Giving Billions Fast, Mackenzie Scott Upends Philanthropy." New York Times, accessed June 11, 2021, https://www.nytimes.com/2020/12/20/business/mackenzie-scott-philanthropy.html

10. "World's Billionaire's List: The Richest in 2021." Forbes, accessed June 11, 2021, https://www.forbes.com/billionaires/

11. "Warren Buffett." The Giving Pledge, accessed June 11, 2021, https://givingpledge.org/Pledger.aspx?id=177

12. Tim Stobierski, "Types Of Corporate Social Responsibility To Be Aware Of." Harvard Business School Online, last modified April 8, 2021 https://online.hbs.edu/blog/post/types-of-corporate-social-responsibility

13. Chris Murphy, "Why Social Responsibility Matters to Businesses." Investopedia, last modified June 29, 2021 https://www.investopedia.com/ask/answers/041015/why-social-responsibility-important-business.asp

14. "Social Impact Challenge" Receiving Through Giving, accessed October 23, 2021, https://www.rtgsocialimpactchallenge.com/

15. "The World's 10 Highest Paid Athletes." Forbes, last modified May 12, 2021, https://www.forbes.com/sites/brettknight/2021/05/12/the-worlds-10-highest-paid-athletes-conor-mcgregor-leads-a-group-of-sports-stars-unfazed-by-the-pandemic/?sh=48d61d9526f4

14. BECOME A MAGNET FOR MORE BUSINESS

1. Jim Collins, *Good to Great* (New York: HarperCollins, 2001), 12-13 & 27.

2. Micah Lally, "Humble Leadership Drives Companies. Learn From the Best of the Best." Bluleadz, last modified July 18, 2019, https://www.bluleadz.com/blog/humble-leadership-why-it-matters-and-examples

3. Amy Y. Ou, David A. Waldman & Suzanne J. Peterson, "Do Humble CEOs Matter? An Examination of CEO Humility and Firm Outcomes." *Journal of Management* 44: no. 3 (September 21, 2015) 1147-1173, https://journals.sagepub.com/doi/10.1177/0149206315604187

4. "C.S. Lewis quote." Goodreads, accessed October 24, 2021, https://www.goodreads.com/quotes/7288468-humility-is-not-thinking-less-of-yourself-it-s-thinking-of

5. "Dr. Howard V. Gimbel, MD, MPH, FRCSC Executive Medical Director; Cataract & Refractive Surgeon." Gimbel Eye Centre, accessed June 12, 2021, https://www.gimbeleyecentre.com/doctors/ophthalmologist-gimbel/

6. Paraphrased from The Holy Bible, New King James Version (Nashville: Thomas Nelson Publishers, 1982), Proverbs 22:29.

7. Jim Collins, *Good to Great* (New York: HarperCollins, 2001), 30

8. Terri Williams, "Why Integrity Remains One Of The Top Leadership Attributes." Economist Education, accessed January 15, 2021, https://execed.economist.com/blog/industry-trends/why-integrity-remains-one-top-leadership-attributes

9. "Integrity." Lexico, accessed June 13, 2021, https://www.lexico.com/definition/integrity

10. "4 Reasons Why You Must Lead With Integrity." LearnLoft, last modified February 1, 2018, https://learnloft.com/2018/02/01/4-reasons-why-you-must-lead-with-integrity/

11. Kate McFarlin, "Morals or Ethics in the Workplace." Chron., accessed January 15, 2021 https://smallbusiness.chron.com/morals-ethics-workplace-11363.html

12. The Holy Bible, English Standard Version, (Crossway: 2001), Matthew 7:12.

13. Chris Voss quote, "Chris Voss Teaches The Art of Negotiation." MasterClass, accessed January 15, 2021, https://www.masterclass.com/classes/chris-voss-teaches-the-art-of-negotiation

15. THE #1 INDICATOR FOR SUCCESS IN BUSINESS

1. Graham Isador, "12 Surprising Entrepreneur Statistics To Know In 2021." NorthOne, accessed October 14, 2021, https://www.northone.com/blog/small-business/entrepreneur-statistics

2. Adda Bjarnadottir, MS, RDN, "How Drinking More Water Can Help You Lose Weight." Healthline, last modified, December 14, 2020, https://www.healthline.com/nutrition/drinking-water-helps-with-weight-loss#TOC_TITLE_HDR_3

3. Alesandra Martelli, "The 7 Characteristics Of Effective Communication." accessed January 18, 2018, https://alessandramartelli.com/en/freebies/characteristics-effective-communication/

4. Chris Voss, "Chris Voss Teaches The Art of Negotiation." MasterClass, accessed January 18, 2021, https://www.masterclass.com/classes/chris-voss-teaches-the-art-of-negotiation

5. "Maya Angelou quote." Goodreads, accessed June 17, 2021, https://www.goodreads.com/quotes/663523-at-the-end-of-the-day-people-won-t-remember-what

6. The Holy Bible, English Standard Version, (Crossway: 2001), Isaiah 30:21.

7. The Holy Bible, English Standard Version, (Crossway: 2001), Jeremiah 29:13.

8. "7 38 55 Rule of Communication." Toolshero, accessed January 18, 2021, https://www.toolshero.com/communication-skills/7-38-55-rule/

9. "The Oprah Winfrey Show Finale." Oprah.com, accessed June 20, 2021, https://www.oprah.com/oprahshow/the-oprah-winfrey-show-finale_1/7

10. Harville Hendrix, Ph.D., *Getting The Love You Want - 20th Anniversary Edition* (New York: St. Martin's Press, 2008), 143-156.

11. Liz Lorge, "11 Brands That Are Teaching Us a Lesson on Empathy." Route for Merchants, last modified August 4, 2020, https://route.com/blog/11-ecommerce-brands-rocking-empathetic-marketing/

12. T.D. Jakes, Don't Drop The Mic (New York: FaithWords, 2021), 34,-35.

16. IT'S ALL GOOD, EVEN WHEN IT ISN'T

1. Paraphrased from The Holy Bible, English Standard Version, (Crossway: 2001), Romans 8:28.

2. "Carbon, the fourth most abundant molecule in the Universe…" ResearchGate, accessed February 8, 2022, https://www.researchgate.net/figure/Carbon-the-fourth-most-abundant-molecule-in-the-Universe-and-the-basis-for-organic_fig1_231078506

3. Michael Fried, "How Diamonds Are Formed." The Diamond Pro, last modified August 31, 2021, https://www.diamonds.pro/education/how-diamonds-are-formed/

4. The Holy Bible, English Standard Version, (Crossway: 2001), Ecclesiastes 3:11.

17. CELEBRATE!

1. Jack Canfield, *The Success Principles* (New York: HarperCollins, 2005), 53-54.

2. "Mother Teresa Quote." Pass It On, accessed October 28, 2021, https://www.passiton.com/inspirational-quotes/4125-there-is-more-hunger-for-love-and-appreciation